The importance of STEM to our society and how we will continue to rebuild our society out of the economic and health crises of the COVID-19 pandemic cannot be understated. I am so pleased to hear that we have people turning their minds to such vital issues of public policy.

Hon Tanya Plibersek, MP, *Shadow Minister for Education and Training*

Building a healthy economy after COVID-19 is a global priority and there will be an emphasis on innovation and entrepreneurial approaches as we seek to create new business opportunities and to strengthen existing industries. Employers are demanding job-ready graduates with transferable skills that can be applied to real-world, contemporary problems and who also have strong understandings of cultural differences and ethical practice. This book is a timely contribution to our exploration of how we can best serve the needs of our students as they prepare for an increasingly dynamic world.

Hon John Gardner, MP, *Minister for Education, South Australia*

There has been widespread enthusiasm, even hype, about the possible benefits of STEM education, but worryingly little careful examination of the issues. This book does a great job of rigorously analysing what STEM integration in higher education might entail and contains helpful examples of actual progress in the field.

Michael J. Reiss, *Professor of Science Education, UCL Institute of Education*

Integrating STEM in Higher Education

This timely book addresses the increasing need for collaboration, innovation and solution-focussed skills by looking at examples of cutting-edge pedagogy that can inform future directions. *Integrating STEM in Higher Education* shows how applying digital innovations that can be generated through the implementation of deliberately designed STEM education can change the world for the better. References to over 45 higher education institutions from around the world are included, where integrated approaches are already occurring. A wide range of teaching strategies and assessment methods are discussed, promoting a transformative method in which students can generate new knowledge within coursework and simultaneously develop skills and attributes for their future careers, lives and the world's needs.

This book is essential reading for STEM educators, administrators and academic leaders, as well as learning designers in higher education.

Lindsey N. Conner is Professor of Digital Education and Innovation, Flinders University, Australia.

Integrating STEM in Higher Education

Addressing Global Issues

Lindsey N. Conner

LONDON AND NEW YORK

First published 2021
by Routledge
2 Park Square, Milton Park, Abingdon, Oxon OX14 4RN

and by Routledge
605 Third Avenue, New York, NY 10158

Routledge is an imprint of the Taylor & Francis Group, an informa business

© 2021 Lindsey N. Conner

The right of Lindsey N. Conner to be identified as author of this work
has been asserted by her in accordance with sections 77 and 78 of the
Copyright, Designs and Patents Act 1988.

All rights reserved. No part of this book may be reprinted or reproduced or
utilised in any form or by any electronic, mechanical, or other means, now
known or hereafter invented, including photocopying and recording, or in
any information storage or retrieval system, without permission in writing
from the publishers.

Trademark notice: Product or corporate names may be trademarks or
registered trademarks, and are used only for identification and explanation
without intent to infringe.

British Library Cataloguing-in-Publication Data
A catalogue record for this book is available from the British Library

Library of Congress Cataloging-in-Publication Data
A catalog record for this book has been requested

ISBN: 978-0-367-67309-3 (hbk)
ISBN: 978-0-367-67308-6 (pbk)
ISBN: 978-1-003-13073-4 (ebk)

Typeset in Bembo
by Apex CoVantage, LLC

Contents

List of figures	xi
List of tables	xii
Foreword	xiii
Acknowledgements	xvi

1 Importance of STEM for social, economic and environmental futures — 1

Introduction 1
Why is STEM so important? 4
Changing world of work 7
Changes due to advances in technology 9
  Introduce data science 9
  Embed ethics for the use of technologies 10
  Make data open and interoperable 11
  Consult social scientists in technology research 11
  Embrace the usefulness of useless knowledge 11
  Find the right role for reskilling 12
Importance of innovation 13
Changing nature of learning and teaching 14
Integrated approaches to STEM 16
  Example 1 – University of Edinburgh and Herriot-Watt University 17
  Example 2 – University of Newcastle 17
  Example 3 – University of Malaya and Universiti Sans Malaysia 18
  Example 4 – Peking University 18
  Example 5 – Grand Canyon University 19
  Example 6 – Flinders University 19
Future educational challenges 19
References 20

viii   *Contents*

2   Role of technology in STEM   23

Introduction 23
Importance of technologies 25
Technologies for solving issues 26
Learning experiences using technology 28
Using specific technologies to develop STEM skills 30
Using technology to support learning 31
   Using technology in specific STEM learning environments 32
   Aligning learning goals, technologies and pedagogies 36
Conclusion 39
References 40

3   Developing a pedagogical framework for STEM   44

Introduction 44
Characteristics of STEM disciplines 46
   Prevailing practices and ways of thinking 46
   Disciplines have cross-cutting concepts 47
   Disciplines have applications 49
Importance of authenticity 50
Driving innovation using STEM 52
Importance of active learning approaches 54
   Challenge-based learning 55
   Problem-solving approaches 57
   Project-based learning 58
   Inquiry learning 59
   Design thinking for innovation 60
   Systems thinking 61
   Analysis 62
STEM learning environments 62
   Learning socially to promote collaboration 63
   Peer learning 64
A framework for integrating STEM 65
Conclusion 67
References 68

4   Designing integrated STEM curriculum   75

Integrating curriculum 75
Understanding by design 76
   Importance of connections to STEM 79
Importance of constructive alignment 80

Contents ix

Developing a theme, context, issue or challenge 81
  Choose a real-world theme, context, issue or
    challenge 83
  Establish learning outcomes 84
  Identify assessment tasks 84
  Identify discipline aspects, skills and capabilities needed 84
  Create learning experiences that enable students to meet the
    outcomes 85
  Identify resources and sources of information 85
  Support students to integrate knowledge and skills 86
Including active learning opportunities 86
  Critical thinking 86
  Creative thinking 87
  Design thinking within challenge activities 88
Supporting effective learning environments 89
Conclusion 90
References 90

5 Assessment   94

Introduction 94
Purposes and outcomes of assessment 96
Authentic assessment 97
Assessing capability 99
Examples of assessing capability 101
  Inquiry and problem-based learning 101
  Communication 103
  ICT 104
  Analytical thinking 105
  Critical thinking 106
  Work-integrated learning (WIL) 106
  Collaboration – peer and self-assessment 107
  Peer review 108
Culminating, enabling and discrete outcomes 109
Designing assessment tasks 110
  Using rubrics 112
Examples of assessment 113
  Case studies 113
  Collating assessment data across outcomes 119
Summary of assessing integrated STEM 119
References 120

x   *Contents*

6   Challenges and professional learning for integrating STEM   124

Introduction 124

Blending discipline and capability 127

  Challenge: educators have knowledge authority 128

  Challenge: accommodate student expectations 129

  *Challenge: adapting pedagogies based on student
    development 131*

  Challenge: students as consumers and producers of knowledge 132

  Challenge: application of evidence-based research 132

  Challenge: valuing ongoing professional learning 133

Professional learning 134

  Scholarship of teaching and learning (SoTL) 136

  Reflective practice 138

  Competencies for using technologies 138

  Collaborating and mentoring 140

Addressing challenges for integrating STEM 140

References 142

**7   Future directions for integrating STEM in higher
    education**   145

Introduction 145

Changing agendas and trends 146

  Drivers in higher education 146

  Changes in HEIs 147

  HEIs and future education 148

  Future of STEM integration 149

Levers for integrating STEM 150

Challenges in designing courses for STEM 152

  Aligning STEM with purposes of HEIs 155

  Discipline challenges 158

  Taking account of changes in technology 159

Taking a systems approach to STEM 161

Future research on integrating STEM 163

Conclusion 164

References 165

Index   169

Figures

3.1	Pedagogical framework for integrating STEM	66
4.1	Pathways for constructing learning experiences	83
5.1	Process of designing assessment tasks	111

Tables

2.1	Examples of enabling technologies for learning in STEM	37
4.1	Steps for planning theme, context, issue or challenge	82
5.1	Rubric for authentic inquiry	114
5.2	Multi-layered rubric for assessing transferable capabilities in group work	115

Foreword

I started my school teaching career as a science, maths and physical education teacher. At the mid-point of my 18-year teaching career, I was at what one might call a "hard to teach at" school. I found myself needing to experiment with my teaching in order to keep the students engaged. Integrating maths, science and physical education, using sport as the stimulus, achieved greater engagement with the things to be learned across the three subject areas. Some years later, I was to teach for a period in a dedicated middle school (Grades 6–9). There was continuous staff professional development on what made middle schooling "different". Integrated curriculum featured prominently in the things that made middle schooling distinctive. Commencing at Flinders University in 2006, I became familiar with work occurring at the Grades 10–12 Australian Science Maths School (ASMS), located on the Flinders University grounds, and the innovative integration of STEM at the core of the school's programme. The teachers at the ASMS have a unique relationship with Flinders University, enabling teacher access to university staff for professional development; ASMS students with merit are able to be accelerated into first-year university courses; and Flinders University pre-service teachers are provided the opportunity for practicum experiences at the ASMS. In recent years, I have provided critical friend support to a secondary school in Adelaide as they developed an inventive STEM–physical education programme for Grades 8–12. These two examples, of secondary schools changing the way curriculum is conceptualised, are responding to the need to close the gap between the knowledge generated in education systems, the skills required by employers and the priority focus on science, technology, engineering and maths to advance the economy and the prosperity of Australia (Australian Government, 2020), while also addressing pressing social and environmental issues.

While integrated curriculum has been proposed as a defining feature of middle schooling (Eichhorn, 1966), the idea of integrating curriculum has a long history. It has been proposed as a feature of progressive education reform for over 100 years (see for example, Dewey, 1916). Broadly, curriculum integration aims to "resituate subject matter into relevant and meaningful contexts" (Dowden, 2007, p. 52) in order to help "students live better lives now as well

xiv *Foreword*

as in the future, not merely gathering more information for possible later use" (Springer, 2006, p. 14). I believe this is what Lindsey has achieved with this book. Focussing on social, economic and environmental imperatives that need responses now and continuing into the future, Lindsey makes the case why it is important to integrate the disciplines that make up STEM – science, technology, engineering and mathematics – in higher education institutions to prepare graduates with the knowledge and skills that contribute to the creative, critical and innovative "joined-up thinking" necessary for the generative mindsets that will bring forward social and economic entrepreneurship. People with these skills are needed to build and contribute to social and economic capital that will generate new opportunities for businesses to grow and new business opportunities to emerge that deal with current and future social, economic and environmental imperatives. Just as is beginning to occur in secondary schools, higher education institutions need to consider how their courses package curriculum to meet the current and developing need for transferable and interdisciplinary skill requirements by employers in the fields of science, technology, engineering and maths.

In this book, Lindsey lays out a path from the "what" – an integrated STEM approach in higher education – to the "why" and "how", using evidence to inform the conversation and examples to illustrate the framing and design of STEM curriculum in higher education. While the concept of curriculum integration is well known in schools, and some schools have developed STEM curriculum (Bissaker, 2014), the concept of integrated curriculum and the potential for interdisciplinary course design to provide it is still emerging in higher education institutions (Akpan, 2019). Lindsey's book is therefore both necessary and timely to inform and lead the field. It will be useful for educators, policy makers and those who wish to promote STEM as an enabler for generating new knowledge and innovation.

Lindsey is the ideal person to be bringing forward this agenda. She is internationally recognised for her research on innovation in education and pedagogy. She has led research on the application of technologies within and across disciplines and teacher education for the future. She has consulted with education departments and ministries and with over 45 higher education institutions and schools globally on science learning and innovative learning environments. I have had the pleasure of working with Lindsey since 2016. I have known her to be committed to initiating, providing and encouraging innovative and entrepreneurial education thinking and providing support to those also interested in this pursuit. This book remains true to Lindsey's belief that through education, social change that provides people with enhanced opportunities and greater life chances is possible. Congratulations, Lindsey, on this important contribution to education literature.

Associate Professor Shane Pill (PhD, MEd, BEd)
Flinders University

References

Akpan, B. (2019). Introduction – a vision of science education 50 years ahead. In B. Akpan (Ed.), *Science education: Visions of the future* (pp. 1–16). Next Generation Education.

Australian Government. (2020). *Why is STEM important? STEM skills are crucial for Australia's changing future.* www.education.gov.au/national-stem-education-resources-toolkit/why-stem-important-0

Bissaker, K. (2014). Transforming STEM education in an innovative Australian school: The role of teachers' and academics' professional partnerships. *Theory into Practice, 53*(1), 55–63.

Dewey, J. (1916). *Democracy and education.* Palgrave Macmillan.

Dowden, T. (2007). Relevant, challenging, integrative and exploratory curriculum design: Perspectives from theory and practice for middle level schooling in Australia. *The Australian Educational Researcher, 34*, 51–71.

Eichhorn, D. H. (1966). *The middle school.* Center for Applied Research in Education.

Springer, M. (2006). *Soundings: A democratic student-centered education.* National Middle School Association.

Acknowledgements

I would like to thank my colleagues at two institutions, Flinders University and the University of Canterbury, for their enduring academic insights into projects and ideas for innovation in teaching and learning through research, particularly in science and technology education. Their support, commitment to academic work and feedback is highly appreciated. In particular, I would like to thank Sue Richards for specific feedback on chapters in this book. Many thanks also to Dr Andreas Schleicher, Director of Education and Skills, OECD, and Professor Michael Reiss, University College London, who both provided highly valuable feedback on specific chapters. Thanks also to politicians who made time to read chapters and provide comments: Hon John Gardner, Minister of Education, and Hon Tanya Plibersek, Deputy Leader of the Labour Party, Australia. I could not have completed this book without the ongoing support of my husband, Dr Richard Draper, who is not only my best friend but also an academic mentor, guide and motivator, whom I adore immensely. Thank you so much, Richy!

1 Importance of STEM for social, economic and environmental futures

Introduction

This book takes a deliberate future focus on learning in STEM because our future depends on the advances we can make in preparing future graduates. It provides a rationale (Chapter 1) for integration, based on the importance of social, economic and environmental imperatives. The shift from more traditional ways of thinking about learning in separate disciplines is necessary to support social development (through emphasising transferable skills) and economic development (through innovation and the creation of new business opportunities) and for addressing the ecological imperatives related to environmental impact and sustainability much more directly.

The discussions throughout the book take into account the trends influencing the availability and transfer of information, which has an impact on the roles of educators and learners. There are consequences of these shifts for pedagogical changes and the need to rethink what higher education institutions (HEIs) offer within coursework for adding value to students in terms of learning gains. These include:

- Appropriating STEM knowledge, technical and practical skills and transferable capabilities towards career orientations.
- Including work-integrated learning (WIL).
- Providing access to the internet, mobile technologies (anytime, anywhere learning with almost unlimited access to information) and a wide range of new immersive technologies (AR, VR, XR).
- Allowing for the impact of ubiquitous computing and differential digital literacy among learners and for emerging domains, such as data science, as fields in themselves.
- Making learning globalised (cloud sharing) and networked, including the availability of open education resources, yet valuing local expertise for co-creating new solutions (knowledge, products and processes).
- Changing to assessment practices that move away from normative testing to problem- and project-based activities for assessing how students combine knowledge, skills and capabilities simultaneously.

2 *Importance of STEM*

- Considering the importance of cultural competencies embedded within cyber citizenship.
- Considering the importance of reflective feedback loops to learning, teaching and organisational development.

Chapter 2 emphasises the important role technologies play in advancing STEM knowledge and understanding in practice. There are specific disciplines or sub-fields that contribute to the design, innovation and evaluation of products, processes and systems. In addition, with increased digitalisation, there has been a burgeoning of technological "tools" that can be used to solve problems through managing large data streams and undertaking simultaneous analysis, controlling things remotely and solving problems through simulations and tools that help to create new solutions to a wide range of environmental issues. Specific examples are given for how relatively new technologies such as virtual reality, gaming, augmented reality, extreme reality and artificial intelligence can be used to provide multi-channel learning experiences that advance knowledge and skills and help to solve problems.

Technologies are also enabling greater access to information and therefore access to education more generally (UN Sustainable Development Goal 4). Communication technologies help to transfer information more quickly so that new knowledge and processes can be shared, compared and revised through crowd sourcing and co-curation.

Throughout the book, there is reference to relevant research, as well as the inclusion of specific examples of where integration is occurring at course, programme and university levels. This has led to the development of a framework of components that are useful to consider in the development of integrated approaches, as shown in Chapter 3. The components of the framework have implications for how to design activities and courses using appropriate technological tools and pedagogies (actions by educators). Chapter 4 provides advice for how to design integrated STEM activities. It considers the appropriateness of a range of teaching and learning approaches relative to the intentions for student learning outcomes, and deliberately focusses on activities that foster the integration of knowledge from several disciplines, the development of skills and the inclusion of transferable skills, concurrently.

Assessment of integrated STEM is discussed in Chapter 5, as assessment tends to drive what is emphasised and hence what students put effort into and what educators promote. The process of designing assessments for integrated approaches is provided along with examples of generic and hybrid assessment rubrics that can be adapted and applied to a range of learning contexts and issues. These provide illustrations of how integrated knowledge can be assessed as well as capabilities (transferable skills) within the same activity.

Importantly, the challenges for implementation are discussed in Chapter 6, including how educators can design and assess integrated STEM, the potential shifts in roles that might be needed for educators and students and a range of types of professional learning and reflective practices for supporting the redesign of activities, courses and assessment. While predetermined content delivery previously dominated, it is time to reconsider what knowledge is useful, how it is acquired and what skills students need (practical, technical and transferable) as we apply more recent findings from learning sciences about how students learn effectively.

Preparing appropriate experiences for future social good is a rather daunting task for educators, given the array of pressures they are under due to institutional financial constraints and consequential increases in teaching workloads and expectations for performance in research. However, building social capital through human skill development should be a core focus for HEIs. As a consequence of graduates gaining transferable skills that contribute to joined-up thinking (creative and critical thinking as well as skills in innovation design), they are more likely to have generative mindsets for contributing to social and economic entrepreneurship. People with these skills are needed to build social capital and to generate new opportunities for businesses to grow.

There are also the dual pressures of meeting the world's demand for higher education provision, yet doing so in a very competitive environment that demands novel qualifications and graduates who are job-ready. As the availability of free online resources and courses increases, students can access information from anywhere around the world without leaving home – at any time and in ways that accommodate other aspects of their lives, such as work and family commitments. They can choose whether they want qualifications as part of this access or not. Higher education in this context is no longer primarily targeted at school leavers, but can and does include further career opportunities for mature students. Students' primary motivation to enrol may be to reskill for future employment. This means HEIs must address the needs of future workplaces, including specific and technical skills, as well as transferable skills such as collaboration, communication and creative and critical thinking.

For this reason, the final chapter synthesises the trends that HEIs are taking into account as they redesign qualifications. There are already multiple massification and boutique opportunities in existence. To enable more widespread, system-wide shifts in higher education, there will need to be substantial changes in thinking about the importance of integrated STEM, professional learning for activity, course and assessment design and collaboration among educators.

The final chapter also promotes the need for integrating STEM to address local and global issues. The effects of not attending to carbon emissions are evident all over the planet. Addressing local and global sustainability of resource use *must* be high on the agenda of every government and therefore drive curriculum changes for addressing the high need for problem-solvers. All governments will need multiple solutions to change the way the Earth's resources are used (or not) and reused. This can be aligned with the concept that HEIs could shift more, to be places of co-creation of knowledge with students through learning experiences within coursework. New knowledge has traditionally been generated through research, with the findings from research used as examples or applications within learning contexts. While this will still be true in the

4   *Importance of STEM*

future, increasingly HEIs are providing opportunities for students to learn and contribute to new knowledge through co-generating new ideas, co-creating curriculum aligned with their interests, questioning current knowledge, using inquiry and problem-solving approaches to seek novel solutions to local or world problems and creating new knowledge and understanding by connecting seemingly disparate ideas. We need much more research to inform future offerings in STEM through systematic evaluation of what works and why.

Why is STEM so important?

There is a worldwide focus on STEM education – science, technology, engineering, mathematics and, sometimes, medicine (National Academies of Sciences, Engineering and Medicine, 2018) – because of the intrinsic value of combining disciplinary knowledge and skills with advances in new knowledge, products and processes (Corrigan, 2020). Associated with this combination is a worldwide trend considering how disciplines can be taught in schools and in higher education by integrating across and within these disciplines, leading to interconnected knowledge, skills and capabilities that are needed in combination for creating innovative solutions to social, economic and environmental issues, locally and globally. In typical fashion, clustering of disciplines has spawned acronyms: STEM stands for science, technology, engineering and mathematics, while STEAM – science, technology, engineering, arts (and humanities) and mathematics – is also gaining popularity. This book is focussed on STEM, as this is emphasised in the compulsory sector and is beginning to be adopted in HEIs.

The intention of this book is to examine available evidence and provide examples of how integration of curriculum in STEM can be implemented. Research findings are used to answer whether integration in STEM leads to improved educational, social and career outcomes for graduates. There is promise of positive outcomes; for example, there has been a move in the compulsory sector to develop a STEM strategy in Australia (Education Council, 2015) and in the USA (National Academies of Sciences, Engineering and Medicine, 2018) as well as in many other countries.

However, in order to answer large-scale questions about improved outcomes, we must start with some specific ones:

- How do we know an integrated STEM approach in higher education will prepare students for future work, life and citizenship?
- How can STEM assist in solving significant problems or developing innovations in future workplaces?
- Under what circumstances is an integrated approach useful?
- What specific examples help to design curriculum in higher education?
- What would be included in a framework for supporting the development of integrated STEM curricula?

- Are there promising pedagogies and assessment methods that could be transferred to multiple learning contexts?
- What are the challenges for implementing STEM in higher education?

These questions will be addressed throughout this book.

A neoliberal rationalisation for emphasising STEM is that it can lead to new knowledge and provide new industries for countries to gain a competitive edge (Yanez et al., 2019). More importantly, there has been a call to address urgent ecological, ethical, technological and social justice concerns prevalent in the world through STEM education (Zeidler, 2016). HEIs have an important role in addressing the great need for social and economic development and to solve people–planet imperatives within an increasingly globalised world, where action within local communities is very important for sustainable futures (Robertson, 2017; Yanez et al., 2019). HEIs are trying to accommodate locality and specific issues and problems of communities, through partnerships with industries who provide students with work-integrated learning opportunities to solve local problems. This enables industry experts to work with and advise students as they collaborate on projects.

Higher education is on the brink of a revolution, one begun relatively recently in response to changes in digitisation and rethinking qualifications more aligned to STEM-related graduate employment. This technological revolution was been termed the "fourth industrial revolution" (Schwab, 2016) and will require workers to think about the interrelatedness of ideas, complexity and multiple layers of understanding and solving problems. Consequently, there is increasing reliance on technological skills and the ability to connect ideas, data and other forms of knowledge.

Skills of acquiring, using and integrating different knowledge sets and skills are vital to this advancement. Integrating knowledge from different disciplines and domains within disciplines is considered desirable for developing solutions to unknown problems and new innovations (Schwab, 2016). Change is often driven by social and economic priorities and new possibilities: take, for example, changes and disruptions derived from the possibilities afforded by electronic hyper-connectedness (Uber and Airbnb) and the effects on more traditional business models, without considering ethics and moral obligations to workers, or any associated legal frameworks. Therefore, there is an urgent need to adapt curricula in higher education to accommodate how technological changes can support future innovation and ethical sociocultural outcomes simultaneously (Yanez et al., 2019; Zeidler, 2016).

As publicly funded organisations and providers of the future workforce, the various types of higher education (such as community colleges, liberal arts colleges, research universities, conservatories, technical colleges and many other categories) are taking notice of comments by the World Economic Forum (2017) that STEM skills will be inherent in approximately 75% of jobs in the future. In response, HEIs are infusing communication, collaboration and critical and creative thinking into STEM discipline offerings and, in some cases,

6 *Importance of STEM*

even combining disciplines. While such skills are not unique to STEM disciplines, they are integral to STEM for developing new innovations and solutions to global issues. For example, global issues that have multiple solutions include poverty, sufficient nutritious food, global warming, disease eradication, housing solutions, automated processing and automated vehicles in relation to job decreases, the use of quantum supercomputers, the increase of robotics and the flow on effects for the need for human skills, genetic edits and neurotechnological developments that enable humans to optimise brain function, as well as other digital human enhancements for increasing our connections with the environment and other people (Schwab, 2016).

Some STEM careers can be directly related to a specific discipline and therefore justify the retention of specific content and technical skills. For example, aerospace engineering graduates expect to gain employment with aircraft designers, such as Boeing and Airbus, or major airline suppliers, such as Rolls Royce. Some STEM-related careers are not so obvious, for example, a special effects technician for a movie company, a designer of smart clothing, a developer of a digital solutions business, applying artificial intelligence to education, a designer of prosthetics or an agricultural engineer who designs irrigation solutions.

At the same time, uncertainty of the future of work is increasing as types of employment are changing with increased adoption of technological solutions. Digitisation and the technologies associated with using digital information (including using sensors and artificial intelligence for many smart functions) make a huge body of information more accessible to more people and will have a far-reaching impact on education and employment (World Economic Forum, 2018). Some types of employment will disappear, while new areas become more apparent with increases in automation. There is therefore an urgent need to support the development of the skills needed for a productive society that focus on humanity's ethical as well as physical well-being.

In 2018, the National Academies of Sciences, Engineering and Medicine (NASEM) found that there were very few research reports that undertook large, controlled and randomised investigations on student outcomes when there was integration of STEM in higher education in the USA (National Academies of Sciences, Engineering and Medicine, 2018). Generally, research studies reporting on student outcomes are in the form of case study narratives, which make it difficult to aggregate disparate cases to draw general conclusions about the effects of curriculum change on students. However, since curricula decisions are determined by faculty rather than by regional or national authorities, NASEM identified pockets of curriculum development that showed promise.

An additional issue is that professional associations tend to prescribe requirements for professionally oriented qualifications, even though many recognise the importance of the development of transferable skills and inter-professional ways of working. Such requirements can therefore somewhat limit the flexibility for some qualifications to be more open in their approaches to learning and teaching.

So, while there is growing interest in the notion of integrating STEM across disciplines in higher education, implementation is still in its infancy. The report of NASEM stated:

> Though causal evidence on the impact of integration on students is limited, it is this committee's consensus opinion that further effort be expeditiously exerted to develop and disseminate a variety of approaches to integrated education and that further research on the impact of such programs and courses on students be supported and conducted.
>
> (National Academies of Sciences, Engineering and Medicine, 2018, p. xi)

Changing world of work

HEIs educate students and these students take their place in the workforce. HEIs have provided education based on current workforce requirements while attempting to "future proof" their graduates, to a lesser or greater extent, for changes in that workforce. This provision is now a requirement, as employers demand transferable skills and expert knowledge from graduates. HEIs have reshaped and positioned their graduate attributes in response to stakeholder input. High on many HEI agendas for curricula reform, then, is the inclusion of innovation: connecting disparate knowledge sources and developing transferable, critical and creative thinking and socio-behavioural skills that can provide the opportunities and credentials for jobs that may not yet be apparent. According to the World Economic Forum's *Future of Jobs Report* (2018), up to 65% of the jobs for Generation Z do not exist yet and up to 45% of the activities for which people are paid could become automated using current technologies. This means that the world of work is changing rapidly, and future jobs will require different skills to those valued previously.

The World Economic Forum's report on human capital (2016) indicated that 38% of employers could not find employees with the required skills. A recent study (Rios et al., 2020) showed, through an analysis of 203,272 job advertisements requiring a college degree, that the skills identified by employers in rank order of importance were oral and written communication, collaboration and problem-solving. These skills, often termed "soft skills", encompass brain power and the ability to accommodate the needs of others. COVID-19 has shown some gaps in people's resilience – the ability to cope with change under pressure – a quality dependent on collaboration and connectedness.

Anticipating key skills needed in the future is critical if higher education is to integrate and emphasise its importance for students to gain employment. In addition, people who can demonstrate "learnability" – the desire and capability to learn skills that are in demand – will likely achieve longer term employment. HEIs have recognised the importance of developing graduate attributes such as critical and creative thinking, complex problem-solving and high-level capabilities in communication, especially as these contribute to developing new

8 Importance of STEM

knowledge – a core purpose of universities. These skills are best developed in real-world contexts.

Many HEIs offer work experience and work-integrated learning (WIL), so that learners can experience and apply their thinking and actions to work situations. As part of this experience, students are supported to reflect on what worked and what could be improved. In addition, the ability to transfer such capabilities from one context to another shows adaptability and agility, also important skills employers desire (Rios et al., 2020). These skills are part of a suite of skills for lifelong learning, alongside social intelligence, self-direction, evaluative capabilities and time management.

The notion of peer review is also developing as part of what it is to "be" a professional. This means that peer feedback is not something "nice to have" in the activities provided for students but rather is actively developed through structured processes as a key professional attribute. This idea will be developed along with others in Chapter 4 of this book, on designing integrated STEM. The development of thinking and reflective skills is seen as very important, as it is not only content knowledge that is applicable and transferable, but also cognitive skills, since they can be transferred to novel contexts.

The need for HEIs to be seen as sites of innovation enables them to have more direct impact on social and economic outcomes. For the last century, there has been some debate about the benefits of a generalist education versus developing specific, specialised professional qualifications in higher education, especially at sub-degree and undergraduate levels. Most economies demand both general and vocational training (World Economic Forum, 2019). With rapid changes in technologies, there is a tendency for lower demand for certain occupation-specific skills, rendering some vocational degrees obsolete and requiring higher education to refresh and renew both the length of offerings and delivery over shorter and shorter qualification cycles. Due to rapid changes in some fields, knowledge within highly specialised, job-specific qualifications may quickly become redundant or subsumed by technologies. Hence, there is a need for HEIs to respond through adapting and changing their curriculum offerings in a timely way.

Even so, vocational training (VET) remains very popular. According to the World Economic Forum Report (2019), the percentage of students engaged in VET was 63% in the Netherlands, 50% in Malaysia and 31% in Kenya. This training tends to meet the current demand for technical skills, including WIL opportunities and apprenticeships, and potentially enables faster training-to-work timelines for some. However, there is now a blurring in the higher education sector between vocational providers and universities, where WIL is becoming common, and degree apprenticeship models are emerging within the university sector because of the increased value placed on combining general and technical skills. Many technical jobs are now valuing higher-order general skills, with consequences for life-wide and lifelong learning skills. There is also recognition that people who have been trained in a narrow skill set could benefit from gaining broader skills. This has led to a wide range of bridging and transition arrangements for retraining in universities and VET sectors.

Changes due to advances in technology

Information technology is increasingly needed in every occupation. The skills of generating, linking data sets, aggregating and interpreting data will become even more important as we move into Web 3.0 and 4.0 eras (Stachowitcz-Stanusch & Wankel, 2015). Semantic web services and artificial intelligence programmes (interactive, self-correcting "agents") are propagating through multiple fields, such as medicine and health sciences, finances, control systems and higher education systems. The scale of these digital developments is increasing, and therefore the demand for developing them will grow. HEIs can play a large role in assisting in the development of technological skills that will support increased applications of digitisation.

At the World Economic Forum Annual meeting in 2019, the global university leader community discussed key aspects that should be focussed on in higher education to meet the changes related to digitisation and the future world of work (World Economic Forum, 2019). They identified the following six areas as being high on the agenda to advance the role of universities in societies of the future:

- Introduce data science.
- Embed ethics for the use of technologies.
- Make data open and interoperable.
- Consult social scientists in technology research.
- Embrace the usefulness of useless knowledge.
- Find the right role for reskilling.

These areas are discussed in the following subsections.

Introduce data science

Data science can act as an integrator for STEM, as it can be applied to all disciplines. While not all graduates gain employment in data-related jobs, many occupations require data literacy skills (Stachowitcz-Stanusch & Wankel, 2015). This is because data is generated through ubiquitous digitisation and is used in a wide range of applications: the number of searches and connections are increasing ever rapidly as the number of internet users increases and storage of data moves to cloud solutions. Universities have recognised the importance of data for learning and communicating in STEM and recommend data science courses and data challenges as essential for STEM and social science candidates.

There is an increasing need for experts in data science: those who can develop software for new semantic and intelligent self-learning systems, as well as those who need to apply data for problem-solving or decision-making

10   *Importance of STEM*

in organisations, businesses, the finance industry and education. Students in higher education can participate in the Semantic Web development of applications in areas such as structuring and representing knowledge within and across discipline boundaries. In fact, the ways in which organisations share and use interactive digital educational tools and community resources (for example, wikis and apps) for creating new innovations are becoming increasingly important as organisations interact more meaningfully online.

Students can use peer-assisted digital mechanisms to mark up their assignments and design their own educational spaces, creating their own learning pathways for exploring how knowledge integration leads to the creation of new knowledge (Stachowitcz-Stanusch & Wankel, 2015). This field is growing, and expanding along with it is the need for people to be curators and influencers who can use these technologies and modify or co-create new digital solutions and processes. Such emergent, digital collaborations can enable the co-creation of new knowledge in any discipline, in a world where face-to-face encounters are downplayed or actively discouraged (as witnessed in the lockdowns associated with the spread of COVID-19).

Embed ethics for the use of technologies

Data can be used to enhance the world we live in, but how data is used should be a serious concern for everyone. People's values, what underpins the technology or drove its acquisition, what assumptions have been made and ethical use of data needs to be embedded into the thinking and use of data or of applications. STEM disciplines tend to use more positivist approaches where specific answers (within tolerance limits) are important. Ethical thinking, in contrast, does not operate in a right or wrong paradigm, but rather relies on attributes such as care, responsibility, considerations of unintended consequences and weighing up risks. The ability to make nuanced judgement and decisions relies on understanding and applying ethical principles.

Embedding values and ethics in relation to the use of data requires students to consider multiple stakeholder perspectives and how the use of the data might impact on people's well-being. This applies especially to STEM disciplines but also to the humanities and social sciences as the digital humanities increase in prominence. With the rise in developments of artificial intelligence, a more human-centred ethical use of ready-made analytics and metrics will become more important (Floridi, 2015; Ravn & Skovsmose, 2019; Walsh, 2018).

In response to the need for graduates to understand and apply ethical principles, many universities are including philosophy teaching in STEM subjects to promote moral imperatives. For example, Harvard University is employing philosophy students to teach philosophy in computer science courses and Princeton (as well as many other universities) is focussing on global issues by creating grand challenges for engineering students to address climate change, water and food security, educational solutions for access to education, data security, the role of artificial intelligence, use of data in health care and developing alternative land vehicle transport that doesn't use fossil fuels.

Make data open and interoperable

Research would be hugely advantaged if data were available and openly accessible, as connecting and aggregating sources of data for systems analysis are possible when data sets are digital and freely available. Increasing data availability can improve the affordability and personalisation of products and services (Lehrer et al., 2018). A reason this hasn't been advanced as quickly as expected is that there needs to be a way to retain control of the underlying data and what it is used for. HEIs could model ways to federate and share data sources and create protocols for use that could be agreeable.

One of the downsides of making data available and openly accessible is the perception of how this impacts individuals or creates inequity issues. For example, already we are seeing some backlash from students when universities use learning analytics for student comparative purposes without considering how this could be demotivating for students (West et al., 2019).

Consult social scientists in technology research

New technologies bring with them concerns, governance issues, trade-offs between benefits and risks and a need for public education about the effects of these technologies. For example, one of the biggest issues in biotechnology has related to the use of genetically modified food (GMO). A lack of knowledge about the technologies, especially understanding about the benefits and risks, has hindered greater acceptance of GMOs for consumption (Ribeiro et al., 2016). This kind of "tech-lash" can be allayed through education and discussion about the affordances and benefits of the use of technology, with risks acknowledged through adequate assessment and clear communication. There is, therefore, a huge need to build in evaluative skills as part of the education agenda (Conner, 2003, 2014), which could include consulting social scientists about pre-empting and managing social and ethical issues. In many countries, for example in New Zealand, considering the social and ethical issues of adopting new technologies has been part of the school curriculum since 1997 (Conner, 2003).

Embrace the usefulness of useless knowledge

In times of tight budgets and stringent accountability, it is difficult to justify research that has no immediate applicability. Yet, good ideas arise from research findings that might seem to be producing knowledge for knowledge's sake. For example, the Institute for Advanced Study, founded by Abraham Flexner in the early 1930s, has become one of the world's leading institutes

12 *Importance of STEM*

for developing curiosity and basic research, promoting academic freedom to undertake research of interest.

Additionally, there are many examples of where a technological invention or innovative process designed for one application has been transferred to another contextual use. Who would have thought that the idea of protecting space vehicles from heat, which led to the invention of Teflon®, would have been applied to cooking utensils? Similarly, Global Positioning System (GPS) was originally developed by the US Department of Defence for assisting space exploration. GPS enables the complex array of satellites to be accessed from smart phones around the globe and, when combined with artificial intelligence, can provide automatic directions anywhere, anytime to anyone with an appropriate device. Given the high demand for this service, especially for tracking services, there is now a range of other satellite systems, such as Galileo in the European Union, Quasi-Zenith Satellite System in Japan and NavIC in India. This is an example of where a technology developed for one use was not only transferred to a new context but was also scaled up to a global level. The importance of this point is that transfer of knowledge and skills is more likely when working in an integrated STEM approach rather than through separate disciplines.

Find the right role for reskilling

As people find their skills no longer "fit" them for new roles, they need to acquire new knowledge and skills. *The Future of Jobs Report* (World Economic Forum, 2018) found that as we approach 2022, approximately 54% of employees will require significant upskilling and reskilling. This will require people to undertake further education and potentially become serial qualifiers.

Higher education has a significant role to play in providing lifelong learning programmes, even though there are many other options for upskilling to occur (especially in self-paced, online educational programmes often provided by employers). There is a shift from four-year programmes prior to graduates entering work, to refresher offerings for Continuing Education and Training (CET). One major example of this is the National University of Singapore (NUS), which launched a lifelong learning programme in 2018 for its 288,600 alumni. Potentially, NUS alumni can undertake CET through any of the 500+ courses on offer for 20 years after their first enrolment. The commitment of NUS to lifelong learning for alumni includes two free modules over a three-year period, and selected modules can contribute to further qualifications. At an institutional level, NUS has created a School of Continuing and Lifelong Education (SCALE), which works with all faculties to offer skills-based and industry-relevant topics, including data analytics, advanced manufacturing, cybersecurity and entrepreneurship. NUS has also developed partnerships with corporate clients so they can offer semi-customised CET courses using modules that target specific skills. CET students can stack short courses (1–5 days) and modules (1 day/week for 13 weeks) into qualifications such as graduate diplomas and master's degrees. Classes are typically held at the weekends or in the evenings to enable working adults to attend, with both NUS staff and partners delivering the courses. The Singaporean government supports this initiative with financial support from the Ministry of Education.

Companies and businesses are not only signalling the need for their employees to gain new skills but also are actively designing and developing multiple opportunities with in-house programmes in partnership with education providers. For example, AT&T in the US has realised that a large proportion of their workers need upskilling and are partnering with multiple institutions and online training providers to assist their employees to gain badges and qualifications to attest to their new capabilities. This trend, as it grows, requires many more educational designers. There is an opportunity for HEIs to ride this trend to enable such small bites of education to be transferrable into larger (or stackable) credentials.

Importance of innovation

We are moving irrevocably into a world where creativity is highly valued because of its role in coming up with novel solutions. Innovation is intrinsically connected to creativity. Whereas cognitive processes help us to synthesise and evaluate information, intentional creativity involves using intuition more and taking risks. A creative mindset asks: What other possibilities are there? How can disparate ideas be brought together to create something new? How can ideas be useful to people or turned into commercially viable products or services? These questions drive "enterprise" approaches for building businesses and hence economies. Linking innovations within STEM is also likely to help create novel solutions to global issues. Therefore, innovation using creative thinking is a crucial element for the advancement of STEM and its impact on social, economic and people–planet futures (Conner, 2020).

Innovation is a buzz word proclaimed by many HEIs. Due to digitisation, new products and services, new ways of developing artefacts and commercialisation of new ideas and products, "innovation" seems somewhat omnipresent. If we take information communication technologies as an example, information is becoming increasingly accessible through fast broadband access to the point of being ubiquitous and indispensable. In the emerging world of interconnectedness, information is freely generated, freely accessible and freely communicated. The skills needed now are no longer about gaining information, but rather about how to use it, in what has been termed "performativity" (Gilbert, 2005). Performativity has a direct connection to innovation in that it is the transfer of knowledge and connecting ideas that creates innovation – something new: ideas, products, systems or services.

In terms of the utility of knowledge and innovation for social good, humanists might ask: How does this information or use of it align with living and being a better human? Innovation can also reduce consumerism, which is unsustainable from both financial and ecological perspectives. Growth for growth's sake in medical terms would be called cancer (Laloux, 2014). Success, Laloux says,

14 *Importance of STEM*

must be measured in more than just money and recognition. It must add value, meaning and reasons for contributing, such as improving life circumstances or support for others. This suggests a more relational, complex way of viewing innovation, rather than as functional or transactional, in what Lepeley (2019) calls "educonomy". An educonomy, according to Lepeley (2019), is where there is a focus on learning for unleashing well-being and human-centred sustainability development. This would seem a very noble aim to have in higher education, especially if it provides the overarching values so important for driving innovation for sustainable futures. To advance this concept, there is a need to consider connections and interactions within STEM systems, since it is systems that lead to sustainability. A systems thinking approach is extended as it applies to STEM education in Chapter 7 of this book.

Changing nature of learning and teaching

Curriculum developers are questioning how knowledge and learning occur effectively in higher education, in response to drivers that are changing the world of work, including changes to technology and the use of automation. Early in the history of universities, learning took a holistic view: that all knowledge and inquiry were essentially connected. People who undertook scholarly work and learned to interweave ideas were considered well prepared for life and participation in society. The current emphasis on skills that include critical and creative thinking and collaboration aligns with previous notions of educated people being those who could sort fact from fiction, detect bias, consider multiple factors and possibilities, synthesise information to provide solutions and work collaboratively with others. How can higher education accommodate changes to thinking about the nature of learning and teaching and apply this to STEM education?

Some HEIs are considering establishing minimum thresholds and expectations for developing cognitive skills, so that students can transfer and apply these skills to other domains in the future. One way is to include general education courses that develop higher level cognitive skills within all undergraduate qualifications. For example, another year of general education was added to all undergraduate programmes in Hong Kong SAR in 2012 to develop thinking skills. This was extended during 2019 to emphasise critical thinking, problem-solving, leadership, communication and lifelong learning.

Another change is to align graduate attributes for an institution with appropriate pedagogies and assessment. For example, challenge activities and short courses, offered in the College of Science and Technology at the University of Rwanda, include a progressive developmental curriculum that promotes embedded learning strategies. These have resulted in improved critical thinking outcomes for students (Staab, 2020; World Economic Forum, 2019). Many universities prefer to embed desired graduate attributes within all courses. Often, there are common undergraduate courses that all students take. For example, at the University of the South Pacific, all undergraduate courses include core courses to ensure students have opportunities to gain the graduate outcomes of communication, creativity, critical thinking and quantitative reasoning, ethics, pacific consciousness, professionalism and teamwork. Unfortunately, there are other examples of where this alignment is not apparent at all (Conner & Kolajo, 2020). Inclusion of skills as outcomes in discipline-specific courses is challenging for educators who may prefer to retain more didactic approaches; this challenge is discussed further in Chapter 6 in this book.

Development of socio-behavioural skills has been ranked as at least as important as technical skills development in employer surveys in Bulgaria, Georgia, Kazakhstan, the former Yugoslav Republic of Macedonia, Poland, the Russian Federation and Ukraine (World Economic Forum, 2019). Teamwork, resilience, self-confidence, negotiation and communication are all considered vitally important for the future workforce. This implies we should be assessing these skills so students can demonstrate their capabilities. Assessing skills alongside integrated content knowledge is detailed in Chapter 5 in this book.

Alongside the inclusion of skills within courses and across qualifications, there is a growing tension between liberal education models that include a range of disciplines and specialist qualifications (National Academies of Sciences, Engineering and Medicine, 2018). Positioning in this debate seems to depend on who is advocating for a particular type of educational change. Professional associations, of course, require their members to be specialists who have met benchmark capabilities and graduating standards that apply directly to those professions. In contrast, high-tech device development companies (who may be employing scientists, engineers, dentists and optometrists) value highly transferable skills, including collaboration, communication, critical and creative thinking, empathy, relationship skills and dispositions, that will help their people learn and relearn well into the future. The ability to be flexible and adaptable, and especially being willing to learn and use new technologies, can be fostered through an integrated approach (National Academies of Sciences, Engineering and Medicine, 2018).

During economic recessions, such as in 2008, there was an increase in demand for vocationally oriented courses and qualifications that supported graduates to gain employment (National Academies of Sciences, Engineering and Medicine, 2018). There is a corresponding trend in higher education more towards what makes graduates employable and work savvy for an uncertain future, as opposed to qualifications that enable students to gain knowledge for its own sake. Employability (having the skills employees need) and employment data are used to rank universities worldwide. Despite this, a more aspirational goal for designing education in the future would be education that helps students to develop their talents and to live good lives (Zhou, 2016).

The concept of lifelong learning assumes that everyone can always learn more and has the need for further learning. Higher education has a huge role to play in support of ongoing adult learning, given people will probably have multiple careers in their lifetime, each requiring refreshing of knowledge, capabilities or upskilling in technical capabilities. Employability of graduates is no

16 *Importance of STEM*

longer dependent on what people know at the completion of a qualification, but rather on their capacity to learn and relearn and may even be based on their potential (given their skill set) and what they are likely to learn. Key standouts are people who have an insatiable curiosity, ask insightful questions and consequently have the potential to unlock further innovation and creativity. So, how can HEIs provide experiences to develop these skills "in time" within qualifications for innovation, and that value agility and are responsive to the changing world of work? One solution might be to develop new approaches to designing and implementing curriculum that enable students to learn transferable skills for their futures and that communities need as well. This is developed further in Chapter 4 on designing an integrated STEM curriculum.

Integrated approaches to STEM

Integrated curricula occur when disciplinary boundaries overlap because there is a focus on a theme or big idea (Stohlmann et al., 2012). In simple form, integration involves connecting ideas and being explicit about the interrelationships of concepts and processes (Drake & Burns, 2004; Stohlmann et al., 2012). Fink (2013) was concerned with a discrete structure for how to design integrated curricula, even though there may be many ways in which disciplines can contribute to content and processes in the broader pursuit of meeting life's problems. Potentially any amount of discipline integration provides opportunities for multiple types of content and methods to contribute to solving problems. These could be within integrated STEM activities that are embedded within courses or they could be whole courses that integrate disciplines or whole programmes.

Intentionally using integrated approaches to learning in STEM comes with challenges because there are a range of ways of considering integration. There may be a perception that content knowledge needs to be "covered" or "delivered" in a didactic sense (Park Rogers & Abell, 2008). When integrating, there may be contestation about "what" content is included. Also, when combining disciplinary knowledge and skills, there may be contesting (disciplinary-bound) ways of thinking and approaches for solving problems. This issue is discussed in more detail in Chapters 3 and 5.

Instead of a single disciplinary approach to a solution or question, the practices undertaken by a range of professionals who work together should be mirrored in coursework to solve real problems using a range of knowledge sources and skills (Crawford, 2000; Colliver, 2000). It may also be useful to focus on developing the skills and expertise as applied to specific issues, contexts, challenges and problems (Becker & Kyungsuk, 2011). Therefore, in integrated STEM, the focus shifts to the theme, issue or challenge, rather than staying on content knowledge, which becomes an "as needed" inclusion. Assessment shifts to focussing on problem-solving processes and solutions and how people collaborate and use technologies to find solutions.

Some examples in the following subsection represent a growing trend in STEM implementation in HEIs. These have taken account of the trends in the world of work and the changing nature of teaching and learning for developing skills deemed essential by employers. In all of these examples there is a blending and use of science, technologies, engineering and mathematics, albeit to different extents of combining content and skills or through specific examples of applications to solve real problems. Additional specific examples are provided throughout this book.

Example 1 – University of Edinburgh and Herriot-Watt University

This is an example of an innovation in higher education that embraces the need for more data science experts within a region. The change in emphasis and collaboration between multiple stakeholders (universities and local authorities) was designed for increasing employment. The University of Edinburgh and Herriot-Watt University partnered with local, regional and UK authorities to drive a regional job growth agenda that infuses the development of data science within multiple curricula. This initiative has the explicit aim of driving social and economic development through skill development and job creation for graduates. Their collective aim is to be the European site for data-driven innovation as it applies to all businesses, health care, science and technology, as well as to the humanities. Such interdisciplinary innovation could potentially be replicated by HEIs in other cities to support employment and the digital revolution. For example, the Universitat Politechnica de Valencia has created a data science qualification because the ideas and processes of data science can be applied to a wide range of disciplines.

Example 2 – University of Newcastle

The University of Newcastle in Australia has developed a STEM precinct to promote cross-campus STEM development, including new qualifications that integrate multiple disciplinary content and approaches. The university recently developed new qualifications that were purposefully designed as interdisciplinary – an online Graduate Certificate of Integrated Science, Technology, Engineering and Mathematics. Their attractor for students to come to the university on their weblink (University of Newcastle, 2020) states:

> The Graduate Certificate in Integrated STEM will equip students with the essential professional skills and knowledge to understand and apply Scientific, Technological, Engineering and Mathematical expertise and significantly, nurture and realise synergies through interdisciplinary knowledge and interaction within and across the interface of these disciplines. Through a collaborative and holistic program approach, the GCISTEM will engage

18 *Importance of STEM*

students with contemporary real–world STEM expertise and practice, interwoven across key endeavours and a variety of contexts and industries.

(University of Newcastle, 2020)

The university appears to take seriously their integrated approach to curriculum development, by offering a Graduate Certificate in Environment and Business Management, a Graduate Certificate in Pollution Impact and a combined Master of Business Administration (Global) and Master of Science (Data Analytics).

Example 3 – University of Malaya and Universiti Sans Malaysia

In Malaysia, the Ministry of Higher Education has a goal to achieve 60% enrolment in STEM disciplines, whether as separate subjects or combinations. The Ministry has taken a long view that includes supporting development of school teachers, so they are skilled at including design thinking and engineering into primary schools, as part of an interdisciplinary school curriculum. The University of Malaya has established eight interdisciplinary research clusters over the last ten years for sustainability science and biotechnology research and development.

The Universiti Sans Malaysia has positioned itself to lead Malaysia for the next 40 years in sustainable development initiatives (Universiti Sans Malaysia, 2020). Through its goal of "Transforming Higher Education for a Sustainable Tomorrow", it emphasises how sustainable development can be integrated through the virtues of equity, accessibility to education (including affordability), appropriateness and quality education with an end point being linked to the quality of life. In order to implement the university's goals, there is advocacy for a STEM approach to build future talent and enable people to transform their lives through socioeconomic well-being. Because of this, Universiti Sans Malaysia has been recognised as a Regional Centre of Excellence on Education for Sustainable Development by the United Nations University in Nagoya, Japan.

Example 4 – Peking University

Peking University in China is building Clinical Medicine Plus X, a research cluster for precision medicine, health, big data and intelligence medicine, clustered because of the interconnectedness of these disciplinary advances. The rationale provided for combining these disciplines for study is that together the disciplines can achieve much more than they could as separate entities, since they inform each other. There are multiple partnerships with industry, government, businesses and other universities to advance both research and coursework within the university to contribute to the generation of new knowledge.

Example 5 – Grand Canyon University

STEM initiatives at Grand Canyon University in Phoenix, Arizona, support school-based STEM, entrepreneurship and extra-curricular activities to create impactful STEM education that helps students to graduate from high school with STEM capabilities for using technologies in the workplace. To facilitate this, the university developed a coalition with local businesses, local authorities (City of Phoenix) and local schools. The initiatives support curriculum and extra-curricular development, especially for coding skills, sports clubs, competitions and collaborative makerspaces for designing and creating artefacts using the most advanced technologies in hands-on, creative experiences. Their goal is to build talents (human capabilities) for the next generation of workers in STEM, including a special emphasis on medical engineers.

Example 6 – Flinders University

Flinders University in South Australia encourages students from multiple disciplines to undertake common STEM courses, including students from science, engineering, nursing and applied medical science qualifications, with common STEM courses for each year of each qualification. In the first year, the focus is on the nature and principles of science, with students being taught how to critically evaluate the strengths and limitations as well as misconceptions about scientific practices. In the second year, emphasis is on innovation in STEM, spanning radical transformative innovation to incremental innovation, social innovation and policy change. There is a focus on problem identification, design thinking, innovation management, intellectual property, advances in manufacturing, commercial viability, partnering and political considerations, negotiation and pitching techniques. In the third year, students are coached to develop connections through preparing a curriculum vitae, a job application and interview, conducting an industry-relevant project and reflecting on their learning. The university partners with a wide range of businesses, industries and government agencies to enable currency and relevancy of the work-integrated learning components included within these qualifications.

Future educational challenges

This chapter has introduced the reasons for integrating STEM curriculum for the development of knowledge and technical, practical and transferrable skills that, together, can help solve problems. Applications for integrated STEM are manifold, and real-life situations are not separated into discrete disciplines. The power of being able to integrate STEM is that it enables problems to be solved because it sanctions the connection of ideas, processes and innovation.

A strong driver for HEIs is the need to differentiate offerings and provide the knowledge and skills people need for a complex future world, as almost everything that was developed for the workforce in the 20th century is being

20 *Importance of STEM*

dismantled and reconstructed. While there is still a place for specialist qualifications to meet the demand for highly applied knowledge and skills, employers are increasingly demanding combinations of skill sets. Integrating STEM within coursework in HEIs supports an innovation agenda through its capacity to draw on multiple sources of knowledge and practical and technical skills and to combine these with transferrable skills. Responding appropriately to these calls from employers will be necessary to advance social and economic agendas.

The importance of technology to STEM relates to digitisation of workplaces and the huge growth in digital tools for representing information, communicating and analysis. It is likely that the number of jobs worldwide will be transformed by technology in the near future, as predicted in the *Jobs of Tomorrow* report (World Economic Forum, 2020). The skills needed most will be related to the use of data, creating digital tools, AI, cloud computing and cybersecurity, as well as product creation and hybrid applied engineering skills. The world of work has changed dramatically; technological innovations surround us whether we like them or not (think satellites or intermediary services).

The implementation of a skills-based learning agenda is not without resistance and challenges, especially around designing integrated curricula. This is because the nature of learning and the expectations of learners are changing, where the expectation is that learning is accessible anytime and from anywhere. Throughout this book, there are specific examples of how STEM disciplines have been integrated and assessed as part of existing courses. Key advances in technology that can be used for integrating STEM and for learning are discussed in Chapter 2.

HEIs are currently in a state of flux in their variable responses to implementing integrated STEM. There are multiple approaches within teaching and learning contexts that take account of the expectations of all stakeholders for what is learned and how learning takes place as part of qualifications. Any curriculum changes will need to support students for problem-solving as a core skill, so that as future citizens they can address local and global issues (especially environmental sustainability) so essential for our future well-being.

References

Becker, K., & Kyungsuk, P. (2011). Effects of integrative approaches among science, technology, engineering, and mathematics (STEM) subjects on students' learning: A preliminary meta-analysis. *Journal of STEM Education: Innovations & Research, 12*(5–6), 23–37.

Colliver, J. A. (2000). Effectiveness of problem-based learning curricula: Research and theory. *Academic Medicine, 75*(3), 259–266.

Conner, L. (2003). The importance of developing critical thinking in issues education. *New Zealand Biotechnological Association Journal, 56*, 58–71.

Conner, L. (2014). Students' use of evaluative constructivism: Comparative degrees of intentional learning. *International Journal of Qualitative Studies in Education, 27*(4), 472–489. http://doi.org/10.1080/09518398.2013.771228

Conner, L. (2020). *Integrating STEMM in higher education: A proposed curriculum development framework*. Paper published in the proceedings of 6th International Conference on

Higher Education Advances (HEAd'20). Universitat Politècnica de València. http://doi.org/10.4995/HEAd20.2020.11058

Conner, L., & Kolajo, Y. (2020). The chemistry of critical thinking: The pursuit to do both better. In E. P. Blessinger & M. Makhanya (Eds.), *Improving classroom engagement and international development programs: International perspectives on humanizing higher education* (Vol. 27, pp. 93–110). Innovations in Higher Education Teaching and Learning. Emerald Publishing Limited. https://doi.org/10.1108/S2055-364120200000027009

Corrigan, D. (2020). *Implementing an integrated STEM education in schools – five key questions answered.* Education Futures Spotlight Report 2. Monash Education Futures. https://educationfutures.monash.edu/all-present/spotlight-report-2-implementing-an-integrated-stem-education-in-schools-five-key-questions-answered

Crawford, B. A. (2000). Embracing the essence of inquiry: New roles for science teachers. *Journal of Research and Science Teaching, 37*(9), 916–937.

Drake, S., & Burns, R. (2004). *Meeting standards through integrated curriculum.* Association of Supervision and Curriculum Development (ASCD).

Education Council. (2015). *National STEM school education strategy: A comprehensive plan for science, technology, engineering and mathematics education in Australia.* www.educationcouncil.edu.au/site/DefaultSite/filesystem/documents/National%20STEM%20School%20Education%20Strategy.pdf

Fink, L. D. (2013). *Creating significant learning experiences: An integrated approach to designing college courses.* Jossey-Bass.

Floridi, L. (Ed.). (2015). *The onlife manifesto: Being human in a hyperconnected era.* Springer Open.

Gilbert, J. (2005). *Catching the knowledge wave: The knowledge society and the future of education.* NZCER Press.

Laloux, F. (2014). *Reinventing organisations.* Nelson, Parker.

Lehrer, C., Wieneke, A., vom Brocke, J., Jung, R., & Seidel, S. (2018). How big data analytics enables service innovation: Materiality, affordance, and the individualization of service. *Journal of Management Information Systems, 35*(2), 424–460. http://doi.org/10.1080/07421222.2018.1451953

Lepeley, M. T. (2019). *Educonomy: Unleashing wellbeing and human centered sustainable development.* Information Age Publishing.

National Academies of Sciences, Engineering and Medicine. (2018). *The integration of the humanities and arts with sciences, engineering, and medicine in higher education: Branches from the same tree.* The National Academies Press. https://doi.org/10.17226/24988

Park Rogers, M., & Abell, S. K. (2008). The design, enactment, and experience of inquiry-based instruction in undergraduate science education: A case study. *Science Education, 92*(4), 591–607. https://doi.org/10.1002/sce.20247

Ravn, O., & Skovsmose, O. (2019). *Connecting humans to equations: A reinterpretation of the philosophy of mathematics.* Springer Nature.

Ribeiro, T. G., Barone, B., & Behrens, J. H. (2016). Genetically modified foods and their social representation. *Food Research International, 84*, 120–127. https://doi.org/10.1016/j.foodres.2016.03.029

Rios, J. A., Ling, G., Pugh, R., Becker, D., & Bacall, A. (2020). Identifying critical 21st-century skills for workplace success: A content analysis of job advertisements. *Educational Researcher, 49*(2), 80–89.

Robertson, S. L. (2017). Colonising the future: Megatrade deals, education services and global higher education markets. *Futures, 94*, 24–33.

Schwab, K. (2016). *The fourth industrial revolution: World Economic Forum.* Crown Business Publishing.

22 Importance of STEM

Staab, L. (2020). *Creating a project-based degree at a new university in Africa.* Paper presented at the 6th International Conference on Higher Education Advances (HEAd'20). Universitat Politècnica de València. http://doi.org/10.4995/HEAd20.2020.11180

Stachowitcz-Stanusch, A., & Wankel, C. (2015). *Emerging web 3.0/semantic web applications in higher education: Growing personalization and wider interconnections in learning.* Information Age Publishing.

Stohlmann, M., Moore, T. J., & Roehrig, G. H. (2012). Considerations for teaching integrated STEM education. *Journal of Pre-College Engineering Education Research, 2*(1), 27–34.

University of Newcastle. (2020). *Graduate certificate in integrated STEM.* www.newcastle.edu.au/degrees/teach-out/graduate-certificate-integrated-science-technology-engineering-mathematics-pre-2021

Walsh, T. (2018). *Machines that think: The future of artificial intelligence.* Prometheus Books.

World Economic Forum. (2016). *The human capital report 2016.* http://www3.weforum.org/docs/HCR2016_Main_Report.pdf

World Economic Forum. (2017). *The global competitiveness report 2016–2017.* www.weforum.org/reports/the-global-competitiveness-report-2016-2017-1

World Economic Forum. (2018). *The future of jobs report.* www.weforum.org/reports/the-future-of-jobs-report-2018

World Economic Forum. (2019). *A global standard for lifelong learning and worker engagement to support advanced manufacturing.* www.weforum.org/whitepapers/a-global-standard-for-lifelong-learning-and-worker-engagement-to-support-advanced-manufacturing

World Economic Forum. (2020). *Jobs of tomorrow: Mapping opportunity in the new economy.* www.weforum.org/reports/jobs-of-tomorrow-mapping-opportunity-in-the-new-economy

Yanez, G. A., Thumlert, K., de Castell, S., & Jenson, J. (2019). Pathways to sustainable futures: A "production pedagogy" model for STEM education. *Futures, 108,* 27–36. http://doi.org/10.1016/j.futures.2019.02.021

Zeidler, D. L. (2016). STEM education: A deficit framework for the twenty first century? A sociocultural socioscientific response. *Cultural Studies of Science Education, 11,* 11–26. http://doi.org/10.1007/s11422-014-9578-z

2 Role of technology in STEM

Introduction

Our understanding of the world and the way we create our futures are both dependent on and limited by the types of technologies we use. For centuries, humans have solved problems and created new knowledge by using technologies. Increasingly, the text we manipulate and the sound and images that we hear and create are generated digitally. This relatively new digital environment to make sense of things or to create new possibilities, especially for knowledge transfer, enables us to analyse and evaluate, to manage systems, to assess learning and to generate new knowledge. Technologies are now such an intrinsic part of the material world in which we live that the utility of technologies is indisputable. Technologies can create "smart" environments through deploying sensors, logistics, control systems and communication networks; philosophers such as Verbeek and Ihde query how these technological environments shape what we do and create (Aydin et al., 2018–2019; Ihde, 1990). Technologies make living easier and can indeed save lives. Using technologies can also reduce the load of undertaking mundane tasks. However, the importance of technology in STEM and its use in problem-solving are closely tied to the huge potential for using technologies to accelerate public good by improving health as well as quality and quantities of food and to address environmental concerns. Through many activities, technologies are integral to STEM and enable application in practice to address local and global issues.

The "T" in STEM refers to the range of disciplinary studies that can be classified as technology. These disciplines specifically study design, innovation and evaluation as applied to developing products, processes and systems. In contrast, technologies (small "t") are also used to enhance and apply good ideas in practice. Technologies play a significant role in solving a wide range of problems through the use of tools and artefacts, enabling access to previous knowledge, sensing things, controlling things remotely, generating and analysing large data sets and communicating through multiple channels. Therefore, in this chapter, technology is also used as a generic term for new devices, hardware and software, as well as for the use of digital representations through a range of media that extend information communication technologies (ICT).

Design and technology, a curriculum area in the compulsory education sector, is considered to be interdisciplinary and process-oriented (Bell et al., 2017). Its higher education equivalent would be applied sciences, such as biotechnology or electrotechnology, in which students undertake inquiry projects that include inherent design processes as students create new products, adapt technologies and investigate technological processes and systems applied in practice to solve an issue. There is an emphasis on problem-solving, reflection and self-management of projects. These disciplines draw on scientific knowledge and mathematical techniques to enable decisions and refinements through iterative testing and confidence measures or tolerance limits. In these STEM disciplines, integrating technological knowledge and processes are core to student outcomes.

When considering integrated approaches to STEM, the power of using technologies as the integrator lies in how computational thinking can span and support interdisciplinary learning. Encompassing this idea, Srisawasdi (2012) indicated that almost every aspect of science incorporates the use of computer technologies (involving computational thinking), providing essential tools for data generation, storage, analysis and simulations; for generating models; and for setting up automatic control of inputs and gathering outputs from instrumentation. Use of computer technologies is therefore inherent in scientific enterprise as part of the processes of investigation, analysis and communication. Also, computerised learning environments provide students with substantially more opportunities to construct understanding of scientific phenomena and principles (Krusberg, 2007), develop inquiry skills (Freidler et al., 1989; Songer, 1998), collaboratively problem-solve (Quellmalz & Silbertglitt, 2018) and potentially increase engagement because there is an inherent novelty factor (Clark & Jackson, 1998). The same could be stated for mathematics and engineering concepts. Therefore, computer-mediated approaches can be seen as integrators in STEM because they are increasingly enabling the development of creativity, collaboration, communication, data manipulation and evaluation skills.

In parallel to the advances in using computations within STEM disciplines, digital access to learning materials and communication that either supports learning remotely or enhances face-to-face learning (as well as the use of different types of visual learning) has become ubiquitous in higher education. Use of video games, virtual reality and augmented reality (multiple modalities) are emerging as extended ways for students to gain knowledge and skills, especially in STEM. The ubiquitous digitisation of information and the proliferation of digital tools are very important vehicles to enable countries to address the UN Sustainable Development Goals (SDG), and SDG 4 in particular: increasing access to education (United Nations, 2020). Technologies have huge potential to support multiple UN SDGs, including building economic growth through data capabilities and job creation as well as adopting strategies for supporting social needs in health and education. This has become an imperative for governments to consider as part of the social and economic recovery from the COVID-19 pandemic (United Nations, 2020).

The ways in which digital tools were infused into teaching and learning experiences during 2020 have been extraordinary. During the COVID-19 pandemic, institutions were forced to adapt very quickly and to provide alternative ways for learning. As a result, there has been greater uptake in the use of collaborative, synchronous video conferencing and other means to collaborate virtually, as well as use of online platforms for creating new types of learning experiences, including virtual simulations. Some of these are likely to be retained as both students and teachers realise the affordances of using digital tools more extensively. However, it should also force higher education to seriously reflect on the value of face-to-face teaching and learning models.

Importance of technologies

Specific technologies are making an impact, and artificial intelligence (AI) is probably the most significant technology because of its infusion into the sciences and medicine (Walsh, 2018). AI is, for example, already used for monitoring personal health analytics to provide advice about daily activities and food we should eat. Fitness watches monitor vital statistics such as pulse, blood pressure, sugar and oxygen levels and can report on sleep patterns and levels of activity. Of the ten predictions that Walsh (2018) makes for the uses of AI in the future, those relating to monitoring and advising on health and well-being are likely to have far-reaching effects. Devices are revolutionising health care for the elderly, enabling them to stay longer in their own homes because the devices can watch for falls and can call for help if required. Toilets can also monitor and analyse urine and stool samples. In the near future, it's likely that phones will be used to monitor health through comparative "selfies" across time, through eye analyses and checking on skin conditions. It is also predicted that personal computers will use sensors to monitor for dementia, Parkinson's disease and general health conditions such as colds and influenza. These types of uses of AI will have huge impacts on not only how STEM becomes more integrated into people's daily lives (and used more frequently for extending human capabilities), but also on the ways that the technologies may enable people to learn more about themselves, their lives and their interactions.

While there are many applications of AI already being applied in STEM contexts, there is likely to be a proliferation and rapid rise in applications of AI to a wide range of services and functions that we haven't thought of yet. The prediction is that the use of AI (and automation more generally) will help people travel (autonomous vehicles), translate languages, write more coherently, reimage images and co-create music. How will mediation of knowledge created by machines change how we come to know about information? What ethical implications arise related to accessing people's information?

26   *Role of technology in STEM*

Another technological advance is the use and importance of digitisation of data and the implications this has for the ability to store, manipulate, analyse and share this data for systems functioning and decision-making. Often AI is applied to digital data sets to generate statistics, and therefore the use of these applications to assist with decision-making is potentially enormous. Consequently, there are huge implications for using AI on how we perceive knowledge, how we use knowledge and its role in human development.

Digital storage of big data sets means that all the works of the mind are potentially available, can be accessed at anytime from anywhere (provided you have electronic connectivity) and can be reproduced and shared easily. As bots and machines reduce the cognitive load for humans through using AI, what does this mean for creativity, given that these machines can assist with digital creations? These types of questions are being asked by philosophers as part of post-humanist considerations (Floridi, 2015), especially given the potential for technological device implants and the augmentation of electronic–nerve interfaces to create cyborgs with super-sense, super-strength and super-data processing capabilities. Philosophically, this raises questions about the future of being human when we realise that we live in a world of hyper-memorise ability, hyper-reproducibility and hyper-diffuse ability (Ganascia, 2015).

Successive technological advances, especially AI, have led to changes in the nature of work, mostly because of the reduction in need for manual processes. This especially applies to industries that use combinations of robotics and AI, such as car manufacturing, that are now more customised due to the ability to programme customer specifications into the assembly line. We are also witnessing changes to business models, for example, online services for banking, finance, travel and accommodation as well as a multitude of social services.

Increasing digitisation will lead to further changes in the use of tools and in work patterns. The National Bureau of Economic Research (DeFilippis et al., 2020) investigated changes in patterns of working behaviour of over 3 million people in 16 cities throughout the world during lockdowns as a result of COVID-19. They found that people were having more, but shorter, meetings online. People adapted to workplaces and time zones and could work together. Digital technologies and particularly video conferencing made this possible. Given the experiences of 2020, many companies are rethinking policies about where and how people work. The National Bureau of Economic Research (DeFilippis et al., 2020) found that online collaboration not only supported local solutions but also enabled people to connect regionally and globally to work on issues together. There are many other ways that devices, artefacts and process solutions can contribute to solving problems. The importance of technology is that it can enable solutions for global problems, as discussed in more detail in the next section.

Technologies for solving issues

The World Economic Forum (2019) posted a list of top 50 companies that were applying technological innovations to solve world issues. These examples

Role of technology in STEM 27

provide a glimpse of how knowledge and skills from STEM fields have been combined to produce the desired solutions and include:

- Chinese company Alesca Life, which creates cloud-connected farms and farm digitisation software to improve the efficiency of food production so that hotels, restaurants or even private homes can produce food in automated "cabinet farms" that it says use up to 25 times less water and land than traditional methods.
- Mexico's Via Verde, which creates vertical gardens in cities – green spaces that generate oxygen, improve air quality, reduce urban heat islands and provide psychological benefits to highly populated cities.
- A US company, Perceptive Automata, combines behavioural science, neuroscience and computer vision to help autonomous vehicles understand how pedestrians, bikes and drivers communicate on the road.

There are many other ways that technology can enable problem-solving. Given the wide range of types of innovation in the business world related to the development and use of technologies, it is not surprising that students frequently see applications in their everyday lives and consequently opportunities for using technology for innovative businesses. As mentioned in Chapter 1, the scope of employment for STEM graduates in the future is probably in this innovation/ entrepreneurial area, in which STEM concepts are applied to create new innovative artefacts and processes that enable us to enhance how we live and solve some very specific challenges for people's health as well. For example, new technological devices are continuing to be invented to enhance people's health. Some devices that have been developed and produced at Flinders University (2020), involving collaboration between a range of STEM professionals and industries, include skates to aid in the recovery of knee-replacement patients; light therapy glasses for resetting sleep patterns for people with insomnia or seasonal affective disorder; a device to find the ends of surgical pins; cheaply produced splints for bone fractures; and a device for detecting the margins of cancerous tissue in breasts. Typical areas where the "makerspace" has developed within educational contexts include developing electronic systems, 3D printing and robotics, as well as where technologies are applied to create a multitude of artefacts, including 360° video and interactive digital objects. Such solutions emerge as people collaborate creatively with industry to address a local need. Therefore, technology can provide solutions that also create job and business opportunities. Technological solutions can create opportunities for entrepreneurship and enterprise that may be able to be scaled globally.

Innovation and technologies are being applied to problems and make living easier on a macro scale, too. Whole cities are being designed and developed from the ground up instead of being allowed to grow in ad hoc fashion. Smart cities are being designed to improve the way we live, work and play. According to the designers, when well designed, user experience is improved, quality of life is enhanced and productivity is increased, thereby leading to increased economic competitiveness. In these cities, greater sustainability and environmental consciousness are promoted, using sensors that provide data for communicating traffic patterns, parking lot emergencies, dust storms, waste management and weather pattern alerts, to name a few. Start-up companies develop and advance technological solutions for transport, more efficient energy use, agricultural and horticultural advances and more sustainable ways of living. In 2019, the United Nations considered the idea of floating cities more seriously as a response to climate change, sea-level rising and the need to build new cities for people, rather than for cars. Such creative solutions have arisen due to the collaboration of designers, engineers, scientists and mathematicians as they consider the interconnections and uses of a wide range of technologies within a system of technologies.

These examples illustrate innovative uses of technology and the importance of technology for solving problems. Technological tools and devices are increasingly becoming essential and will play an ever more important role in integrating across the STEM disciplines to solve problems, generate new knowledge and connect people and components within systems. The idea of using systems thinking is developed further in Chapter 7. Because of the prevalence of technology and its importance to STEM, the next section considers the increasing impact technology is having on what and how people learn.

Learning experiences using technology

Technology has an increasing impact on education through its capacity to manipulate and manage environments, including learning environments. In STEM, there are two components to the affordance of technology for learning that overlap. These are:

- Use of devices and customised tools, including computer programmes, that are specifically designed for developing practical applications in STEM (for example, computer science).
- Integration of ICT, visual and emerging technologies such as augmented reality (AR) and virtual reality (VR) that are inherent in the design of learning activities for enabling specific outcomes.

At the same time, technology is enabling education to become more accessible for more people through the huge increase in digital learning resources, objects and world wide web sources. Digital technologies enable students to connect, interact, track, share and build on previous knowledge in new ways, including transforming information to make it into something new; using or recombining ideas to solve a problem; linking previously unlinked information; and reflecting on ideas, processes and interconnections. Learning in HEIs has shifted to multimodal and hybrid versions of online support, with direct instruction through video and synchronous digital connections. We have been catapulted into this space by the 2020 COVID-19 outbreak with what amounts to a great pivot to online education.

The current generation of school leavers entering higher education have been exposed to a multitude of technologies and consequent representations of the world and, for this reason, have been called Net Gen (Koh, 2015). Engagement with anything digital means that they have grown up participating in more immersive and experiential ways of interacting with digital worlds. The global pandemic will further cement these experiences and expectations. This is in contrast to the more traditional, passive-recipient way of learning promoted by a didactic approach to teaching and learning in higher education. Net Gen are more accustomed to working socially, interactively and through networking where they can contribute short byte reactions. Undoubtedly, if student expectations (including learners in addition to Net Gen) have changed in orientation, then teaching and learning experiences should move to accommodate these changes. Students therefore expect there to be multiple digital channels using smart gadgets as part of learning in higher education (Koh, 2015).

In addition, Net Gen learners seem to have more capacity to connect ideas in multiple dimensions rather than just linearly (Prensky, 2005). Their ability to multitask and switch from one task to another, as well as their relative comfort with working in visually rich and virtual environments, tends to help them to be adept visual communicators (Oblinger & Oblinger, 2005). Learning experiences can accommodate visual aspects and utilise a range of sources that can be collected and re-synthesised by the students into something new. The ability to create new knowledge, as part of learning experiences, is a core skill to being innovative and so is crucial to advancing the applications and solutions arising from integrating STEM.

Online learning communities now abound. Ganascia (2015) indicates that the hyper-connectivity era into which we have entered means that it is possible, through networks and social media, to connect simultaneously with hundreds of people who live all around the world. This means we can share specialised information at high speed and access many brains within a network, giving us huge potential for knowledge creation, curation and connectivity. Utilising such networks will also advance capabilities and capacities for dissemination and peer review of STEM innovations.

The importance of technology use in STEM curriculum in HEIs is that it can help to develop knowledge and skills. In particular, data manipulation and the use of digital technologies will be extremely important and in-demand skills. Assessing digital skills may need to occur within contexts where they are required. It is important that technological skills are contextualised through being embedded appropriately within learning situations and specific contexts (Mishra & Koehler, 2006). Then, the use and assessment of technological skills, including digital literacy, become integral to enabling and advancing STEM knowledge, processes and systems. Some specific examples in STEM will be discussed next to provide more evidence of its importance.

Using specific technologies to develop STEM skills

Using specific technologies can enable more connected and sophisticated ways to learn that support students to gain specific STEM knowledge and skills. There is increasing access to a range of technological tools and digital applications for manipulating images, data, analysis and representation of concepts and processes (info graphics). Learners can use technologies to make meaning by using text, symbols, images and apps, and they are able to share and explain these experiences in a range of multimodal formats. Newer representations of information that use AI, AR, VR, mixed reality (XR) and 360° video are infusing learning systems and are being used for enhancing learning experiences through connected digital worlds (Southgate et al., 2016). While enhancement often arises from increased motivation of students, it is the quality of learning and the learning of transferable skills through the use of technologies that is important (Schrum, 2011).

The top ten digital technologies identified by New Media Consortium (2017) as most influencing higher education in the early 2020s were 3D printing, cloud computing (access and storage), digital games, learning analytics, mobile learning, massive open online courses (MOOCs), open content sources, augmented and virtual (wearable) reality and remote laboratories. For example, virtual laboratories have been used in universities in Bolivia (Vargas, 2020) to enable 3D problem-solving that integrates the use of differential equations, matrix algebra and physics.

The increased use of virtual simulations for scientific, technological and medical procedures is also helping to prepare students with practical skills through virtual practice. An example is in Thailand where students experimented on an olfactory system using simulations (Srisawasdi, 2012) and used statistical trends to draw conclusions and identify possible errors in hypothetical investigations. As a result of these activities, students also gained an appreciation of the interconnections between science, statistics and technology and the application to human health (Srisawasdi, 2012). Simulated practice may be safer when done digitally than with real objects. However, simulations should be considered as complementary to real experiments, rather than substitutes for them. There is huge scope to develop and use digital tools for supporting such context-based learning in the future.

As a result of these trends, new contexts for learning are emerging, particularly those inclusive of interdisciplinary approaches and the use of multiple technologies simultaneously. Of importance to the development of student outcomes is that multiple technologies can enable students to create and critically evaluate STEM content and to develop capabilities. The idea is that students are empowered when they are valued as creators and curators of new knowledge. Student views indicate that this approach influences their work life after graduation (New Media Consortium, 2017). The concept of students as co-creators of new knowledge is developed further in Chapter 7.

Using technology to support learning

There have been developments in pedagogy in higher education related to blended learning, and in particular to "flipping" models of content (Reidsema et al., 2017; Parappilly et al., 2019). Research indicates that when using blended or "flipped" approaches, there is a need for both faculty and student expectations to be clarified and understood. For example, a study of first-year biology students by Mackinven (2015) showed that blended learning provided benefits, such as supporting the visualisation of abstract biological processes (especially through animations and videos) and critical thinking. Unfortunately, students' lack of skills to be self-starting and their mismatch in expectations for teaching and learning, compared to lecturers' expectations, obviated the effectiveness of the "flipped" approach. Students did not value reading and analysing online materials prior to class. Mackinven's (2015) study concluded that faculty need to align learning activities and resources much more closely with purpose and make this alignment explicit to students. When there is not alignment between the use of technology and purpose, using technology can be a distraction (Hunter, 2015). Educators can also be supported through professional learning to implement questioning protocols, cues and prompts and to assist students in making more effective use of learning materials and out-of-class learning time. Please see Chapter 6 in this book for further discussion of professional learning opportunities.

At the Universidad Politécnica de Madrid, a "flipped" approach was used in engineering courses that considered the circular economy for environmental sustainability (Rodríguez-Chueca et al., 2019). As a consequence, class time was used to share and discuss the theoretical concepts that students studied outside of class time, using videos of the content posted online. These videos included information on industrial ecology, ecosystems, sustainable development, circular economy innovation and environmental management (Rodríguez-Chueca et al., 2019). In addition, scientific manuscripts and case studies were provided to students through a learning management system (LMS) for reading ahead of the discussion. Students were required to summarise ideas and have debates about them in groups during class time. Again, in this study, the approach was not as successful as hoped due to students' lack of readiness to be self-directed learners: they tended not to spend enough time reading the materials before class and exhibited low levels of creativity, teamwork and planning strategies in class. The implication is that educators may need support in designing and enabling changed learning environments, especially if they are new for students. For this reason, there is more detail about designing integrated learning experiences within supportive learning environments in Chapters 3 and 4.

Despite challenges, though, viewing technologies as tools that support and enable learning has become more prominent. In a report on the use of AI and emerging technologies in schools, Southgate et al. (2016) evaluated a range

32   *Role of technology in STEM*

of resources and modalities such as AI, VR and AR, haptics, tangibles (smart sensors that link to virtual objects for providing sensory feedback) and new video media. Haptics, as used to enhance other technologies, provided sensory feedback to mimic physical changes in the virtual environment. They are often used in medical simulation software to help medical students learn a procedure, such as feeling resistance when inserting a needle into a virtual arm (Xia & Sourin, 2012). These feedback responses help to create the feeling of being immersed in the situation through multi-sensory inputs.

Learning technologies can offer students the chance to experience more open-ended activities and potentially to develop multi-literacies, enabling students to co-generate knowledge through shared experiences in using technologies. A simple example is teaching students how to use Excel as a tool to support the recording and reporting of experimental outcomes. This approach enables students to collaboratively contribute to the data and to visualise trends in the data analysis. The inbuilt (potentially dynamic) functionality in Excel enables graphs to be generated much faster digitally than by hand with graph paper. There is no need for students to focus on tedious manual graphic processes that are no longer used by scientists, technologists, engineers or mathematicians. In this way, students' use of digital tools and visualisation of experimental results may reduce cognitive load and develop digital literacy and analysis skills simultaneously.

Technologies are making it easier for students to learn key concepts, connect ideas and perform tasks as part of developing capabilities, although the research evidence that identifies the affordances for learner outcomes and transfer of knowledge is still emergent (Schrum, 2011; Southgate et al., 2016). There is no doubt that the wealth of digital resources for higher education represent a huge opportunity to include content of very high quality (UNESCO, 2020). Networks can also assist students in connecting and collaborating through social media channels and video conferencing, an approach that enables globalisation and an expectation that higher education will equip students with the capabilities and competencies to contribute to issues of importance and, especially, to the UN Sustainable Development Goals (UNESCO, 2020). Some of the more emergent technologies have been applied in specific STEM learning contexts, as highlighted in the next section.

Using technology in specific STEM learning environments

This section discusses the application of technology within integrated STEM learning environments, including the use of emergent technologies for practical experiments, simulations and work-integrated learning experiences (WIL), AR, VR and serious gaming.

Practical experiments

In 2020, during COVID-19-related considerations for reducing face-to-face contact, a human physiology teaching team at Flinders University shifted their practical curriculum to the cloud and involved 475 students (nurses, medics and biologists) linked through the university's online LMS. The change shifted activities from being group-based to individual learning, but with online shared question and discussion spaces. Teaching included instructional videos on how students could collect their own physiological data and was complemented by a series of online lectures that were designed to help students analyse and interpret their own bio-data and then apply their understandings to other problems (that had data embedded for students to process). Helper videos showed students how experiments were performed and how data had been collected and could be used to inform decisions. Benefits of this shift to online instruction for remote data gathering and analysis could be seen in how well individual students engaged with the practical activities because the data was personally relevant. The importance of authentic learning contexts for integrating STEM is developed further in Chapter 3.

Simulations

Simulations are being used in specific STEM learning contexts, especially for systems modelling that cannot be replicated through practical experiments and for virtual WIL. In the compulsory sector, examples include Model-IT (Fretz et al., 2002), which enables an investigation of a model environmental system, and Virtual Solar System (Barab et al., 2000). These simulations helped students to identify key variables and relationships between variables in systems that were manipulated and tested through simulations (Tsurusaki et al., 2003).

Simulated practice with stakeholders is emerging for developing communication skills for a range of professional WIL experiences in higher education. Actors are often trained by tutors to record video situations, problems and issues to be used as part of these simulations. Large and small groups, in an online environment, discuss situations posed in the videos. In pairs, one student takes on the role of stakeholder, while the other interviews and seeks more information about the issue or project. They can record this process as a video session and gain feedback from each other on their approaches and communication skills using provided assessment rubrics. Self-assessment is very important in these simulated interactions with stakeholders, especially to build reflective skills and to take account of peer feedback as part of cyclical development as a professional. Students practise looking for non-verbal clues (as part of the video analysis) and can comment on how they responded to both verbal and non-verbal communication. Tutors can also provide written, audio and video feedback to students about aspects that need development and further ideas for enhancing communication skills.

Augmented reality

Augmented reality (AR) involves the layering of objects and information (voice threads and visual objects) on top of other objects. The value of AR as a visual

34   *Role of technology in STEM*

display for learning is that it can layer very complex ideas in 3D space that can change over time. For example, astronomers have been using innovative ways to share their knowledge about star cluster formations using AR. Taking inspiration from a magic trick, researchers from the University of Leeds use 3D holograms to help people learn about massive stars and star clusters that form before their eyes. This kind of visual representation helps to explain the complex phenomenon of star formation, making it much easier to understand. The teaching/research team at Leeds is developing a digital app for smart phones or tablets to provide learning experiences about astrophysics.

AR is also being used in a range of ways for teaching engineering. For example, Luwes and Van Heerden (2020) reported on how AR using smart phones is being used to teach complex threshold concepts in engineering, specifically for students to learn about digital logic gates and their applications in electrical engineering. Almost 90% of students in this study reported that they were more likely to remember and use logic gates following use of AR and, further, that they found this way of learning to be engaging (Luwes & Van Heerden, 2020).

In process engineering, computer images are generated as dynamic augmented visual models to show chemical changes in large batch industrial reactors. The ability to visualise changes in fluid dynamics using sensors and algorithms has huge applications in the industrial processing of food and pharmaceutical production (Koulountzios et al., 2019). Viewing what is happening inside industrial reactors and crystallisers during production can be used to teach about how important it is to monitor changes in products.

Virtual reality

Education that is fully immersed in a digital world can connect learners to a virtual environment in which learning can take place safely or in contexts that would not otherwise be possible for practising, collecting or measuring data. Virtual reality (VR) can provide experiences for practising skills that might be risky, expensive or dangerous, such as practising using heavy machinery, developing intricate technical or surgical skills and practising rescue missions that might be needed due to natural disasters.

Virtual fieldtrips can transport learners to places that are unsafe to travel, such as erupting volcanoes, coal mines and so on (see LEARNZ.org.nz). Simulations can also be created using VR, in which people can take a role using an avatar to undertake decision-making and simulate consequences. A collaborative problem-solving task called Tetralogue is designed to assess collaboration through a digital chat box, in which students discuss how they will make a forecast, based on data they collect in the virtual world, for a volcano eruption alert and at what level of activity the alert should be activated (Liu et al., 2016). In this example, paired student discussions were analysed using Amazon's Mechanical Turk to automatically evaluate students' collaboration in solving problems. It is likely there will be developments of additional analytic tools designed to log student interactions in virtual spaces and how students working in these environments are enabled to develop collaborative problem-solving.

The University of Leiden has set up a centre of research whose members investigate the didactic value of prototypes for VR and AR. VR can enable students to visit distant environments, create scenarios and measure objects using expensive equipment from the comfort of the classroom. For example, during environmental science classes, VR enabled students to be immersed in a lifelike virtual forest so they could experience and develop skills for collecting data remotely (Timmermans, 2019). In this small group of students, Timmermans (2019) found that the students were able to understand complex concepts faster by using the VR app for remote sensing than through more traditional ways of teaching and learning. Developments for more sophisticated skill development in remote sensing includes using combinations of technologies to monitor and make sense of environmental data inputs. These can include combinations of using drones with cameras and heat sensors, satellites, radar and computing to collect and analyse data about remote environments. Even so, the considerations and research on appropriate pedagogies for virtual learning are just beginning.

As virtual worlds become incorporated more into mainstream learning experiences, the types of activities, affordances and outcomes will need much more investigation (Bannan, 2015; Dalgano & Lee, 2010; Fowler, 2015). The importance of this growing field of virtual experience is exemplified by large investments of major technology and entertainment companies, including social media magnates. Although many uses of AI, AR, VR and XR will be apparent in entertainment, business, health care and the military, many devices and software will be developed and adapted for enhancing learning, for both formal and on-the-job learning or reskilling. For example, there has been an estimation (Goldman Sachs Group, 2016) that the market for head-mounted displays and associated software will be worth $80 US billion by 2025, with potentially 15 million users in educational contexts. Therefore, there will be a need for software and hardware developers and learning designers to address the support needed to implement these modes for learning as they become more prevalent.

Serious gaming

There is also an emergence of online gaming using concepts of discovery, innovation and reflection as learning experiences. Discovery involves learners being immersed in situations in which they explore possibilities and experience consequences of decision-making. For example, SimCity: Pollution Challenge (GlassLab, 2014) is a social geography online game for reducing pollution in pre-constructed cities. Success in this game is determined by those who can use green technologies and rezone areas within the cities, all the while supporting the city's growth, especially in employment. As students progress through the missions, they are introduced to themes of human impact leading to pollution,

36 Role of technology in STEM

as well as systems modelling. This technique for learning, serious gaming, could be extended to business developments that include blending disciplinary expertise in STEM to develop innovative business solutions that take humanistic and ethical aspects into account.

An example of serious gaming was applied through online crowd sourcing to understand the structure of protein folding in the HIV–AIDS virus. As reported by Buck (2013), student engagement in learning through gaming was linked to participants feeling positive emotions such as joy, relief, love, surprise, pride, curiosity, excitement, awe, wonder, contentment and creativity. When these emotions are "in play", they can counteract depression and support resilience and persistence to achieve, despite failure. Gaming can also be used as a strategic vehicle for inventing the future or trialling possible futures (Buck, 2013).

There is a move in the compulsory sector (in New Zealand) to encourage students to create games (Bolstad & McDowall, 2019), which is difficult, especially in generating choices, feedback response loops and alternatives. However, there is high interest in this pursuit, and gaming is likely to increase in its influence in digital learning environments. More game developers will be needed for developing games as learning tools.

Despite the positive experiences students have when playing games, Slota and Young (2017) caution us about the difficulties of demonstrating learning gains in students who play games. This is because gaming is a highly customised experience (even when played in teams). It is messy, with potentially alternative interpretations of players, even when they have the same sequence within a game. Instead of trying to analyse learning outcomes using conventional testing, they say gaming should be viewed more ecologically and target the player–game interactions and the skills that are developed through playing (Slota & Young, 2017). Like using other technological tools for learning in STEM, the use of serious gaming really needs to be aligned with whether participation enables the desired learning outcomes, as elaborated on in the next section.

Aligning learning goals, technologies and pedagogies

Using technologies for enabling learning in STEM involves more than just using tools. It also requires educators to think deeply about the purpose of using technology and then appropriating pedagogies they use to support the conversion of learning goals to learning outcomes. Some examples of how technologies can be used for enabling the development of transferable skills are provided in Table 2.1. The pedagogies associated with developing these skills when using technologies are also indicated in Table 2.1. These pedagogies are very important, as they contribute to creating a learning environment that supports student learning gains, as emphasised in Chapter 3, that move beyond just using technological "tools".

Role of technology in STEM 37

Table 2.1 Examples of enabling technologies for learning in STEM

Learning goals	Enabling technology	Associated pedagogy
Collaboration and communication	Learning management system (LMS), video conferencing, chats, instant text messaging, polling tools.	Explores knowledge as contestable, bounded, partial and contextual. Uses substantive and sustained dialogue and educator uses examples to model critical/creative thinking. Highlights connections between ideas and processes, Provides structured support using questions, prompts and feedback, Ensures there is a rotation process as to who provides the small group feedback to the larger group (online), Promotes collaboration and clear communication that is valued in assessments,
Problem Solving • Individual • Peers • Groups	LMS, creative apps for brainstorming, wikis, Padlet, eportfolios, digital search engines, data analysis software, presentation software, photos, interactive digital objects, interactive videos, AR, VR, XR, serious gaming.	Guides development of disciplinary foundations and processes for problem-solving. Assists students to build on prior knowledge and skills. Provides support for students to make links between ideas and testing solutions. Explores knowledge as contestable, bounded, partial and contextual.
Inquiry • Individual • Peers • Groups	LMS, inspiration tools for brainstorming, wikis, project management tools (e.g. Trello®), online survey tools, eportfolios, digital search engines, data analysis, presentation software, photos, videos, audio files for interviews with stakeholders.	Assists students to build on prior knowledge and skills. Supports development of deep contextual knowledge and specific information technology skills. Highlights connections between ideas and processes. Provides students with choice and responsibility for their own learning, leading to graduated autonomy. Includes structured support, for example, questions as prompts and clear chunking of tasks.

(*Continued*)

38 Role of technology in STEM

Table 2.1 (Continued)

Learning goals	Enabling technology	Associated pedagogy
Design or process Developing creative thinking and innovation Including simulation	Design software, ideation processes, digital hackathons, computerised adaptive testing, polling tools, LMS, video conferencing, audio capture, animations, videos, branching scenarios, serious gaming, 360° video, AR/VR/ MR/XR, interactive digital objects, data analysis, data visualisation programmes and apps.	Stimulates creative thinking and risk taking. Enables reflection on professional behaviours. Allows for co-construction. Enables structured peer review and evaluation that is embedded in tasks.
Case-based Evaluation • Individual • Peer–peer	LMS, interactive platforms, data bases, sequencing programmes, data analysis, simulations and visualisations, wikis, blogs, vlogs, eportfolios, presentation software, photos, videos, interactive videos (e.g. H5P).	Assists students to build on prior knowledge and skills. Provides clear instructions and feedback. Provides access to statistical tools.
Ethical thinking	Tools for linking ideas, simulations.	Discusses positive and negative ethical dimensions related to STEM. Considers social impact of STEM. Considers environmental impact of STEM.

Choosing appropriate technology and pedagogies to support desired learning outcomes is very important and has been called technological, pedagogical and content knowledge (TPACK) (Mishra & Koehler, 2006). The TPACK concept and its applications are important for designing activities because all of the sub-components of TPACK need to work together to ensure that the purpose and use of technologies coalesce synergistically. Effective use of technologies for learning relates to applying technologies appropriately for more effective or creative outcomes (Hunter, 2015; Mishra & Koehler, 2006). For example, it is important to use technologies that enable students to collaborate if the transferable skill desired is the ability to work with others.

Taking this a step further, it can be challenging to teach using digital platforms when there is a large number of students in a class, especially as it is very difficult to see and gauge reactions while teaching in online environments. To get around this to some extent, students can be asked to use a status indicator in a video conferencing tool, such as Collaborate, as a quick way to provide instant feedback on whether the session was going too fast, too slow or just right. Other solutions include dividing a class into chat groups (six to eight students), to set up separate group (video conferencing) sessions and to allow groups to have alternative means of communicating through video conferencing apps of their choice. One of the issues of using team-based learning online may be in engaging quieter students and enticing them to contribute, especially when there are large groups. To help to distribute engagement, educators can require each group to rotate which person in the group provides a group response to the class. This tends to foster accountability, collaboration and communication skills.

There is a need to provide much more professional learning for educators in relation to how they align pedagogies (what they do to support learning) with the use of specific technologies for developing student learning outcomes (Kirkwood & Price, 2014). HEIs have the technologies to provide very rich, interactive and creative learning experiences (Picciano, 2017), as explored in this chapter. More research on the benefits of using technologies for learning is warranted since the use of technologies for learning in STEM contexts is still emergent.

Conclusion

This chapter discussed the role of technology in STEM, particularly how technology can assist in solving significant problems locally and globally. Design and technology processes are crucial for the innovation that is so essential for social and economic advances. Technological tools can support the creation of new knowledge, new products and processes that can enhance living and create employment. Technology helps our knowledge and understanding to grow, especially as more sophisticated digital technologies are used to view, design, gather data, refine and evaluate techniques and so on.

Because of the importance of technology, particularly AI, for supporting more efficient and effective systems (e.g. growing food, disposing of waste, organising traffic for less carbon emission), the links between the design of learning activities or experiences and the use of technology and creating innovative solutions must be integrated into problem-solving in STEM. As such, technology acts as an integrator between the sciences, mathematics and engineering. A wide range of examples were given in this chapter to support this idea.

Providing and designing contexts for learning in STEM would be difficult if technology was not a core element. Digital sources of information and software have the capacity to support learning through a range of tools and experiences that are moving into immersive worlds. Siemens (2005) was clear that students need to be provided with experiences that help them not only to understand knowledge but to create new knowledge as well. In the current

40 *Role of technology in STEM*

age of information ubiquity, knowing *what* and *how*, is being replaced with knowing *where* to find and *connect* information (resource foraging and curation of knowledge sources). Assessment practices related to capturing learner behaviour while participating in digital tasks is also expanding, as assessments become more adaptive and are provided digitally (Agard & von Davier, 2018). Since learning technologies are continually evolving, there is no single technology for advancing learning, but rather a huge growth in the development of technologies to support multiple modes for learning.

Given that multiple modalities for teaching and learning are emergent in higher education, students need to be confident with using technologies to be successful in applying them to their learning in STEM and to their future careers. There are a range of ways of using learning technologies that span drill and practise memorisation to authentic, high-interest, adaptive gaming and immersive VR technologies (Southgate et al., 2016). As growing, emerging academics, technical experts and professionals, students need to be able to read, synthesise, curate, create and perform a range of skills in a variety of contexts for different purposes and audiences. Research from the learning sciences indicates that using multiple modalities can enhance student learning outcomes (Southgate et al., 2016).

Any use of technology must enable students to meet desired learning outcomes. This also requires considering the types of pedagogies (what educators do) to support students, as indicated in Table 2.1. However, since many technologies and software are new to the higher education sector, often their use is preliminary, experimental and not proven as being effective. Student satisfaction surveys are also revealing gaps in the support provided by their teachers, the lack of development of pedagogies appropriate for applying the technology and the need for greater understanding about how the use of technological tools actually enhances learning outcomes more directly. The effectiveness of any technology for learning depends on how it is used, how tools are appropriated to specific learning contexts (Owusu et al., 2015) and particularly how technologies help to address the needs and characteristics of each learner (National Academies of Sciences, Engineering and Medicine, 2018). Ongoing research on the effectiveness of using technologies for enhancing learning is needed. There will be a growth in jobs related to designing technological tools for learning and especially for learning how to use a range of technologies that are becoming increasingly essential for solving problems in STEM contexts.

References

Agard, C., & von Davier, A. A. (2018). The virtual world and reality of testing. In H. Jiao & R. W. Lissitz (Eds.), *Technology enhanced innovative assessment: Development, modelling and scoring from an interdisciplinary perspective.* IAP.

Aydin, C., Woge, M. G., & Verbeek, P. P. (2018–2019). Technological environmentality: Conceptualizing technology as a mediating milieu. *Philosophy & Technology, 32*, 321–338. https://doi.org/10.1007/s13347-018-0309-3

Bannan, K. (2015). Is virtual reality for everyone? *Edtech Magazine.* https://edtechmagazine. com/higher/article/2015/08/virtual-reality-everyone

Barab, S. A., Hay, K. E., Squire, K., Barnett, M., Schmidt, R., Karrigan, K., Yamagata-Lynch, I., & Johnson, J. (2000). Virtual solar system project: Learning through a technology-rich, inquiry-based, participatory learning environment. *Journal of Science Education and Technology, 9*(1), 7–25.

Bell, D., Wooff, D., McLain, M., & Morrison-Love, D. (2017). Analysing design and technology as an educational construct: An investigation into its curriculum position and pedagogical identity. *Curriculum Journal, 28*(4), 539–558. http://doi.org/10.1080/09585 176.2017.1286995

Bolstad, R., & McDowall, S. (2019). *Games, gamification, and game design for learning innovative practice and possibilities in New Zealand schools.* NZCER Press.

Buck, T. (2013). The awesome power of gaming in higher education. *EdTech Focus on Higher Education.* https://edtechmagazine.com/higher/article/2013/10/awesome-power-gam ing-higher-education

Clark, S. A., & Jackson, D. F. (1998). *Laboratory technology and student motivation in a conceptual physics classroom: A year-long case study.* Paper presented at the Annual Meeting of the National Association for Research in Science Teaching, San Diego, CA.

Dalgano, B., & Lee, M. J. (2010). What are the learning affordances of 3-D virtual environments? *British Journal of Educational Technology, 42*(1), 10–32.

DeFilippis, E., Impink, S. M., Singell, M., Polzer, J. T., & Sadun, R. (2020). *Collaborating during coronavirus: The impact of COVID-19 on the nature of work.* www.nber.org/papers/ w27612

Flinders University. (2020). *Brave minds.* www.flinders.edu.au/braveminds/5-revolutionary-medical-technologies-changing-lives

Floridi, L. (2015). *The onlife manifesto: Being human in a hyperconnected era.* Springer Open.

Fowler, C. (2015). Virtual reality and learning: Where is the pedagogy? *British Journal of Educational Technology, 46*(2), 412–422.

Freidler, Y., Nachmias, R., & Songer, N. (1989). Teaching scientific reasoning skills: A case study of a microcomputer-based curriculum. *School Science and Mathematics, 89*(1), 272–284.

Fretz, E. B., Wu, H., Zhang, B., Davis, E. A., Krajcik, J. S., & Soloway, E. (2002). An investigation of software scaffolds supporting modelling practices. *Research in Science Education, 32*(4), 567–589.

Ganascia, J. G. (2015). Views and examples of hyper-connectivity. In L. Floridi (Ed.), *The onlife manifesto: Being human in a hyperconnected era* (pp. 65–85). Springer Open. http://doi. org/10.1007/978-3-319-04093-6_13

GlassLab. (2014). *SimCity: Pollution challenge.* www.gamesforchange.org/game/simcityedu-pollution-challenge/

Goldman Sachs Group. (2016). *Virtual and augmented reality: Understanding the race for the next computing platform.* www.golmansachs.com/our-thinking/pages/technology-driving-innovation-folder/virtual-and-augmented-reality/report.pdf

Hunter, J. (2015). *Technology integration and high possibility classrooms: Building from TPACK.* Routledge.

Ihde, D. (1990). *Technology and the lifeworld: From garden to earth.* Indiana University Press.

Kirkwood, A., & Price, L. (2014). Technology-enhanced learning and teaching in higher education: What is "enhanced" and how do we know? A critical literature review. *Learning, Media and Technology, 39*(1), 6–36. http://doi.org/10.1080/17439884.2013.770404

42 Role of technology in STEM

Koh, C. (2015). Understanding and facilitating learning for the net generation and twenty-first-century learners through motivation, leadership and curriculum design. In C. Koh (Ed.), *Motivation, leadership and curriculum design: Engaging the net generation and twenty-first century learners* (pp. 1–12). Springer.

Koulountzios, P., Rymarczyk, T., & Soleimani, M. (2019). A quantitative ultrasonic travel-time tomography to investigate liquid elaborations in industrial processes. *Sensors, 19*(23), 5117. http://doi.org/10.3390/s19235117

Krusberg, Z. A. C. (2007). Emerging technologies in physics education. *Journal of Science Education and Technology, 16*(5), 401–411.

Liu, L., Hao, J., von Davier, A. A., Kyllonen, P., & Zapata-Rivera, J. D. (2016). A tough nut to crack: Measuring collaborative problem-solving. In Y. Rosen, S. Ferrara, & M. Mosharraf (Eds.), *Handbook of research on computational tools for real-world skill development.* IGI-Global.

Luwes, N., & Van Heerden, L. (2020). *Augmented reality to aid retention in an African university of technology engineering program.* Paper presented at the 6th International Conference on Higher Education Advances (HEAd'20). Universitat Politècnica de València. http://doi.org/10.4995/HEAd20.2020.11103

Mackinven, K. (2015). *Blended learning in tertiary education: A science perspective* [Unpublished MEd thesis]. University of Canterbury.

Mishra, P., & Koehler, M. J. (2006). Technological pedagogical content knowledge: A framework for teacher knowledge. *Teachers College Record, 108*(6), 1017–1054. http://punya.educ.msu.edu/publications/journal_articles/mishra-koehlertcr2006.pdf

National Academies of Sciences, Engineering and Medicine. (2018). *How people learn II: Learners, contexts and cultures.* The National Academies Press.

New Media Consortium. (2017). *Digital literacy in higher education, part II: An NMC horizon project strategic brief.* https://library.educause.edu/resources/2017/8/digital-literacy-in-higher-education-part-ii-an-nmc-horizon-project-strategic-brief

Oblinger, D., & Oblinger, J. (2005). Is it age or IT: First steps toward understanding the net generation. In D. G. Oblinger & J. L. Oblinger (Eds.), *Educating the net generation* (pp. 2.1–2.20). EDUCAUSE. www.educause.edu/educatingthenetgen/

Owusu, K., Conner, L., & Astall, C. (2015). Contextual influences on science teachers' TPACK levels. In M. Niess & H. Gillow-Wiles (Eds.), *Handbook of research on teacher education in the digital age* (pp. 307–333). IGI Global.

Parappilly, M., Woodman, R., & Randhawa, S. (2019). Feasibility and effectiveness of different models of team-based learning approaches in STEMM-based disciplines. *Research in Science Education.* https://doi.org/10.1007/s11165-019-09888-8

Picciano, A. G. (2017). Theories and frameworks for online education: Seeking an integrated model. *Online Learning Journal, 21*(3), 166–190. http://doi.org/10.24059/olj.v21i3.1225

Prensky, M. (2005). Listen to the natives. *Educational Leadership, 63*(4), 8–13.

Quellmalz, E. S., & Silbertglitt, M. D. (2018). SimScientists: Affordances of science simulations for formative and summative assessment. In H. Jiao & R. W. Lissitz (Eds.), *Technology enhanced innovative assessment: Development, modelling and scoring from an interdisciplinary perspective* (pp. 71–94). IAP.

Reidsema, C., Kavanagh, L., Hadgraft, R., & Smith, N. (2017). *The flipped classroom: Practice and practices in higher education.* Springer.

Rodríguez-Chueca, J., Molina-García, A., García-Aranda, C., Pérez, J., & Rodríguez, E. (2019). Understanding sustainability and the circular economy through flipped classroom and challenge-based learning: An innovative experience in engineering education in Spain. *Environmental Education Research, 26*(2), 238–252. http://doi.org/10.1080/1350 4622.2019.1705965

Schrum, L. (2011). Revisioning a proactive approach to an educational technology research agenda. In L. Schrum (Ed.), *Considerations on educational technology integration: The best of JRTE* (pp. 1–8). International Society for Technology in Education.

Siemens, G. (2005). Connectivism: A knowledge learning theory for the digital age. *International Journal of Instructional Technology and Distance Learning, 2*, 1–8. https://lidtfoundations.pressbooks.com/chapter/connectivism-a-learning-theory-for-the-digital-age/

Slota, S. T., & Young, M. E. (2017). The inevitability of epic fail: Exploding the castle with situated learning. In M. Young & S. Slota (Eds.), *Exploding the castle: Rethinking how video games and game mechanics can shape the future of education* (pp. 271–284). Information Age Publishing.

Songer, N. B. (1998). Can technology bring students closer to science? In B. J. Fraser & K. G. Tobin (Eds.), *International handbook of science education* (pp. 333–347). Kluwer.

Southgate, E., Smith, S. P., & Cheers, H. (2016). *Immersed in the future: A roadmap of existing and emerging technology for career exploration.* DICE Research. http://dice.newcastle.edu.au/DRS_3_2016.pdf

Srisawasdi, N. (2012). Introducing students to authentic inquiry investigation using an artificial olfactory system. In K. Chwee, D. Tan, & M. Kim (Eds.), *Issues and challenges in science education research* (pp. 93–106). Springer.

Timmermans, J. (2019). *This is how virtual reality brings education to the next level.* www.universiteitleiden.nl/en/news/2019/12/this-is-how-virtual-reality-brings-education-to-the-next-level

Tsurusaki, B., Amiel, T., & Hay, K. (2003). Using modelling-based inquiry in the virtual solar system. In D. Lassner & C. McNaught (Eds.), *Proceedings of EdMedia: World conference on educational media and technology* (pp. 2237–2240). Association for the Advancement of Computing in Education (AACE).

UNESCO. (2020). *Digital higher education.* https://en.unesco.org/themes/higher-education/digital

United Nations. (2020). *The sustainable development goals: Our framework for COVID-19 recovery.* www.un.org/sustainabledevelopment/sdgs-framework-for-covid-19-recovery

Vargas, F. (2020). Virtual laboratories as strategy for teaching improvement in math, sciences and engineering in Bolivia. *International Journal of Engineering Education, 2*(1), 52–62.

Walsh, T. (2018). *Machines that think: The future of artificial intelligence.* Prometheus Books.

World Economic Forum. (2019). *These are the World Economic Forum's technology pioneers of 2019.* www.weforum.org/agenda/2019/07/meet-the-tech-pioneers-at-the-vanguard-of-science-and-innovation

Xia, P., & Sourin, A. (2012). Design and implementation of a haptics-based virtual venepuncture simulation and training system. In *Proceedings of the 11th ACM SIGGRAPH international conference on virtual reality continuum and its application in industry* (pp. 25–30). ACM Press.

3 Developing a pedagogical framework for STEM

Introduction

Higher education institutions (HEIs) are essential for making broad educational changes in STEM education because HEIs provide knowledge, create new knowledge and enculturate students into careers through providing exemplars and applications to practice. Coursework contributes knowledge by using recent developments and new perspectives on how theories and practices can be applied to problem-solving. More importantly, HEIs can endorse and support the relevance and value of new forms of knowledge. This includes being clearer about how knowledge sources overlap and combine, since more and more emphasis is being placed on the efficacy and benefits of joining up information for creating meaning, developing capabilities, applying learning in practice to real situations and enhancing life experiences.

HEIs play a key role in preparing graduates for developing the types of thinking they will need to create the new knowledge and innovation essential for solving humanity's issues. Integrating disciplinary knowledge and approaches to learning contributes to this preparation (Feldon et al., 2013).

Future graduates, as citizens of the world, will need to be competent in constructing their futures and fortunes. While HEIs have been in the business of creating new knowledge through research for undergraduates, especially in apprenticeship models (e.g. Gentile et al., 2017), more attention must be paid to design and innovation for STEM coursework to develop interdisciplinary understanding and to create new knowledge and products as solutions to issues or problems. An emphasis on creating humanistic solutions must be high on the agenda in HEIs for developing new courses. However, issues and their solutions are not bounded by disciplines, so we need to consider what and how knowledge and processes can be integrated.

Each academic STEM discipline has its own constructs of knowledge, with associated academic language and key processes underpinning each discipline's philosophy (Goldman et al., 2016; National Research Council, 2005, 2007). More recently, boundaries between disciplines have been blurred, especially when using inquiry and problem-solving in authentic, real-world themes

Developing a pedagogical framework 45

and contexts. This blurring has led to a greater emphasis on interdisciplinary understanding, which has been described as

> that capacity to integrate knowledge and modes of thinking in two or more disciplines or established areas of expertise to produce a cognitive advancement – such as explaining a phenomenon, solving a problem, or creating a product – in ways that would have been impossible or unlikely through single disciplinary means.
>
> (Boix Mansilla & Duraising, 2007, p. 219)

The connections between concepts, processes and methods enrich how learners use multiple lenses to view themes, problems, issues and challenges. Nissani (1995) extended the idea of integrated curriculum to include a range of levels of richness that depend on the extent of integration. Any richness depends on how well concepts and methodologies are blended, how many disciplines are involved, the novelty of combining specific disciplines and what is actually integrated. Therefore, it is important to begin this chapter with the characteristics of STEM disciplines that lend them to being integrated.

In STEM coursework, the intention to integrate disciplines, processes and transferable skills must build on the interconnectedness present in the current world in which students live (Schneider et al., 2019), often called authentic contexts (Conner, 2020). The skills and processes students learn while participating in problem-solving, inquiry approaches, challenges and design thinking help to develop skills and capabilities identified by employers as essential for employment (Rios et al., 2020), particularly in communication and collaboration. Interdisciplinary approaches can support development of synthesising, thinking critically and creatively and making complex ideas more visible and understandable (Boix Mansilla, 2010; Repko et al., 2014), but only if teaching and learning promote thinking. Active engagement by learners, that is, engaging minds to think and develop their autonomy as learners, should be an inherent part of any undergraduate learning experience (Davis et al., 2008). For this reason, active learning approaches, rather than content-centred and direct instruction, are discussed in this chapter.

An integrated approach to STEM entails combining content and capabilities so they are integrally embedded (or integrated) and assessed. In contrast to planning by courses, curriculum integration in STEM can take a variety of forms, from coherent alignment with professional standards through to highly complex collaborations within interdisciplinary teams, creating new knowledge, innovations, processes and products. A key part of designing an integrated curriculum is to start with what needs to be assessed in mind and with a learning environment that supports student success.

For over 20 years, there has been a growing body of research evidence on STEM integration in the compulsory sector, into which STEM has been integrated more widely than in the higher education sector. Questions around the

46 *Developing a pedagogical framework*

"how" of integrating STEM disciplines has been of great interest. This chapter uses some of that evidence, along with examples from the higher education sector, to provide insights into what works and why. First, the characteristics of disciplines that enable integration are discussed. Then, a range of factors that can be considered for effective integration of STEM for addressing global issues are provided, including the importance of authentic learning contexts, driving innovation, students' active engagement in learning and the creation of learning environments that support development of transferable skills. A synthesis of literature is provided, culminating in a pedagogical framework for integrating STEM in coursework in higher education. The benefit of interdisciplinary understanding in STEM is that it enables students to identify broader patterns and connections across and within STEM that go beyond how separate disciplines could by themselves contribute to solutions (Conner, 2020).

Characteristics of STEM disciplines

An integrated approach to STEM does not negate the value of separate disciplinary knowledge and epistemologies but rather seeks to use authentic contexts and applications of complementary and multiple sources of knowledge in tandem. Strober (2011) indicated that activities that integrate STEM can coexist with separate disciplinary models of teaching and learning. That is, interdisciplinary approaches and pedagogies focussed on in this book can be complementary to individual disciplinary approaches, rather than substituting for them.

To integrate disciplines effectively, there needs to be a consideration of the prevailing practices and ways of thinking that are discipline-specific and of those that cut across STEM disciplines. In addition, all STEM disciplines can contribute to problem-solving for humanistic solutions. The applications of different forms of knowledge also influence what is included in integrated learning experiences. These are discussed in more detail in the three subsections that follow.

Prevailing practices and ways of thinking

STEM disciplines have characteristic ways of thinking; beliefs about the nature of knowledge; specific language and concepts; forms of representing knowledge; specific research practices; and methods of inquiry and discourses (Goldman et al., 2016). They may differ in their use of logic, observation and evidence, such as privileging either inductive (data-driven) or deductive (theory-driven) approaches to reasoning (Bauer, 1992). For example, science uses empirical evidence and logical inference to explain ideas, phenomena and processes in the natural world. In science, replicability determines quality, and often the aim is for parsimony, so that an empirically supported theory can simply explain the widest range of instances of a phenomenon (Blackburn, 1999). Engineering also makes use of empirical evidence leading to logical

Developing a pedagogical framework   47

inferences, striving to find solutions within constraints of reliability, cost and speed (Koen, 1985). In engineering, designed solutions are often specific to the context and connected to a range of acceptable parameters that are required to determine failure rates (Kroes, 2012). Such an approach does not scientifically validate cause-and-effect relationships but instead can provide validation of a function or product that signifies an endpoint for an engineering specification, with limitations.

Across the STEM disciplines, there are many overlaps, connections and dependencies. For example, science and technology are connected to one another, in that advances in technological capabilities enable scientists to investigate phenomena and uncover details that were previously inaccessible, and advances in science contribute to new technological innovation. Please see Chapter 2 in this book for more detail on the role of technology in STEM.

Disciplines have cross-cutting concepts

There are cross-cutting concepts that enable people to interpret, relate and extend specific concepts across multiple fields of study (National Academies, 2012). For example, in the Next Generation Science Standards for compulsory schooling in the USA (Next Generation Science Standards, 2013, p. 3), examples of cross-cutting concepts include patterns, cause and effect, scale, proportion and quantity, systems and system models, energy and matter: flows, cycles and conservation, structure and function, stability and change. Examples of science, technology and engineering practices include asking questions, developing and using models, planning and carrying out investigations, analysing and interpreting data, using mathematics and computational thinking, constructing explanations (for science) and designing solutions (for technology and engineering), engaging in argument from evidence and obtaining, evaluating and communicating information (p. 3).

It is highly likely that cross-cutting concepts, such as those identified by the Next Generation Science Standards, could be reinforced through elaborative interrogation techniques, in which students are prompted to ask themselves questions that invoke deep reasoning, such as why, how and what-if (Gholson et al., 2009). Self-explanation of steps in the problem-solving process may include students responding to open-ended prompts to generate their reasoning capabilities (National Academies of Sciences, Engineering and Medicine, 2018).

There are also common practices within the disciplines that contribute to STEM. For example, mathematical concepts and processes, and indeed the data sciences more generally, can be applied to all fields of science, technology and engineering. Using data is potentially the most promising focus for integrating STEM disciplines (Czerniak, 2007). Interestingly, Pang and Good (2000) found that mathematics was often integrated with science, but commonly as an adjunct to science content. While science and mathematics share common

48 *Developing a pedagogical framework*

aspects for problem-solving, purposeful integration of the disciplines of science and mathematics is relatively rare (Bush & Cook, 2019).

A likely trend is that computational thinking and the application and use of data will become a key digital capability (Wing, 2011). This will be because there is high demand for people who can use computations and digital visual representations to solve problems (Brunetto et al., 2020; The Royal Society, 2011). Computational thinking has been aided by the ubiquity of digital devices that can assist in understanding science and technologies by providing access to data analysis with a virtual flick of a finger. Even though computational thinking is closely linked with computer science, it should be considered as separate from it (Mishra et al., 2013). Computer science involves programming, hardware design, networks, graphics, data bases and information retrieval, computer security, software design, programming languages, logic, artificial intelligence, limits of computations, applications of information systems and social issues (internet security, privacy and so on). In contrast, computational thinking involves problem-solving using algorithms, switching between abstract and tangible concepts, analysis and debugging. Computational thinking has been summarised as a way to systematically process information and tasks (Voogt et al., 2015).

Bundy (2007) argued that computational thinking is important for every discipline, as it is part of problem-solving. The National Research Council (2010) suggested that everyone should learn to think and understand how to use data and equations to help solve problems, create new innovations through abstractions, consider layers within systems, evaluate the consequences of scale of changes over time and come up with new questions to be explored. In this way, computational thinking is regarded as being important for creativity (Mishra et al., 2013), in that it not only enables students to be consumers of technologies and evaluate claims but also supports the creation of new technologies and processes. It is likely that data sciences and computational thinking skills are the integrating "glue" that can connect STEM disciplines.

There are many examples of the application of computational thinking in higher education learning contexts. One is where computations have been applied to the study of landforms. Geographic information technologies (for example Google Earth, Adobe Acrobat Reader and image viewers) can be used to develop 3D, photorealistic images of landforms using photogrammetric techniques that can be viewed in stereoscopic mode, offering new opportunities in geology and geography education (Sanchez, 2009). Another example is in the emerging field of robotic psychology (companion robots), which calls on combinations of computations related to behavioural responses, AI and synthetic sensory feedback systems (Libin & Libin, 2004). In chemical engineering, operations, reactors, fluid mechanics, process control and optimisation rely on analysing the effect of changing variables, modelling and software to help solve problems.

Often visualisations and graphic representations are used to show applications and to integrate knowledge sources, as seen in real-time sports events (for example in the America's Cup) and in reporting comparisons of COVID-19 outbreaks. Understanding how phenomena are represented using data and analysis is important, especially for visualising how changes in variables or inputs alter these representations. Many applications occur as integrated approaches, for example in multiple applications in astronomy (e.g. *The Atlas of Moons*, National Geographic, 2019), environmental monitoring (*Drowning in Plastic*, Reuters Graphic, 2019) and agriculture, forestry and horticulture, where growth, soil water and deforestation can be monitored over time and data captured by geospatial positioning systems of these environmental changes are represented visually over time. These examples show how computations provide information that can be transformed using digital imaging (technologies that use interactive software applications) to support problem-solving and decision-making.

Digital and visual applications of processes can also support the creation of "new" knowledge and artefacts. Such tools are evolving quickly in the form of apps and simulations, with great promise for how students transfer ideas to create entrepreneurial opportunities. Potentially, blending of human intuition and creativity with computing (in STEM contexts) will support future human endeavours (Mishra et al., 2013), including learners creating their own future employment.

Disciplines have applications

Application in education involves taking knowledge out of its setting and making it work beyond that setting, translating ideas and concepts into actual or simulated practice. The process of applying knowledge and skills requires transferring knowledge and skills from one context (or situation) to another in order to transform, reinvent or retest validity of inferences. Application of knowledge and skills to the real world is what confers authenticity (rather than memorising discrete facts and abstract theories). Transfer may be cued (such as "use Boyle's Law to explain . . .") or accomplished through questioning or by relying on students to make their own connections using prior knowledge and skills. As such, transfer and application are crucial for the adaption and adoption of ideas and practices and for innovation more generally.

The challenge in creating authentic learning experience is in planning for how students will develop their knowledge and skills simultaneously, as they deliberately make connections between disciplines and between disciplines and skills within situated learning experiences (activities that solve real problems) (Putnam & Borko, 2000). Such planning may require letting go of some prescribed disciplinary-specific content. Educators can guide students regarding transferring or applying particular ways of thinking. For example, design thinking in engineering can be applied to a range of innovation contexts. Transfer of types of thinking can be assisted by prompting students to recall a previous use of a thinking process. Application of specific content knowledge and skills to new contexts, often through discussion, becomes critical for developing

50 *Developing a pedagogical framework*

students' deeper understanding of the importance of connecting ideas and processes. Then understanding (rather than recalling facts) is what becomes valued through applying knowledge and skills within an inquiry, problem-solving, a challenge or a work experience (Comer & Brogt, 2010). Educators who plan with this in mind tune the learner into the distinctions between concepts and theoretical ideas; between transferability and appropriateness of processes for learning and thinking; and in terms of how to apply learning skills in practice. This shift in focus, away from just imparting facts, is core to the integration of STEM and requires educators to think about their pedagogies very carefully. The need for professional learning for appropriating pedagogy to new ways for learning is discussed in Chapter 6.

Also important is that educators provide specific questions and activities to enable students to transfer knowledge and skills, simulating contexts as proxies for workplaces and requiring students to discern when it is appropriate to generalise. The reverse is also true, in which a general case or practice might be given and students have to come up with specific examples to illustrate the concept or phenomenon. By applying knowledge and skills to a problem or issue, learners can purposefully develop new concepts and new procedures and create innovative artefacts or processes.

Within any group of learners, there will be a range of experiences, prior knowledge and skill sets. Individuals interpret instructions and cues differently depending on prior experience and level of attainment. Therefore, educators cannot assume students have a grasp of the important concepts, processes and skills that can be applied to different contexts. Students may need structured support to make connections and to apply concepts and skills appropriately.

Importance of authenticity

John Dewey (1938) was an advocate of the view that education should be grounded in experience, so that students could connect meaningfully with content rather than using disciplinary inventories that educators have imposed on them, as if there were a bucket of information to be learned. Since then, more authentic approaches to education have evolved as an alternative to didactic approaches that are more teacher-directed and content-centric. Authentic experiences for learning embody relevance and timeliness of introducing content, processes and skills by linking with real-world examples that matter to students. In authentic learning contexts, there are positive learning effects when interest in the subject matter is high, and for some students, this contributes to persistence and better performance (Brown et al., 1989; Conner, 2014; Linnenbrink-Garcia & Patall, 2016).

During the 20th century, there were many attempts to realise the benefits of authentic learning that connected with student interest. For example, Kilpatrick advocated for project-based learning in which students undertook projects of value to them and that helped to determine their own learning processes and outcomes (Kilpatrick, 1918). Pedagogies used in higher education have not

Developing a pedagogical framework 51

always appreciated the importance of linking with student interest and prior understanding.

Constructivism, as a learning theory, promotes the importance of connecting to prior knowledge to help make sense of new knowledge, which can be declarative, procedural or conditional forms of knowledge (Conner, 2014). This requires prior knowledge to be revealed. After all, advancing learning can't be designed if what students know already is unknown. Comprehension, understanding and transfer require linking ideas, analysis, logical sequencing and evaluation of evidence. Learning in this conception is active meaning-making through processing information, rather than just memorising facts. Students may not do this for themselves unless they have had some guidance and have a chance to self-assess their knowledge and skills through actively thinking for themselves, or with others, including reflection on their experiences (Kolb, 2015).

Authentic (relevant) themes are those that are useful and inventive or that matter because they are socially relevant and important in current times. When knowledge is embedded within a theme or context that is relevant to students, learning is more meaningful because of its direct application to understanding (Brown et al., 1989). Zeidler (2016) indicated that it is fundamentally important for students to be able to learn in STEM through personally relevant themes or contexts, because these enable students to take on more humanistic perspectives, potentially leading to contributions to their future lives and their world. As such, interdisciplinary approaches that support situated, immersive and personally meaningful content have been shown to engender student interest and therefore motivation (Barab & Landa, 1997) and willingness to invest energy to stretch their learning (Conner, 2014).

In support of this idea, Biggs (2003) stated in relation to learners in universities:

> With a history of successful engagement with content that is personally meaningful, the student both builds up the knowledge base needed for deep learning and, motivationally, develops the expectations that give confidence in future success.
>
> (p. 59)

An integrated approach plans for teaching in and by use of themes, contexts, projects, issues and challenges. Such approaches to curriculum design have been implemented in the compulsory education sector for some time. For example, in the mid-1990s, the Science–Technology–Society movement advocated that science content should be embedded in social–technological themes and contexts that were meaningful to students (Aikenhead, 1994). In short, themes, contexts and situations for learning STEM matter (Suchman, 2007; Bliss et al., 1999; Singleton, 1998).

Work-integrated learning (WIL) and internships are examples of learning environments that provide ample opportunity for students to learn "on the job"

52 *Developing a pedagogical framework*

and to apply their knowledge and skills to relevant problems. Goodenough et al. (2020) found that students enrolled in a Bachelor of Science degree who participated in an internship had significantly higher adaptability and challenge orientation compared with students who did not. This finding applied across students majoring in biology, geographical information systems and biogeography at the University of Gloucestershire. In this study, adaptability, optimism, purposeful direction and ingenuity improved in students who participated in internships.

Connecting with industry may also yield benefits in developing socially responsible citizens. A recent study conducted at the Contamination Lab at the Politecnico di Torino found that collaboration with companies assisted multidisciplinary teams of students to shift their thinking from a product–design logic to a product–service system (Remondino et al., 2020). The challenge approach used in this case required students to find multiple solutions for disposal of food waste.

To further highlight the importance of actual experience, a recent study of WIL in engineering in a Saudi Arabian university (Hussain & Spady, 2020), which moved online in response to social distancing requirements, found that remote and virtual experiences did *not* provide students with sufficient experience with industry in order to confer positive comprehensive technical and transversal skills expected for graduating engineers. However, when virtual alternatives were created for WIL, with outcome-based activities and assessments using a state-of-the-art digital support together with entrepreneurship, these seemed to provide a reasonable *temporary* alternative to face-to-face, work-integrated experiences.

Using a thematic approach creates complexities as well as advantages for assessment (Draper, 2009). An integrated approach to STEM implies that content and capabilities are embedded and are valued by being assessed. Well-designed assessments with clear intentions that focus on personally and socially relevant themes, problems, issues and challenges can increase student motivation to learn (Draper, 2009). This is discussed further in Chapter 5 in this book, which focusses on assessment in STEM.

Driving innovation using STEM

Creating innovative solutions is a key driver for integrating STEM curriculum in higher education to create new knowledge, processes, products and systems. It is important to note that it is very difficult to be creative or inventive without a good foundation of discipline knowledge. This does not negate integration but instead requires identifying what knowledge students might need prior to demonstrating innovation as an outcome.

STEM innovation is often exhibited in one of the following forms (Feldon et al., 2013, pp. 359–360):

- A novel strategy is applied to solve a previously intractable problem.
- Knowledge – strategic, procedural, conceptual, or factual – from one field or discipline is effectively applied to an existing, previously intractable problem in a different field or discipline.

Developing a pedagogical framework 53

- A new conceptualisation or framing of an existing, intractable problem provides better progress toward its resolution.
- A new problem is identified whose resolution will enable significant theoretical advance.

Given this range for innovation, it is not surprising that there are a range of types of learning experiences that can assist students in developing innovations in STEM. These all accommodate the idea that new problems always have constraints and that real-world problems are often not well structured and are potentially highly complex, with variables or parameters that may not be malleable. Collectively, these types of learning involve students in problem-solving and inquiry that integrate content knowledge from one or more disciplines and develop thinking, including reflective and metacognitive skills and intuition simultaneously. These experiences are generally clustered (Feldon et al., 2013; Fink, 2013) and should be frequent, rather than one-off opportunities, so that students can expand both repertoire and outcomes.

Learning experiences may include students making authentic artefacts in response to solving problems and design challenges (de Castell, 2016; Yanez et al., 2019). In these instances, learning includes undertaking a situated exploration and iteratively critiquing several possible methods to create or refine artefacts or processes. A critique often involves considering the impact of a product or process and its worth, benefit and meaning to the user (de Castell, 2016). Students may present and publish their findings, indicating the connections and applications for communities beyond the institution.

One of the challenges for designing STEM experiences for innovation is in setting up activities that are flexible and open-ended enough using a theme or solution orientation, yet include boundaries in relation to resources and outcomes (Sawyer, 2011). Completely open-ended activities are difficult to resource. Since innovation is only as good as the next good idea, there is also a need to capture and connect the next "good ideas" in order to gain the synergies that lead to innovations. Designing effective activities may involve considering the major ways scientists, mathematicians and engineers leverage what they know already, adding reasoning, experimentation, tinkering and reflecting in order to solve novel problems innovatively. Such innovation requires a critical evaluation of information and sufficiency of all possible solutions, identifying next steps, seeking peer review and working with people as resources.

In the digital learning era, the large volume of dynamically evolving information available, and its ready accessibility, means that sorting and sifting information is incredibly important. Learners need ways to establish reasonable and reliable information management so that they can quickly filter and select appropriate sources. Research on how people learn has indicated that when learners incorporate ideas and process the information in some way through making connections (e.g. synthesise, analyse, look for patterns, evaluate), they

54 *Developing a pedagogical framework*

are more likely to retain an understanding (National Academies of Science, Engineering and Medicine, 2018). Activities such as participating in discussions, arguments, creating visual representations, analysing and interpreting data and constructing reasoning, as well as creating products, are all important in connecting ideas and transferring knowledge to real-world contexts. Therefore, in integrated STEM, it is important to provide students with opportunities to make links and to connect ideas, processes and theories with applications as they arise. These links and connections lead to innovation.

There are inherent tensions within STEM that may be difficult to resolve, as there are different ways of gaining and processing knowledge. Dealing with such tensions requires skill for teachers and learners (Henriksen et al., 2020). Kuhn's idea of essential tension refers to the inherent incongruities, paradoxes and contradictions that may obviate innovation (Kuhn, 1977). These could relate to drivers for change versus maintaining the status quo, or for developing skills for collaboration versus developing innovation for competitive advantage. Tensions are not necessarily resolvable because we might need to use *and* thinking rather than *either/or* thinking. This played out in the race for developing vaccines for COVID-19, in which multinational sponsors wanted to be the first to create a successful vaccine, despite a call for international collaboration to develop multiple vaccines for different strains of the virus. These tensions reflect innovation for social good versus commercial advantage. The latter also creates jobs. However, the point here is that often there are conflicting agendas which influence what is included in STEM learning experiences, why it is included and how connecting ideas and people (collaboration) can lead to innovation that supports both social *and* economic innovation.

Importance of active learning approaches

Associated with developing an integrated STEM curriculum are approaches that promote more student-driven, self-conscious and reflective learning (Conner, 2014; Sawyer, 2011). Embracing these approaches wholeheartedly and applying a student-centred philosophy to curriculum design in higher education is still emergent (Coll & Taylor, 2008). This is because, in many institutions, there has not been a shift from content-specific assessment that acts as a gatekeeper and rewards memorisation (Hume & Coll, 2005). The goal is to create a more open-ended problem-solving and inquiry-related outcome that incorporates transversal thinking skills with levels of attainment.

In active learning approaches, students deliberately choose learning tactics and thinking strategies that they can appropriate for the demands of their learning experiences. Even very young children have been shown to be able to use appropriate learning tactics (Hussain, 2011). In a meta-analysis of 225 studies on active learning, Freeman et al. (2014) found that active learning contributed to improved student performance on examinations and that concept inventories increased on average by 0.47 SDs ($n = 158$ studies). Failure when lecturing approaches were used was 50% higher than when active learning approaches were used (Freeman et al., 2014). In addition, examination scores improved on average by almost 6% when active learning was incorporated.

Class size is often given as an excuse for not including active learning. However, Freeman et al. (2014) showed that class size did not seem to have an effect on the benefits of active learning, presumably because a larger group can have subgroups of appropriate size for feedback and collaboration that maximises participation. These results raise questions about the continuance of only using teacher-directed lecturing.

Benefits of active learning approaches are provided in more detail in the following subsections. Additional benefits of active learning can include opportunities to be mentored by experts who are engaged in real-world consultancies and research related to the problems being addressed. Students may also need to complete a professional internship as part of their coursework, possibly including assessments that require active learning approaches.

Challenge-based learning

Challenged-based learning is an interdisciplinary approach often linked to addressing compelling issues from multiple perspectives and to taking action (Apple Education, 2010; Gibson et al., 2018). It is similar to project-based learning in that students collaborate and reflect on their learning and on the impact of their potential solutions or actions. Research on challenge-based approaches in STEM has shown that students increase the amount of time they spend on activities, develop creative uses for technologies and have increased engagement and satisfaction with their learning (Johnson & Adams, 2010; Roselli & Brophy, 2006).

Although in a challenge there may be individual tasks driven by ideation processes and guiding questions, as well as collaboration with peers, educators and other experts as appropriate, tasks are very student-centric in that students drive their own progress (with support). This approach has often been used to immerse students in solving environmental issues and in designing technological solutions (Harris & Nolte, 2007; Rodríguez-Chueca et al., 2019).

Usually a challenge starts with a definition or description of the challenge (Challenge-Based Learning, 2020). This can lead to a "generating" challenge that is relatively open-ended and which may spawn focussing questions. For example, a challenge provided to engineering students (Rodríguez-Chueca et al., 2019) was to find ways to reduce the environmental impact of the pulp and paper industries. Questions that were developed for responding to the video materials included (p. 242):

- How can sustainable development create value for a company?
- What are the four forms of savings in the phases of the production–consumption process proposed by the circular economy?
- What is the difference between creativity and innovation?

56 *Developing a pedagogical framework*

During this challenge, although students highly rated the opportunity to apply their learning to real situations, they reported difficulties in finding technical solutions to the challenge itself (Rodríguez-Chueca et al., 2019). Therefore, educators may need to provide sufficient technical information as part of the challenge materials.

Often, as part of challenges, students not only learn content and ways to solve problems but also develop transversal skills and competencies in planning, finding sources, collaboration, creativity and communication (Gibson et al., 2018). Since challenges can be set up as gaming sequences for completion of tasks, there may be built-in feedback responses, points, leader boards and levels of attainment, all of which can contribute to motivation (Gibson & Grasso, 2007). In order to develop skills that can be applied to the "real world", students need opportunities to connect with people in industry and in local communities (Compton, 2005). These people can assist students to develop key ideas and ask probing questions, and can direct students towards possible resources, thereby supporting them in meeting evaluation and assessment criteria.

As outcomes, students may be required to present or pitch their ideas for their solution locally or through using digital platforms for greater sharing and impact, and for getting feedback on their potential solutions globally (Gibson et al., 2018). A pitch can be higher stakes for relevance and impact if students are judged by stakeholders from local businesses, government agencies and industries (Johnson et al., 2009).

In Australia, a yearly event, the National Innovation Games, brings together a range of stakeholders to participate in a challenge to solve an issue or problem, using a hackathon in which government, businesses and not-for-profits collaborate with students and faculty to generate solutions (Paddl, 2020). In 2020, the driving question was: "How might you use digital solutions to engage with your customers and your community?"

The brief on the website for this challenge stated (Paddl, 2020):

> This event will be particularly relevant to students in agricultural and environmental sciences, tech-based disciplines, business and tourism. However innovation requires people from different backgrounds to work well, so all disciplines are welcome! The Challenges will require you to think "outside of the box", brainstorm, ideate and design innovative ideas for the future. They will also require you to be agile in how you communicate and interact virtually!

Challenge events are important to focus students on real situations, to provoke compelling investigation and to provide a vehicle for evaluating solutions given resourcing constraints (Quigley et al., 2019). When students are given opportunities to examine problems, connect meaningfully with application and contingencies of a problem and take multiple factors related to a challenge into account (in situ if possible), they gain an understanding of the importance of

Developing a pedagogical framework 57

how inputs from different disciplinary fields can work together synergistically to derive solutions (Sánchez Tapia, 2020).

Challenge activities require students to perform to criteria (similar to a performance assessment or a capstone topic), aiming to deliver relatively narrow yet integrated content, focussed on what is relevant, without covering all competencies. Knowledge gained spans declarative, procedural and conditional types of knowledge, with high engagement because of the richness and relevance of the issue or problem. Even more importantly, internationally connected challenge activities have been shown to provide symbolic hope for the future and a vehicle for students' ideas to have impact, especially if a new solution could change the world (Gibson & Grasso, 2007).

Problem-solving approaches

Problem-solving approaches that use real-world problems automatically position learning in an authentic context that often requires connections across disciplines. In problem-based learning (PBL), student choice and intentions, coupled with their own sense of agency, drive inquiry-based learning (Conner, 2014). In a meta-study of PBL, over 35 research publications conducted in 19 different institutions, PBL was found to be superior with respect to student opinion about their courses and measures of student performance in clinical medicine and aspects of humanism (Vernon & Blake, 1993). However, PBL can be challenging for students who are not comfortable with high levels of autonomy and choice.

One example of PBL was where scientists were struggling (over a 15-year period) to discover the crystal structure for the virus that causes AIDS (Khatib et al., 2011). The solution to how the protein could fold into its lowest possible energy state came from a computer-based game called Foldit (https:fold. it/portal), a "serious game" that engages participants in finding solutions to protein folding. Scientists were able to analyse the solutions from many players, including science students, and to apply these solutions in the understanding of manipulating proteins in the real world. Another example using the Foldit game involved players collaboratively developing a construction plan for an enzyme for accelerating biosynthetic reactions, used in many cholesterol medications, by up to 2,000% (Hersher, 2012)! Research on the key factors that led to the success of players revealed that they created new "tools" (computer programme codes) and learned collaboratively through working in teams to share code (or protocols) and to update team members on their failures and successes as they tinkered with refinements (Khatib et al., 2011). Such use of serious gaming could be applied to a range of authentic STEM issues.

Application of knowledge to a problem or challenge does not necessarily occur naturally. Students may need guidance and support to apply what they know and to identify and find out what they don't, in terms of background facts and processes for problem-solving. It is also highly likely that students

58 *Developing a pedagogical framework*

come with the variable skills to be able to call on prior knowledge and develop investigative skills using a range of disciplinary approaches. Timely assistance with scoping a problem becomes very important (Kluger & DeNisi, 1996) and may include elaboration on procedures (Moreno et al., 2009). For example, students designing plants for specific climates who were given evaluative feedback about their problem-solving strategies out-performed students who were given less feedback (Moreno, 2004).

Project-based learning

PBL has been widely adopted in many higher education institutions due to its benefits. However, Biggs (2003) suggested that the reason why problem- and project-based approaches are not used more often in universities is because they require institutional and teacher flexibility. That is, it requires less effort for experts to provide direct instruction in their specialty, leaving integration up to students – perhaps years later – rather than integrating and applying knowledge sources within a problem-based frame. Given the importance of solving problems in STEM, not using PBL really needs to be questioned.

Marx et al. (1997) indicated that some of the benefits for students participating in PBL include:

- Developing a deeper, more integrated understanding of content and processes.
- Learning to work collaboratively and cooperatively.
- Promoting responsibility within a group, as well as independent learning.

In a six-week study conducted by Lai (2013), students from an experimental group used a digital project-based approach to understand electric circuits. These students demonstrated significant improvement in understanding and had a more positive attitude, compared to those from a control group that received direct instruction. Another study carried out by Sema et al. (2009) with physics students showed that PBL enhanced student learning and improved attitudes towards physics, including the importance of developing inquiry skills.

PBL can include aspects of inquiry using text sources and practical or technical work. In some instances, it may be helpful for students to follow a simulation of discovery, as was set up for an integrated biology course for students to learn about the discoveries of cell theory (Danilov & Danilov, 2013). This approach helped students understand logical progression and analysis of the sort that leads to theory generation. Using simulations also enabled students to connect their knowledge of the chemistry of cell membranes to constructing models of membranes by using virtual representations of lipids, proteins and carbohydrates.

PBL is also becoming more commonly associated with WIL. The German VET sector is the envy of the world in this regard, where the Federal Bundes Institut für Berufsbilfung (BIBB) has created a dual pathway in its higher education system that enables students to undertake highly skilled trades or move into universities. It leverages key partnerships with large industries and schools to assist in providing education on essential job skills for students. Participants engaged in the trades with large employers, such as VW and Bosch, are paid while in training. This model attracts people into highly skilled training and contributes to Germany's high-tech economy talent pipeline.

Inquiry learning

Inquiry approaches have mostly been developed in the sciences and mathematics, in which students undertake a collaborative investigation of a phenomenon or issue and come up with evidence and reliable sources to support their claims. Research on inquiry models for learning indicate that students may need to understand the nature of disciplines before they can successfully develop in-depth inquiry skills (Wilson et al., 2012). Conversely, learning to undertake inquiry does not ensure students acquire an understanding about the nature of disciplines (Thoermer & Sodian, 2002; Samarapungavan et al., 2006).

Despite these constraints, inquiry approaches are used when students have access to a wide range of information sources and use collaborative learning opportunities combined with hands-on activities for immersive experiences. These include undertaking physical experiments, digital simulations, use of avatars and gaming, discussed in more detail in Chapter 2 on the role of technologies in STEM.

The rise in availability of digital sources of information on the internet has created opportunities for collaborative inquiry on a larger scale through social and institutional networks. For example, inquiry need not be restricted to one class or institution but could be opened up through online networks for more varied and considered solutions from a wide range of learners, within and across national borders. In fact, a case was made that large-scale networks make it possible for people and organisations to manage and analyse large sets of information (Stephenson, 1998). Learning in higher education can therefore model and reflect the world of work that requires social interaction and harnesses the power of networking.

A key pedagogical practice in inquiry models is to link concepts and problems with prior knowledge and understanding and to include an evaluative component that requires students to think about these connections (Conner, 2014; Willison, 2020). Links between the familiar and unfamiliar become important, with metacognitive reflection built in. In authentic inquiry, students determine the questions to be investigated and also have some agency over the inquiry process. Like collaborative problem-solving, inquiry can support development of knowledge and critical and creative thinking, alongside communication skills (Willison, 2020).

A specific example is a course at the University of Western Sydney that addresses major global sustainable challenges. In this course, students critically examine cases related to climate change, indigenous health, medical

60 *Developing a pedagogical framework*

intervention and discovery, the implications of a loss of biodiversity, environmental sustainability and human–animal interactions. Students evaluate evidence and bias in decision-making by producing a newspaper article about a real case. Through such interdisciplinary approaches, problems can be studied along with actions as human behaviour, advocacy and social justice are taken into account.

Design thinking for innovation

Design thinking, as a learning process, has been used extensively as an art form and in engineering. It employs approaches, tools and thinking to devise better creative solutions (Kelley & Kelley, 2013) and is an iterative, reflective process, informed by evaluation at each step. Design thinking may result in new ideas, systems solutions, material artefacts, devices, processes and systems (Henriksen et al., 2019). In this sense, it is very future-oriented and is useful in combination with PBL, inquiry and challenge approaches.

Design thinking is developed through ideation processes in which creative ideas are collected, selected and applied to situations that may contain uncertainty, instability and value conflict. During an ideation process, students are introduced to a specific problem to be addressed, initial concepts are created, basic solution developments might be trialled, modelled or simulated and the results are used to "tinker" with multiple iterations of potential solutions.

Henriksen et al. (2019) claimed that design thinking is important for learners as it enables them to grapple with complex subject matter by capitalising on using both analytical and intuitive thinking. In design thinking, students can make inferences based on data analysis and can take account of real-world complexities. While analytical thinking requires breaking up content and ideas into constituent parts or data and considers how these parts relate to one another, intuitive thinking is more about bringing forth ideas from people's unconsciousness about what might work or whether people would like and use this idea, product or process.

The design process is useful in interdisciplinary studies. For example, in Iceland, the national curriculum in schools assumes that everyone can be innovative using ideation processes (Thorsteinsson, 2013). Consequently, innovation education is integrated into multiple disciplines in Iceland. As well as stimulating and developing skills of innovativeness, Icelandic teachers encourage students to apply the processes, from concept development to realisation, to everyday life, while simultaneously increasing student awareness of ethical issues, especially related to environmental sustainability (Thorsteinsson, 1998).

At the Middlebury Institute of International Studies at the University of California Santa Cruz, a team of experts developed virtual reality experiences in a project called "The Virtual Planet" to help students and the community understand and model future changes in the coastline that may occur due to climate change and consequent sea level rise (Christopherson, 2019). This team included a scientist and data expert, a certified drone pilot, a senior VR developer and game designers. The development involved flying drones over specific areas of land, taking hundreds of photos, then working with "photogrammetry" (which uses GPS, triangulation and geometry) to identify 40,000 points of similarity between the photos. The software incorporates wide-ranging data sets to create 3D layers, which are developed into a VR experience that students can use for modelling and predicting sea level rise and its effects. Such design thinking may assist with transfer of knowledge or application of ideas from one context to another, especially when students are assisted in considering conditional aspects of data. Application and transfer can be fostered by educators as part of developing reflection on the design thinking process.

Systems thinking

Systems thinking provides a perspective (view, process or approach) that enables participants to understand complexity in systems in which multiple factors or elements influence that system. It is not just about applying ideas from one discipline to another, but rather about considering how interactions within multiple levels (or layers) of influence can be used to expand understanding of a phenomena, going beyond simple combinations of concepts to include multiple interactive effects.

In STEM, there are a range of types of systems, including natural systems; defined physical systems that have been consciously designed and created for a purpose; and abstract systems for explanatory purposes, as in mathematical models and human activity systems (Frank & Kordova, 2015). Components within a system, when acting together, confer synergistic advantages such that the properties and behaviours of the system are more than the sum of its components. Systems thinking can be used to focus on the bigger picture, of reciprocal relationships and interactions within a system, rather than focussing on components and events in isolation (Frank & Kordova, 2015). This is especially important in engineering and technology contexts.

According to Senge (1994), good systems thinkers consider how levels operate simultaneously, where levels are events, patterns of behaviour of substances, systems and mental models. Because there is no direct method of measuring systems thinking, Frank and Kordova (2015) recommended using an indirect method of measurement that uses four logic layers: cognitive capabilities, abilities, individual traits and multidisciplinary knowledge and experience. Kordova (2020) described how students from medicine, mathematics, biotechnology, engineering and computer science completed high-tech industry projects, improving their logical and systems thinking through participation in these multidisciplinary projects.

In biological systems thinking approaches, connections can be made between interacting components, whether for plant systems, natural or artificial ecosystems and animal systems, such as in mammals, where cells, organs and organ systems interact and provide feedback for biochemical and behavioural self-regulation. Systems thinking is especially important when considering

62   *Developing a pedagogical framework*

environmental, biochemical and physiological impacts of chemical components of fertilisers, herbicides and pesticides, including their flow through levels of food chains. Links can be made between methods of artificially supplying essential elements for plant growth in hydroponics and soil fertility; using soil analysis for contaminants; diagnosing nutrient deficiencies in plants; and other plant pathology preventative activities. Such systems thinking has huge implications for communities wishing to develop more effective ways of generating food.

In making systems thinking relevant to students, Danilov and Danilov (2013) cited examples and practical work that examined healthy versus diseased or unhealthy tissue, organs, endocrine and immune systems, as a means to indicate how human systems were affected by behaviours such as drinking alcohol and smoking. This is an example of coursework helping to promote healthy lifestyles and the consideration of consequences of some behaviours, thus making learning incredibly relevant to major human health issues. Such principles were also used to construct curriculum and assessments in human biology courses in New Zealand (Hipkins & Conner, 1986).

Analysis

Analysis involves an examination of cause and effect, structure and function and the relationships between entities. It leads to reasoning and development of logical arguments. Analysing may also involve identifying a purpose and interpreting a range of perspectives and intentions and the values and interests any decisions might serve. Analysing critically interrogates purposes, intentions and interests, and evaluates experimental outcomes and functionality of processes related to the design of new products.

In a study that integrated biology concepts (Danilov & Danilov, 2013), analytical skills were developed using a computer-based learning system. In this system, tasks were built in to be personally relevant. As well as studying chemical and physical properties of water and why it is essential for life, students were asked to use the software to analyse their own daily water use and compare the water components of a range of substances in humans. This enhanced students' analytical skills (Danilov & Danilov, 2013).

STEM learning environments

Learning environments establish modes for student engagement by determining the types of interactions between individuals and resources (including other people) and depending on discipline practices, affordances of any identified focus for learning, expected outcomes and a culture that supports learning and learner motivation to succeed (National Academies of Sciences, Engineering and Medicine, 2018). Designing and providing an effective learning environment may also involve considering the optimum use of resources, how well

Developing a pedagogical framework 63

models and tools support solving problems, the extent of applicability and the evaluation of outcomes and projects undertaken in work situations (Brown et al., 1989; Lave & Wenger, 1991).

Structuring and supporting learning in STEM through specific activities and feedback (experiences) is key for creating positive learning environments for students so they can progress and demonstrate the desired learning outcomes. The concept of providing "scaffolding" for learners within a learning environment was first used by Bruner in the 1950s and refers to structural elements that help learners to navigate and acquire concepts and skills with which they may be unfamiliar, followed by gradual, faded input from the instructor as learners become more confident and autonomous (Willison, 2020). With scaffolding, educators support learners through providing appropriate resources, guiding instructions, tools and provision of cues, prompts, questions and types of activities and interactions. It may involve providing exemplars, procedural clues (especially for integrating knowledge sources), chunking tasks or creating opportunities for collaboration (Conner, 2014) and constructing peer feedback, since this is a core skill in STEM-embedded professions.

The amount of guidance students need will vary. For example, in inquiry approaches, students can develop academic judgement in relation to discipline knowledge, but will vary in capability depending on prior experience, skill level and reflective capability. The idea is that educators help students apply filters for relevance and usefulness of information and learning approaches. This can be done by providing descriptive, layered questioning sequences to support students in critiquing and integrating disciplinary knowledge sources (Nokes-Malach & Mestre, 2013) and to provide descriptive criteria in the form of rubrics to guide students to achieve desired outcomes.

Learning socially to promote collaboration

There is considerable research on how learning socially has improved student learning outcomes (Brown & Campione, 1995; Freeman et al., 2014; Johnson et al., 2000). Affective outcomes can also be improved when learning is socially mediated. Students tend to be more engaged, interested and active in their contributions to learning and possibly more accountable to their peers in collaborative models (Bonwell & Eison, 1991). This is likely the result of greater task orientation and increased awareness of different perspectives and ways to solve problems, as students may gain nuanced understandings of concepts, reinforce ideas and ask questions of each other (Boud et al., 2001; Hake, 1998). Further, during group work, there may be more opportunities through cooperation to allocate and contribute to parts of tasks and to navigate the demands of tasks together, which helps to reduce task demands on individuals (Leisman et al., 2018).

The processes for teaching and learning are becoming more complex and are contingent on social interactions and relational factors. The pace of change

64 *Developing a pedagogical framework*

mandates we respond to the need to be faster, smarter and more connected with knowledge and each other. As Beverley and Etienne Wenger-Trayner (2015) stated:

> We're living in a time when things are moving fast. The rules of the game are changing. Science is changing. Technology is changing. Geo-politics is changing. Learning fast is the only mode of survival. But here's the crazy thing: our models of learning have not kept up. For many people, learning starts with something that's known. It's then transmitted to someone who doesn't know it. But for the projects we're involved in, this simple view doesn't work. In the real world, things are too dynamic and complex.
>
> (para. 1)

In this sense, connections and interactions change as new technologies and ways of communicating become more commonplace and complex socially through using digital media. Students are finding ways to sort through huge bodies of knowledge, learn about how to harness knowledge as it is created and be the creators of new knowledge.

Social practices have been described as those that are shared, developed and negotiated within specific communities of knowing (Bowen et al., 1999). Community of inquiry models, developed for online environments (Garrison et al., 2000), support the notion of "active" learning that depends on participants sharing their emerging learning and understanding. This interaction often occurs through collaboration forums on learning management systems, discussion boards, wikis, blogs and videoconferencing (Picciano, 2017).

Professionals working in STEM-related professions are often required to work in teams. One consequence is that physics and engineering education (Parappilly et al., 2019) and technology education (Bailee & Catalano, 2009) have been undergoing reform that includes members of the profession contributing as experts to coursework for inquiry and problem- and project-based learning to model how professionals use social practice to inform and peer review their work. This approach leveraged the professional practice of scientists, technologists and engineers to collaborate with universities in using innovative collaborative problem-solving and in developing cutting-edge breakthroughs. In these cases, boundaries between engineer, technologist and scientist were blurred as they solved open-ended problems together (Parappilly et al., 2019).

Peer learning

In a large study of the effects of small group learning on undergraduate outcomes in science, mathematics, engineering and technology university courses, Springer et al. (2013) found that a range of small-group learning approaches was effective in promoting greater academic achievement, more favourable attitudes towards learning and increased persistence. As Boud et al. (2001) showed, when students had access to a study group and peer feedback, they were more likely to reflect on their learning.

Peer review is developed as a core part of becoming a biochemist in a course at Flinders University. Students are required to provide a review of two project plans and construct at least three questions that will help their peers to think about content-based, procedural or technical issues related to their plans. Students are given credit in the course for their reflection on the value and usefulness of the feedback and questions they received from peers and how they will incorporate these into revised project plans. Here, building in peer review supports students to advance their thinking, understanding and practical skills simultaneously.

A framework for integrating STEM

This section pulls together all the other sections in this chapter to develop a new pedagogical framework for integrating STEM. In the last two decades or so, there has been significant investment in and effort towards educational reforms within STEM disciplines (American Association for the Advancement of Science, 1989, 1993; International Technology Education Association, 1996, 2007; National Council of Teachers of Mathematics, 2000; Next Generation Science Standards, 2013), producing competing agendas that have confused educators. As a result, Kelley and Knowles (2016) developed a conceptual model for integrating STEM, indicating that educators lacked a cohesive framework for understanding how to construct integration and that much more work was needed in curriculum design. Many educators struggle to make connections across disciplines, especially in integrating mathematics or using data and analytics. Consequently, students may miss cross-cutting concepts that would help them understand real-world situations.

The Kelley and Knowles (2016) framework connected disciplinary concepts in STEM but did not include pedagogical enablers or aspects required to create effective learning environments. The need to develop pedagogies that enable content connections across STEM disciplines, and an application of skills and transferable capabilities to STEM processes, should not be underestimated (National Research Council, 2005). Therefore, there is still a need to consider an expansive pedagogical framework to enable integration of disciplines, specific skills and general capabilities simultaneously.

More effective integration is likely if educators have a framework within which to make decisions about domain pedagogical content knowledge (Nadelson et al., 2012). The framework presented in Figure 3.1 can be used to support considerations for designing interdisciplinary coursework in STEM in the following ways:

- Create learning experiences for students that support a holistic active learning environment that weaves in the development of problem-solving.
- Plan, teach and assess learning in STEM (see Chapters 4 and 5).

66 *Developing a pedagogical framework*

- Indicate aspects for potential professional learning for educators (see Chapter 6).
- Provide aspects to focus on for further research (see Chapter 7).

The core of the intent for integration is for students to derive innovative, humanistic solutions to real problems (Figure 3.1). In an array of combinations, processes such as collaboration, making iterative changes, reflection, evaluation, synthesis and authentic assessment help to drive student outcomes. Consideration is also given to prior knowledge, active learning, authentic contexts, learning environments and systems thinking. These dimensions are not mutually exclusive, as the components within dimensions may interact and influence each other. The components of the framework can be thought of as interdependent and contingent on each other.

In Figure 3.1, the *prior knowledge* dimension implies that educators and students are aware that students already possess knowledge or know how to find it. Students need to be supported to use analytic and intuitive thinking as well as to manage learning progressions effectively. This affects what learning approaches are used and how educators plan and choose appropriate pedagogies or what they do as teachers to support ongoing learning. *Student support* includes providing facilities, technical resources and learning technologies. Support necessitates helping students to establish clear goals for learning, providing high interest and modelling curiosity through questioning, so that students invest effort towards the criteria on which they will be assessed. The *learning environment* includes the mode of student engagement (for example,

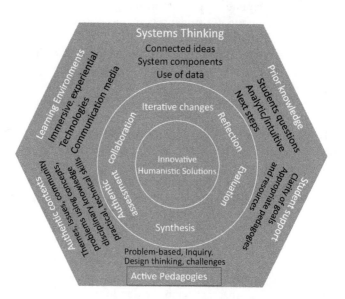

Figure 3.1 Pedagogical framework for integrating STEM

immersive and experiential), where collaborative and team contributions can contribute to innovations for humanistic solutions. This dimension also includes how educators encourage students to manage their time effectively, develop a positive mindset about their choices, appreciate differences and create solutions for their communities (Schreiner et al., 2012). As described previously in this chapter in the section on the importance of using active learning approaches, *active pedagogies* are those that purposively engage students in thinking (for example, PBL, using scenarios, challenges, simulations and inquiry learning) in real-world situations. *Authentic contexts* for learning that matter to people are those that provide a theme or address a real issue or relevant problem using disciplinary knowledge, concepts and practical, technical and thinking skills. Students are encouraged to think about connections, to transfer knowledge and skills and to use analytical and intuitive thinking, practices essential to systems thinking and innovation. *Systems thinking* also sanctions tinkering and evaluating changes through trialling or prototyping iterations in order to develop the best possible solutions.

In the framework (Figure 3.1), interactions between components and relative weighting depend on the focus for the learning (theme, context or issue), which may lend itself to greater emphasis on a particular discipline, thinking skill or systems approach. The assessment dimension needs to be authentic, with a focus on the outcomes and processes for problem-solving. The desired learning outcomes and consequent assessments will determine the choice of appropriate learning experiences. Chapter 4 provides specific steps for designing curriculum, using backwards design processes (Vasquez et al., 2017; Tomlinson & McTighe, 2016), by starting with the desired outcomes and determining how they will be assessed. Chapter 5 provides more detail related to how assessment can support ongoing development and demonstration of learning outcomes by students.

Conclusion

In a world in which knowledge is ubiquitous and accessible, there is a need to rethink what knowledge is included and how that knowledge is used, generated, co-created and connected as part of STEM coursework in higher education that has, as its core, problem-solving for humanistic solutions. In addition to providing human capital for the future, supporting people to have the skills deemed important for future development and sustainability, interdisciplinary approaches can provide authentic, contextual and situated examples for learning that is engaging and transformative and can serve public good. Expectations of society itself for innovative solutions are also driving the need for rethinking learning in STEM, which diverges from single-disciplinary thinking.

A focus on local relevance has not been the case for many HEIs, which rely on international connections, high tuition fees, research funding and rankings. However, paying attention to local needs and creating innovative solutions in partnership are crucial for HEIs to inspire the next generation of graduates to address issues of importance.

68   *Developing a pedagogical framework*

The principles for integrating STEM have been discussed in this chapter and are embodied in a pedagogical framework, presented in Figure 3.1. This framework leverages the complexity of designing integrated STEM in higher education, using themes, scenarios, challenges and projects to enable learning situated in authentic contexts that use collaborative inquiry, problem-solving and design-based approaches. In combination, the components shown in Figure 3.1 sanction creativity and flexibility for integrating STEM that can capture student and educator interest and contribute to solving local and global issues.

Educational researchers can use the framework to investigate implementation in practice in relation to student outcomes. There is a huge need to research how intersections between disciplines, cross-cutting ideas and practices, types of thinking, pedagogies and learning activities enable students to construct humanistic solutions to address global issues. Reforming STEM education, said Yanez et al. (2019), should not just involve considering instructional units, but should also position STEM education such that students are enabled to develop critical and agentic roles as citizens of the future and can negotiate real challenges and controversies using appropriate tools.

References

Aikenhead, G. S. (1994). What is STS science teaching? In J. Solomon & G. Aikenhead (Eds.), *STS education international perspectives on reform* (pp. 47–59). Teacher's College Press.

American Association for the Advancement of Science. (1989). *Science for all Americans.* Oxford University Press.

American Association for the Advancement of Science. (1993). *Benchmarks for science literacy.* Oxford University Press.

Apple Education. (2010). *Challenge based learning classroom guide.* Apple, Inc. http://cbl. digitalpromise.org/wp-content/uploads/sites/7/2016/08/CBL_Classroom_Guide 2010.pdf

Bailee, C., & Catalano, G. (2009). *Engineering and society: Working towards social justice, part I: Engineering and society.* Morgan & Claypool Publishers. https://doi.org/10.2200/S00136 ED1V01Y200905ETS008

Barab, S. A., & Landa, A. (1997). Designing effective interdisciplinary anchors. *Educational Leadership, 54*(6), 52–55.

Bauer, H. H. (1992). *Scientific literacy and the myths of the scientific method.* University of Illinois Press.

Biggs, J. (2003). *Teaching for quality learning at university* (2nd ed.). The Society for Research into Higher Education and Open University Press.

Blackburn, S. (1999). *Think: A compelling introduction to philosophy.* Oxford University Press.

Bliss, J., Saljo, R., & Light, P. (1999). *Learning sites: Social and technological resources for learning.* Elsevier.

Boix Mansilla, V. (2010). *MYP guide to interdisciplinary teaching and learning.* International Baccalaureate Organization.

Boix Mansilla, V., & Duraising, E. D. (2007). Targeted assessment of students' interdisciplinary work: An empirically grounded framework proposed. *The Journal of Higher Education, 78*(2), 215–237.

Bonwell, C., & Eison, J. A. (1991). *Active learning: Creating excitement in the classroom*. ASHE-ERIC Higher Education Report No. 1. https://www.asec.purdue.edu/lct/HBCU/documents/Active_Learning_Creating_Excitement_in_the_Classroom.pdf

Boud, D., Cohen, R., & Sampson, J. (2001). *Peer learning in higher education: Learning from and with each other*. Stylus Publishing, Kogan Page.

Bowen, M., Roth, W. M., & McGinn, M. K. (1999). Interpretations of graphs by university biology students and practising scientists: Towards a social practice view of scientific representation practices. *Journal of Research in Science Teaching, 36*, 1020–1043.

Brown, A. L., & Campione, J. C. (1995). Guided discovery in a community of learners. In E. McGilly (Ed.), *Classroom learners: Integrated cognitive theory and classroom practice* (pp. 229–249). The MIT Press.

Brown, J. S., Collins, A., & Duguid, P. (1989). Situated cognition and the culture of learning. *Educational Researcher, 18*, 32–42.

Brunetto, D., Marchionna, C., & Repossi, E. (2020). *Supporting deep understanding with emerging technologies in a STEM university math class*. Paper presented at the 6th International Conference on Higher Education Advances (HEAd'20). Universitat Politècnica de València. http://doi.org/10.4995/HEAd20.2020.11109

Bundy, A. (2007). Computational thinking is pervasive. *Journal of Scientific and Practical Computing, 1*(2), 67–69.

Bush, S. B., & Cook, K. L. (2019). Structuring steam inquiries: Lessons learned from practice. In M. S. Khine & S. Areepattamannil (Eds.), *Steam education: Theory and practice* (pp. 19–35). Springer Nature.

Challenge-Based Learning. (2020). www.challengebasedlearning.org/

Christopherson, R. (2019). *Virtual reality "sea level rise explorer" helps the city of Santa Cruz*. www.middlebury.edu/institute/academics/centers-initiatives/center-blue-economy/cbe-news/virtual-reality-sea-level-rise-explorer

Coll, R. K., & Taylor, N. (2008). The influence of context on science curricula: Observations, conclusions and some recommendations for curriculum development and implementation. In R. K. Coll & N. Taylor (Eds.), *Science education in context: An international examination of the influence of context on science curricula development and implementation* (pp. 355–362). Sense Publishers.

Comer, K., & Brogt, E. (2010). Student engagement in relation to their field of study. In A. Radlof (Ed.), *Student engagement in New Zealand universities* (pp. 11–21). Ako Aotearoa. https://akoaotearoa.ac.nz/ako-aotearoa/student-engagement

Compton, V. (2005). Futureintech: The story so far. In D. Fisher, D. Zandvliet, I. Gaynor, & R. Koul (Eds.), *Proceedings of the fourth international conference on science, mathematics and technology education* (pp. 1–11). Key Centre for School Science and Mathematics, Curtin University of Technology.

Conner, L. (2014). Students' use of evaluative constructivism: Comparative degrees of intentional learning. *International Journal of Qualitative Studies in Education, 27*(4), 472–489. http://doi.org/10.1080/09518398.2013.771228

Conner, L. (2020). *Integrating STEMM in higher education: A proposed curriculum development framework*. Paper published in the proceedings of 6th International Conference on Higher Education Advances (HEAd'20). Universitat Politècnica de València. http://doi.org/10.4995/HEAd20.2020.11058

Czerniak, C. N. (2007). Interdisciplinary science teaching. In S. K. Abell & N. G. Lederman (Eds.), *Handbook on research on science education* (pp. 537–560). Routledge.

Danilov, S., & Danilov, O. (2013). In an integrated approach to the study of biology. In L. V. Shavinina (Ed.), *The Routledge international handbook of innovation education* (pp. 396–403). Routledge.

70 *Developing a pedagogical framework*

Davis, B., Sumara, D., & Luce-Kapler, R. (2008). *Engaging minds: Changing teaching in complex times* (2nd ed.). Routledge.

de Castell, S. (2016). *A pedagogy of production: An introduction.* New Media Files [Video]. https://vimeo.com/181978126

Dewey, J. (1938). *Experience and education.* Collier Books.

Draper, S. (2009). Catalytic assessment: Understanding how MCQs and EVS can foster deep learning. *British Journal of Educational Technology, 40*(2), 285–293.

Feldon, D. F., Hurst, M. D., Rates, C. A., & Elliot, J. (2013). Innovation in science, technology, engineering, and mathematics (STEM) disciplines: Implications for educational practices. In L. Shavinina (Ed.), *The Routledge international handbook of innovation education* (pp. 359–371). Routledge.

Fink, L. D. (2013). *Creating significant learning experiences: An integrated approach to designing college courses.* Jossey-Bass.

Frank, M., & Kordova, S. K. (2015). Four layers approach for developing system thinking assessment tool for industrial and systems engineers. *Industrial Engineering & Management, 4.* http://doi.org/10.4172/2169-0316.1000178

Freeman, S., Eddy, S., McDonough, M., Smith, M., Okoroafor, N., Jordt, H., & Wenderoth, M. (2014). Active learning increases student performance in science, engineering, and mathematics. *Proceedings of the National Academy of Sciences.* https://doi.org/10.1073/pnas.1319030111

Garrison, D. R., Anderson, T., & Archer, W. (2000). Critical inquiry in a text-based environment: Computer conferencing in higher education. *Internet and Higher Education, 2*(2–3), 87–105.

Gentile, J., Brenner, K., & Stephens, A. (2017). *Undergraduate research experiences for STEM students: Successes, challenges and opportunities.* The National Academies Press.

Gholson, B., Witherspoon, A., Morgan, B., Brittingham, J. K., Coles, R., Graesser, A. C., Sullins, J., & Craig, S. D. (2009). Exploring the deep-level reasoning questions effect during vicarious learning among eighth to eleventh graders in the domains of computer literacy and Newtonian physics. *Instructional Science, 37*(5), 487–493.

Gibson, D., & Grasso, S. (2007, November). The global challenge: Save the world on your way to college. *Learning & Leading with Technology, 5191,* 12–16.

Gibson, D., Irving, L., & Scott, K. (2018). Technology-enabled challenge-based learning in a global context. In M. Shonfeld & D. Gibson (Eds.), *Collaborative learning and a global world* (pp. 25–40). Information Age Publishers.

Goldman, S. R., Britt, M. A., Brown, W., Cribb, C., George, M. A., Greenleaf, C., Lee, C. D., & Shanahan, C. (2016). Disciplinary literacies and learning to read for understanding: A conceptual framework for disciplinary literacy. *Educational Psychologist, 51*(2), 2019–2246. http://doi.org/10.1080/00461520.2016.1168741

Goodenough, A. E., Roberts, H., Biggs, D. M., Derounian, J. G., Hart, A. G., & Lynch, K. (2020). A higher degree of resilience: Using psychometric testing to reveal the benefits of university internship placements. *Active Learning in Higher Education, 21*(2), 102–115. https://doi.org/10.1177/1469787417747057

Hake, R. (1998). Interactive-engagement versus traditional methods: A six-thousand-student survey of mechanics test data for introductory physics courses. *American Journal of Physics, 66*(1), 64–74.

Harris, D., & Nolte, P. (2007). *Global challenge award: External evaluation year 1 2006–2007.* Vermont Institutes Evaluation Center.

Henriksen, D., Jordan, M., Foulger, T. S., Zuiker, S., & Mishra, P. (2020). Essential tensions in facilitating design thinking: Collective reflections. *Journal of Formative Design in Learning, 4,* 5–16. https://doi.org/10.1007/s41686-020-00045-3

Henriksen, D., Mehta, R., & Mehta, S. (2019). Design thinking gives STEAM to teaching: A framework that breaks disciplinary boundaries. In M. S. Khine & S. Areepattamannil (Eds.), *STEAM education: Theory and practice* (pp. 57–78). Springer Nature. http://doi-org-443.webvpn.fjmu.edu.cn/10.1007/978-3-030-04003-1_4

Hersher, R. (2012, April 13). FoldIt game's next play: Crowdsourcing better drug design. *Spoonful of Medicine: A Blog from Nature Medicine.* http://blogs.nature.com/spoonful/2012/04/foldit-games-next-play-crowdsourcing-better-drug-design.html?WT.mc_id=TWT_NatureBlogs

Hipkins, R., & Conner, L. (1986). *Alive and well II: A systems approach.* Longman.

Hume, A., & Coll, R. K. (2005). *The impact of a new assessment regime on science learning.* Paper presented at the 34th Annual Conference of the Australasian Science Education Research Association, Hamilton, New Zealand.

Hussain, H. (2011). *Complicity in games of chase and complexity thinking: Emergence in curriculum and practice-based research* [Doctor of Philosophy]. University of Canterbury.

Hussain, W., & Spady, W. (2020, November 5–6). *Accreditation during and post COVID19: A new reality.* Paper published in Proceedings of the 6th International Symposium on Accreditation of Engineering and Computing Education, 2020 ICACIT Virtual Symposium. ICACIT.

International Technology Education Association. (1996). *Technology for all Americans: A rationale and structure for the study of technology.* International Technology Education Association.

International Technology Education Association. (2007). *Standards for technological literacy: Content for the study of technology.* International Technology Education Association.

Johnson, D. W., Johnson, R. T., & Stanne, M. E. (2000). *Cooperative learning methods: A meta-analysis.* University of Minnesota Cooperative Learning Centre.

Johnson, L., & Adams, S. (2010). *Challenge based learning: The report from the implementation project.* New Media Consortium.

Johnson, L., Smith, R., Smythe, J., & Varon, R. (2009). *Challenge-based learning: An approach for our time.* New Media Consortium.

Kelley, T. R., & Kelley, D. (2013). *Creative confidence: Unleashing the creative potential within us all.* Crown Business.

Kelley, T. R., & Knowles, J. G. (2016). A conceptual framework for integrated STEM education. *International Journal of STEM Education, 3*(1), 1–11.

Khatib, F., Dimaio, F., Cooper, S., Kazmierczyk, M., Gilski, M., Krzywda, S., Zabranska, H., Pichova, I., & Thompson, J. (2011). Crystal structure of a monomeric retroviral protease solved by protein folding game players. *Nature Structural & Molecular Biology, 18*(10), 1175–1177.

Kilpatrick, W. H. (1918). *The project method: The use of the purposeful act in the educative process.* Teachers College.

Kluger, A. N., & DeNisi, A. (1996). The effects of feedback interventions on performance: A historical review, a meta-analysis, and a preliminary feedback intervention theory. *Psychological Bulletin, 119*(2), 254–284. http://doi.org/10.1037/0033-2909.119.2.254

Koen, B. V. (1985). *Definition of the engineering methods.* American Society for Engineering Education.

Kolb, D. A. (2015). *Experiential learning: Experience as the source of learning and development.* Pearson Education Press.

Kordova, S. (2020). Developing systems thinking in a project-based learning environment. *International Journal of Engineering Education, 2*(1). https://doi.org/10.14710/ijee.v2i1.4

Kroes, P. (2012). *Technical artefacts: Creations of mind and matter: A philosophy of engineering design.* Springer.

Kuhn, T. S. (1977). *The essential tension: Selected studies in scientific tradition and change.* University of Chicago Press.

72 Developing a pedagogical framework

Lai, C. S. (2013). A study of computer project-based learning on electric circuits for 4th graders. *The Journal of Human Resource and Adult Learning, 9*(1), 55–61.

Lave, J., & Wenger, E. (1991). *Situated learning: Legitimate peripheral participation.* Cambridge University Press.

Leisman, G., Mualem, R., & Mughrabi, S. K. (2018). *How people learn II: The science and practice of learning.* The National Academies Press.

Libin, A., & Libin, E. (2004). Person-robot interactions from the robopsychologists' point of view: Invited paper. *Proceedings of the IEEE, 92*(11), 1789–1803. http://doi.org/10.1109/JPROC.2004.835366

Linnenbrink-Garcia, L., & Patall, E. A. (2016). Motivation. In E. Anderman & L. Como (Eds.), *Handbook of educational psychology* (3rd ed., pp. 91–103). Taylor & Francis.

Marx, R. W., Blumenfeld, P. C., Krajcik, J. S., & Soloway, E. (1997). Enacting project-based science. *The Elementary School Journal, 97*(4), 341–358.

Mishra, P., Yadav, A., & Deep Play Research Group. (2013). Rethinking technology and creativity in the 21st century: Of art & algorithms. *TechTrends, 57*(3), 10–14. http://doi.org/10.1007/s11528-013-0655-z

Moreno, R. (2004). Decreasing cognitive load for novice students: Effects of exploratory versus corrective feedback in discovery-based multi-media. *Instructional Science, 32*(1–2), 99–113. http://doi.org/10.1023/B:TRUC.0000021811.66966.1d

Moreno, R., Reisslein, M., & Ozugul, G. (2009). Optimising worked example instruction in electrical engineering: The role of fading and feedback during problem-solving practice. *Journal of Engineering Education, 98*, 83–92.

Nadelson, L., Seifert, A., Moll, A., & Coats, B. (2012). i-STEM summer institute: An integrated approach to teacher professional development in STEM. *Journal of STEM Education, 13*(2), 69–83.

National Academies. (2012). *A framework for K-12 science education: Practices, cross-cutting concepts and core ideas.* Committee on Conceptual Framework for the New K-12 Science Education Standards, National Research Council of the National Academies.

National Academies of Sciences, Engineering and Medicine. (2018). *The integration of the humanities and arts with sciences, engineering, and medicine in higher education: Branches from the same tree.* The National Academies Press. https://doi.org/10.17226/24988

National Council of Teachers of Mathematics. (2000). *Principles and standards for school mathematics.* www.standards.nctm.org

National Geographic. (2019). *Atlas of the moons.* https://nerdist.com/article/interactive-atlas-solar-system-moons/

National Research Council. (2005). *How students learn: History, mathematics and science in the classroom.* The National Academies Press.

National Research Council. (2007). *Taking science to school: Learning and teaching science in grades K-12.* The National Academies Press.

National Research Council. (2010). *Report of a workshop on the scope and nature of computational thinking.* The National Academy Press.

Next Generation Science Standards. (2013). *Next generation science standards: For states, by states.* The National Academies Press.

Nissani, M. (1995). Fruits, salads, and smoothies: A working definition of interdisciplinarity. *Journal of Educational Thought, 29*(2), 121–128.

Nokes-Malach, T. J., & Mestre, J. P. (2013). Toward a model of transfer as sense-making. *Educational Psychologist, 48*(3), 184–207.

Paddl. (2020). *Students/grads for (virtual) innovation challenge.* www.paddl.com/jobs/860

Pang, J., & Good, R. (2000). A review of the integration of science and mathematics: Implications for further research. *School Science and Mathematics, 100*(2), 73–82.

Parappilly, M., Woodman, R., & Randhawa, S. (2019). Feasibility and effectiveness of different models of team-based learning approaches in STEMM-based disciplines. *Research in Science Education*. https://doi.org/10.1007/s11165-019-09888-8

Picciano, A. G. (2017). Theories and frameworks for online education: Seeking an integrated model. *Online Learning Journal, 21*(3), 166–190. http://doi.org/10.24059/olj.v21i3.1225

Putnam, R., & Borko, H. (2000). What do new views of knowledge and thinking have to say about research on teacher learning? *Educational Researcher, 29*(1), 4–15.

Quigley, C. F., Herro, D., & Baker, A. (2019). Moving toward transdisciplinary instruction: A longitudinal examination of STEAM teaching practices. In M. S. Khine & S. Areepattamannil (Eds.), *Steam education: Theory and practice* (pp. 143–164). Springer Nature.

Remondino, C. L., Fiore, E., & Tamborrini, P. (2020). *CLab Torino: A transdisciplinary environment to provide a challenge-based teaching model.* Paper presented at the 6th International Conference on Higher Education Advances (HEAd'20). Universitat Politècnica de València. http://doi.org/10.4995/HEAd20.2020.11197

Repko, A. F., Szostak, R., & Buchberger, M. P. (2014). *Introduction to interdisciplinary studies.* Sage Publications.

Reuters Graphic. (2019). *Drowning in plastic.* https://graphics.reuters.com/ENVIRONMENT-PLASTIC/0100B275155/index.html

Rios, J. A., Ling, G., Pugh, R., Becker, D., & Bacall, A. (2020). Identifying critical 21st-century skills for workplace success: A content analysis of job advertisements. *Educational Researcher, 49*(2), 80–89.

Rodríguez-Chueca, J., Molina-García, A., García-Aranda, C., Pérez, J., & Rodríguez, E. (2019). Understanding sustainability and the circular economy through flipped classroom and challenge-based learning: An innovative experience in engineering education in Spain. *Environmental Education Research, 26*(2), 238–252. http://doi.org/10.1080/1350 4622.2019.1705965

Roselli, R., & Brophy, S. (2006). Effectiveness of challenge-based instruction in biomechanics. *Journal of Engineering Education, 95*(4), 311–324.

The Royal Society. (2011). *Shut down or restart? The way forward for computing in UK schools.* https://royalsociety.org/~/media/education/computing-in-schools/2012-01-12-computing-in-schools.pdf

Samarapungavan, A., Westby, E., & Bodner, G. (2006). Contextual epistemic development in science: A comparison of chemistry students and research chemists. *Science Education, 90*(3), 468–495. http://doi.org/10.1002/sce.20111

Sanchez, E. (2009). Innovative teaching/learning with geotechnologies in secondary education. In A. Tatnall & A. Jones (Eds.), *Education and technology for a better world: WCCE 2009* (Vol. 302). IFIP Advances in Information and Communication Technology. Springer. http://doi.org/10.1007/978-3-642-03115-1_7

Sánchez Tapia, I. (2020). Introduction: A broad look at contextualization of science education across national contexts. In I. Sánchez Tapia (Ed.), *International perspectives on the contextualization of science education* (pp. 1–17). Springer.

Sawyer, R. K. (2011). *Structure and improvisation in creative teaching.* Cambridge University Press.

Schneider, B., Krajcik, J., Lavonen, J., & Salmela-Aro, K. (2019). *Learning science – crafting engaging science environments.* Yale University Press.

74 Developing a pedagogical framework

Schreiner, L. A., Louis, M. C., & Nelson, D. D. (2012). *Thriving in transitions: A research-based approach to college students' success*. National Resource Centre for the First-Year Experience and Students in Transition.

Sema, A., Ümit, T., & Erdoğan, B. (2009). The effect of project based learning on science undergraduates' learning of electricity, attitude towards physics and scientific process skills. *International Online Journal of Educational Sciences*, *1*(1), 81–105.

Senge, P. M. (1994). *The fifth discipline: The art and practice of the learning organization*. Doubleday.

Singleton, J. (1998). *Learning in likely places: Varieties of apprenticeship in Japan*. Cambridge University Press.

Springer, L., Stanne, M. E., & Donovan, S. S. (2013). Effects of small-group learning on undergraduates in science, mathematics, engineering, and technology: A meta-analysis. *Review of Educational Research*, *69*(1), 21–51.

Stephenson, K. (1998). *Internal communication, no 36: What knowledge tears apart, networks make whole*. www.netform.com/html/icf.pdf

Strober, M. H. (2011). *Interdisciplinary conversations: Challenging habits of thought*. Stanford University Press.

Suchman, L. (2007). *Human-machine reconfigurations: Plans and situated actions* (2nd ed.). Cambridge University Press.

Thoermer, C., & Sodian, B. (2002). Science undergraduates' and graduates' epistemologies of science: The notion of interpretive frameworks. *New Ideas in Psychology*, *20*, 263–283. http://doi.org/10.1016/S0732-118X(02)00009-0

Thorsteinsson, G. (1998). Innovation in the elementary school. *Uppeldi*, *6*(1), 140–148.

Thorsteinsson, G. (2013). Developing and understanding of the pedagogy of using a virtual reality learning environment (VRLE) to support innovation education. In L. Shavinnia (Ed.), *The Routledge international handbook of innovation education* (pp. 456–470). Routledge.

Tomlinson, C. A., & McTighe, J. (2006). *Integrating differentiated instruction and understanding by design*. Association for Supervision and Curriculum Development.

Vasquez, J. A., Comer, M., & Villegas, J. (2017). *STEM lesson guideposts: Creating STEM lessons for your curriculum*. Heinemann.

Vernon, D. T., & Blake, R. L. (1993). Does problem-based learning work? A meta-analysis of evaluative research. *Academic Medicine*, *68*(7), 550–563.

Voogt, J., Fisser, P., Good, J., Mishra, P., & Yadav, A. (2015). Computational thinking in compulsory education: Towards an agenda for research and practice. *Education and Information Technologies*, *20*, 715–728. https://doi.org/10.1007/s10639-015-9412-6

Wenger-Trayner, B., & Wenger-Trayner, E. (2015). *Planning and evaluating social learning*. https://wenger-trayner.com/resources/planning-and-evaluating-social-learning/

Willison, J. (2020). *The models of engaged learning and teaching: Connecting sophisticated thinking from early childhood to PhD*. Springer Open. https://doi.org/10.1007/978-981-15-2683-1

Wilson, A., Howitt, S., Roberts, P., Åkerlind, G., & Wilson, K. (2012). Connecting expectations and experiences of student in a research-immersive degree. *Studies in Higher Education*, *38*(10), 1562–1576. http://doi.org/10.1080/03075079.2011.633163

Wing, J. M. (2011). Research notebook: Computational thinking – what and why? *The Link (Magazine of Carnegie Mellon University's School of Computer Science)*, *6*, 1–32. https://www.cs.cmu.edu/~CompThink/resources/TheLink Wing.pdf

Yanez, G. A., Thumlert, L. K., de Castell, S., & Jenson, J. (2019). Pathways to sustainable futures: A "production pedagogy" model for STEM education. *Futures*, *108*, 27–36. https://doi.org/10.1016/j.futures.2019.02.021

Zeidler, D. L. (2016). STEM education: A deficit framework for the twenty first century? A sociocultural socioscientific response. *Cultural Studies of Science Education*, *11*, 11–26. http://doi.org/10.1007/s11422-014-9578-z

4 Designing integrated STEM curriculum

Integrating curriculum

Curriculum design is a key element in determining what students experience as part of their coursework. There is no silver bullet for designing opportunities to learn through integrated STEM. As indicated in the previous chapter on developing a framework for integrating STEM, curriculum can be integrated at various levels, including but not limited to:

- Separate events and challenge tasks.
- Content knowledge from a discipline topic, integrated with technical and thinking skills.
- Integrated content knowledge from more than one topic within a discipline.
- Integrated content knowledge from more than one discipline.
- Content knowledge from more than one discipline, integrated with technical and thinking skills.
- Process orientation, using a theme or context to solve a problem or undertake guided inquiry.
- Designing and developing technologies, products and processes using a multidisciplinary perspective to test and trial solutions.

Park Rogers and Abell (2008) undertook a review of the benefits of integrated studies, including how good design can create efficiencies in instructional time, reinforcing key ideas, learning big concepts, connecting disparate ideas and developing skills. However, concerns were noted, such as potentially emphasising one discipline more than another and potential for the lack of strong instruction in any one topic of interest due to the blurring of discipline boundaries. These concerns related to expectations about what content was covered, rather than what experiences and skills were being developed. The concern by faculty to "cover" content knowledge was a barrier (Park Rogers & Abell, 2008), along with other constraints, such as educator knowledge and effort required to construct new activities (Treacy & O'Donoghue, 2014), that will be discussed further in Chapter 6, which considers the challenges of integrating STEM.

Suggestions in this chapter support teaching practice reform in higher education to enable students to build the capability needed for future employment. The

76 *Designing integrated STEM curriculum*

impact of coursework should last for multiple years beyond its completion, and what students demonstrate as outcomes should distinguish them from students who have not completed these courses. Capabilities identified by Goldsprink and Kay (2018) and Rios et al. (2020) as being needed for a changing world are the ability to solve real and complex problems that address local and global issues; possession of effective communication skills; the ability to cooperate and collaborate; and the ability to think critically and creatively in order to develop innovative solutions. Frameworks for integrating STEM therefore need to include these skills and capabilities and to assess them (see Figure 3.1, Chapter 3).

The goal of any frameworks or models for designing creative, engaging, integrated STEM coursework must be to embed knowledge, skills and capabilities in authentic learning contexts (for example, Treacy & O'Donoghue, 2014; Conner, 2020). Sadly, this goal has rarely been achieved in HEIs, possibly because there are deeply held views about the importance of retaining specialist knowledge associated with disciplines. Most likely, educators do not know how to design a curriculum that integrates content and thinking skills (Conner & Kolajo, 2020). Despite this, in higher education around the world, there is a growing enhancement and more expansive view of integrated curriculum (Fink, 2013; National Academies of Sciences, Engineering and Medicine, 2018).

Pedagogical approaches for integration often involve developing contexts and themes for focussing learning and use inquiry, problem- or project-based approaches, case study analyses, scenario evaluations and challenges. These approaches have often been included within or alongside more conventional or more discipline-focussed teaching methods. However, educators need a more structured process for *designing curriculum* that integrates content, skills and capabilities simultaneously to enable students to meet the desired learning outcomes (Kelley & Knowles, 2016; Koh & Chai, 2016), especially if the ultimate goal is to address global issues.

This chapter focusses on how to design integrated STEM curriculum. It considers the steps involved and how to make multiple connections between curriculum elements, based on the desired outcomes and appropriate pedagogies and resources. It indicates how educators can create more effective learning environments by selecting and appropriating support for learning within meaningful, real-world learning contexts.

Understanding by design

This section explains the components of understanding by design models of curriculum design, as they can support a process for choosing what is included, why it is important and how content and skills can be integrated, which is useful when applied to integrated STEM curriculum. According to Tomlinson and McTighe (2006), quality curriculum design should:

- Develop and deepen student understanding of knowledge.
- Enable students to apply understanding by transferring knowledge and skills to authentic situations.

Designing integrated STEM curriculum 77

- Build in evidence of progress, allowing for variations in proficiency (at the beginning, during and at the end).
- Follow backwards design by starting with desired outcomes and purposes of the learning experiences provided.
- Provide sufficient support and challenge to enable students to think in complex ways.
- Provide opportunities for students to self-assess progress ("good at", "need help with").
- Develop strengths towards students becoming experts in using both specific and generic performance indicators (PIs).
- Use technologies that enable sharing collaborative design and critiquing of ideas and outcomes.
- Build in review processes to enhance quality of instruction and assessment.

Understanding by design models comply with these principles (Tomlinson & McTighe, 2006), which can be used to construct curriculum. These models tend to value backwards design principles that start with and develop alignment between student outcomes, course learning outcomes, performance indicators, assessments, teaching and learning experiences.

Given that a key aim of education is to strengthen knowledge acquisition and use, as well as to apply knowledge in new situations, research findings have clarified that different settings and pedagogies tend to promote different types of learning and ways to improve learning performance (Leisman et al., 2018). Research on integrating STEM in schools indicates that a range of pedagogies, including those that promote inquiry and social discourse, is important, especially in studies integrating math and science (Stohlmann et al., 2012; Treacy & O'Donoghue, 2014; Zemelman et al., 2005). There are likely to be advantages if the design for STEM is agile enough to include student and staff interests and is socially enabling yet is goal-oriented enough for the intentions to be clear and feasible given available resources. Approaches should not be completely open-ended, as these tend to cause confusion and misdirected effort.

Therefore, any design for *learning* really needs to be structurally aligned and to take account of what combination of outcomes are expected, what students can do to demonstrate these outcomes and what kind of learning support is required for effective learning. More briefly, three general steps in backwards curriculum design process include:

- Identify desired outcomes.
- Consider possible acceptable alternatives as evidence for assessment.
- Plan learning experiences and any necessary student support (including resources) to enable students to achieve the outcomes.

Guiding frameworks based on educational theory and practice inform curriculum design. In the framework presented in Chapter 3 (Figure 3.1), students *actively* develop knowledge and skills simultaneously through the range of focussed learning experiences provided for them (Fink, 2013). In this approach,

78 *Designing integrated STEM curriculum*

curriculum is dynamic (ever-evolving) and student-centred, in that it accommodates student interests, levels of prior knowledge, expertise and attainment, and is adapted appropriately to the resources and pedagogies available (Stenhouse, 1975). There is flexibility and therefore multiple ways to support students to achieve desired outcomes (Istance & Paniagua, 2019), including establishing what students are good at and need help with (Conner, 2014).

Constructing curriculum may also require considerations around how important the following components are in determining what is designed (Sniedze-Gregory, 2018; Stohlmann et al., 2012):

- What discipline ideas will be used as a base for interdisciplinary understanding – what is core (for example, demonstration of logical reasoning, proof or practical investigative skills)?
- What discipline components will be deliberately used for integration (see Figure 3.1 in Chapter 3)?
- How will academic, collaborative, communication and other technical and transferable skills be included?
- What opportunities will be included for students to contribute to advancing new knowledge and understanding (including innovation for new products or processes)?

Educators who followed the ADDIE instructional design concept (Branch & Kopcha, 2014) used it to construct courses that were more learner-centred (Kaminski et al., 2018; Seel et al., 2017) and were able to create appropriate teaching and learning materials through each of five processes:

- **A**nalyse learner needs.
- **D**esign an effective learner environment.
- **D**evelop learning materials.
- **I**mplement instructional strategies.
- **E**valuate results of development.

These processes inform each other during the curriculum design process and therefore can occur linearly, concurrently and recursively as iterations are made.

Guidelines for constructing integrated STEM curriculum have been based on Sniedze-Gregory (2018) but are extended here for guiding various levels of embedded skills development and include:

- Situate learning in contexts or themes that cross disciplinary boundaries (for example, environmental, technological contexts or systems).
- Provide opportunities to learn and extend key concepts (for example, applying data visualisations to modelling of the production of products from algae in biochemistry, peer reviewing and communicating possible modifications to inputs for growth systems).

Designing integrated STEM curriculum 79

- Connect disciplinary ways of working (for example, in electrical engineering connecting physics concepts, developing practical and technical skills, using design thinking, evaluating prototypes, problem-solving and working with challenges to invent and critique).
- Use appropriate technologies for STEM learning experiences (see Chapter 2).
- Use inquiry to promote relentless curiosity (student-directed and educator-supported identification of sub-questions and resources needed, student reflection on the quality of connections and development of communication skills).
- Embed work within authentic projects to develop content and skills to derive an outline or brief (development of communication, collaboration, creative and critical thinking and understanding of validity, risk evaluation and reliability).
- Assess concept understanding, process skills and argumentation in authentic ways based on evidence, ideation, insight and explanations.
- Require students to self-assess values and take a critical stance or actions measured against purpose and quality criteria to reflect on aspects of their progress.

There is clearly a huge range of means to design curriculum and learning experiences. The framework presented in Figure 3.1, Chapter 3, is an important reminder of the components that are most likely to achieve the anticipated outcomes, including appropriate supports for the range of student needs. Substantive research has revealed that, if recall of facts is desired, a different approach to learning is required than approaches required for transferring and applying knowledge (Biggs, 2003; Koedinger et al., 2013; Marton & Saljö, 1976). Approaches that improve memory recall include practice over time and practising ways to link retrieval in a range of ways. In contrast, approaches that are more likely to lead to understanding for transfer to new situations are providing multiple examples of concepts and requiring students to reflect on why a phenomenon might occur; being clear about conditional aspects related to a concept; developing models, re-synthesising information and applying it. The usefulness of memorising facts, in an era of ubiquitous digital access to knowledge sources, needs to be seriously questioned. It is what people can do with knowledge and skills to connect ideas for creative outcomes that is becoming increasingly important.

Importance of connections to STEM

Connecting ideas, practices and processes is fundamentally important to integrated STEM curriculum. There are several learning theories that discuss the importance of utilising networks and connected forms of learning, such as "actor–network theory" (Bell, 2011), "heutagogy" (Phelps et al., 2005) and

80   *Designing integrated STEM curriculum*

"connectivism" (Siemens, 2005). These theories describe how learning occurs through linking ideas, processes, people and communities, reminding us how important it is to take connectivity into account when designing curriculum and for using systems approaches for learning and connecting, potentially for generating new knowledge. The guiding principles of connectivism (Siemens, 2005) may be useful for integrating STEM and include:

- Learning and knowledge rest in diversity of opinions.
- Learning is a process connecting specialised nodes or information sources.
- Learning may reside in non-human appliances.
- Capacity to know more is more critical than what is currently known.
- Nurturing and maintaining connections is needed to facilitate continual learning.
- Ability to see connections between fields, ideas and concepts is a core skill.
- Currency (accurate, up-to-date knowledge) is the intent of all "connectivist" learning activities.
- Decision-making is itself a learning process.

More recent models of curriculum design include using digital tools for curriculum mapping as well as automated systems that help to streamline collation of student assessments for continuous quality improvement (CQI) cycles that inform accreditation processes. For an example in engineering and ABET accreditation, see Hussain et al. (2020).

Importance of constructive alignment

Constructive alignment refers to the level of congruence between course organisation, teaching and learning activities, appropriate support for learners (including feedback and assessment) and any other aspects that the educator needs to take into account to make learning more effective (Biggs, 2003). Constructive alignment is important for considering how conventions and values of disciplines are incorporated alongside any challenges for student learning.

Designing an integrated STEM approach assumes that teachers understand how the choice of pedagogy influences learning. It also assumes that teachers in higher education take the stance of an expert professional, using the art, science and scholarship of teaching (Paniagua & Istance, 2018), in which evidence related to student outcomes informs change, especially in terms of support for learners. Educators can refresh promising pedagogies to enable *learning*, rather than taking a technical or functional approach towards designing content delivery. This is discussed further as part of the challenges of integrating STEM, in Chapter 6.

In a report on the redesign of curricula that embraced the concept of participatory practice and the situated nature of learning at UniSIM in Singapore,

Lim and Cheah (2015, p. 173) recommended the following principles for designing authentic curricula:

- Connect learners to authentic workplaces.
- Engage learners in occupational dispositions (i.e. values) in the same way as those of practitioners in the field.
- Embed content in the context of workplace use.
- Develop discursive capacity for learners to engage in the same ways as practitioners.
- Develop cognitive (thinking) skills in learners.
- Develop learning-to-learn skills in learners.
- Use technological tools to promote work-based learning.

Authentic activities include inquiry, themed assignments and projects, with guides for students in the form of assessment rubrics to indicate levels of proficiency such as introductory, reinforced, mastery, outstanding and so on.

Alignment may include constructing assessment maps to indicate which activities contribute to specific aims and outcomes. These can be constructed through using a layered workbook that aligns activities (learning experiences) with assessments, as described for combining engineering and science courses by Easa (2013). In its simplest form, an assessment map is a matrix in which rows indicate learning experiences (for example, specific content focus, collaborative inquiry, situated problem-solving, internships) and columns relate to outcomes within a specific course. Such mapping helps to identify sequencing within courses and whether students have had sufficient opportunities to attain mastery for specific skills. When managed as a system of collated performance indicators, a map can provide cohort information related to outcomes-based assessment (Hussain et al., 2020).

Developing a theme, context, issue or challenge

Planning for integration is best done by developing a theme, context, issue or challenge in which knowledge and processes are drawn from more than one discipline. These need to be authentic, real-world and relevant to students. Themes, contexts, issues and challenges can be broad enough to enable multiple pathways and choices for students yet have specific-enough outcomes to enable connections to be demonstrated from at least two disciplines. It is important that quality resources are available to support the theme, context, issue or challenge. Some steps for developing them are provided in Table 4.1.

There may be variable contributions from each of the STEM disciplines in this approach, as there is no rule for parity nor specified combinations: this is not an "anything goes" approach. Rather, it works best when bounded and when students are guided by the criteria on which they will be assessed. This is why it is important to start planning by considering how students will demonstrate the end point.

82   *Designing integrated STEM curriculum*

Table 4.1 Steps for planning theme, context, issue or challenge

Step	Guiding questions
1 Choose real-world theme, context, issue or challenge	Why is this focus important? What problem or issue needs to be solved?
2 Establish learning outcomes	What are the learning outcomes? (for example, solve a problem, create a product, explain connections and/or communicate new understandings)
3 Create assessment tasks for demonstrating the learning outcomes	What knowledge, skills and capabilities should be demonstrated?
	How will students demonstrate their understanding, their creation of new knowledge or products and skills?
	What rubrics are needed to support student development and progress?
	What levels of performance will indicate student success? What performance indicators (PIs) for proficiency and sufficiency will be used?
4 Identify discipline aspects, skills and capabilities needed	Which disciplines will contribute and to what extent? How are they connected? (see previous section on cross-cutting concepts)
	What discipline objectives will be achieved? (key concepts, processes or discipline approaches)
	What skills do students need to develop to connect their knowledge, understanding and skills from a range of sources?
5 Identify possibilities for integration	Educators work together to uncover meaningful links within a theme, context, issue or challenge. How will students be guided to see connections between disciplines, so they become mutually supportive and are synergistically generative?

In backwards curriculum design frameworks, themes are developed with the desired learning outcomes in mind (Vasquez et al., 2013). In higher education, these outcomes are often standards, recommended prescribed knowledge, performance indicators or skill levels. Starting with the potential ways that outcomes could be assessed, both formative (for informing students' progress and development) and summative (for completion outcomes) are therefore very important. Obviously, there are a range of outcomes, kinds of artefacts and products that could demonstrate learning outcomes as part of assessment. Further examples are provided in Chapter 5.

Activities that allow students to choose how to frame aspects of tasks seem to enhance student engagement, probably because enabling choice supports student autonomy (Schmidt et al., 2018). Providing open-ended tasks with bounded guidelines enables student choice, which can lead to increased motivation (Glasser, 1998).

Big ideas and concepts for a theme are identified alongside the associated skills students are expected to demonstrate in assessment tasks (International Baccalaureate Organization, 2017). Themes can be advanced by identifying the essential or key questions that will foster inquiry and build understanding. Figure 4.1 shows pathways for constructing possible learning experiences associated with a theme, context, issue or challenge. Within the learning experiences, students can determine what they already know, what sources of knowledge they need and how they will connect ideas to solve the issue, problem or challenge to demonstrate the desired outcomes.

Figure 4.1 indicates steps and iterations for developing active learning experiences within a theme, context or issue as follows:

1. Choose a real-world theme, context, issue or challenge.
2. Establish learning outcomes.
3. Identify assessment tasks that enable students to demonstrate the outcomes.
4. Identify discipline aspects, skills and capabilities needed.
5. Create learning experiences that enable students to meet the outcomes.
6. Identify resources and sources of information (including appropriate people).
7. Support students (through feedback) to integrate knowledge and skills.

These steps are described in the following subsections.

Choose a real-world theme, context, issue or challenge

The chosen context, theme, issue or challenge should be relevant to students, so that they can make connections with it at a personal, institutional or social level. It could be a current issue or problem for students, the institution or

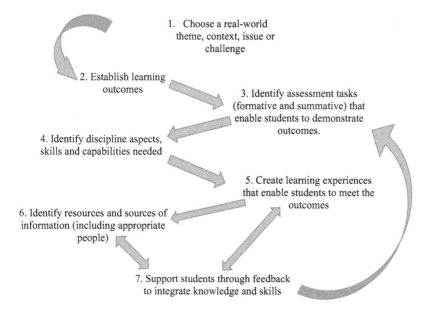

Figure 4.1 Pathways for constructing learning experiences

84 *Designing integrated STEM curriculum*

the local community. It is useful to identify the key concepts (big ideas) that provide the focus for problem-solving. Ideally, the big idea or issue is one that could be solved in a number of ways. This then provides choice for students in how they can solve the problem and evaluate possibilities. Some inquiry and problem-solving activities can be launched by posing an overarching question.

Establish learning outcomes

Learning outcomes could be content-related, problem-related or skills-oriented. It is useful to include specific statements such as "demonstrate . . ." and broader outcomes beyond those of "understand and recall", such as "connect and evaluate . . .". The intention is to integrate more than one STEM discipline and to develop skills and capabilities simultaneously. Statements for learning outcomes need to be specific enough to reflect the focus and student accomplishment yet broad enough to enable students to have some choice in how they can demonstrate achievement.

Identify assessment tasks

The third step is to identify assessment tasks (formative and summative) that enable students to demonstrate outcomes. So, how will students demonstrate outcomes? Assessment tasks should link to concepts, big ideas and practices, so that students are required to demonstrate how they have used, applied or linked these. Be open and creative in terms of the range of assessment tasks that could be used. Whatever is focussed on must be measurable and feasible given the resources available.

The language used for learning outcomes is very important, as it indicates the performance levels required. The levels of acceptable student performance can be clearly indicated using a range of levels of performance indicators (PIs), which can be quite specific in naming techniques, identifying the specific connections between key concepts, use of methodologies or levels of thinking, analysing, synthesising, evaluating, classifying and so on. For example, creating a video presentation and sharing this online to demonstrate key concepts and thinking processes has become more common recently in the confines of social distancing. This kind of assessment also allows for self and peer review and provides opportunities for students to ask each other for elaboration or extended explanations. Consider whether presentations are for triads, larger groups or the whole class, whether in-person or online and whether assessments contribute to eportfolio items.

Identify discipline aspects, skills and capabilities needed

Authentic contexts tend to be open-ended and complex. Many different skills may be needed for different pathways in solving the same problem, including knowledge from different disciplines and skills to curate and synthesise information. This kind of learning requires agility on the part of learner and educator, adapting to the theme, context, issue or challenge and resources available. It is useful to become relatively comfortable with uncertainty and potential ambiguity, as this is often inherent in authentic and real-world issues. If present, uncertainty can be investigated itself and can be linked to the tentative nature of STEM knowledge or the limitations bounded by current technologies. It is important to embrace complexity and model evaluative inquiry with students by asking lots of questions, demonstrating enduring curiosity and the need for rigour and reflection on evidence (Conner, 2014). This will demonstrate the type of thinking that helps learners develop resilience within uncertain futures.

Create learning experiences that enable students to meet the outcomes

Learning experiences are important because they enable students to integrate knowledge and skills to achieve desired outcomes. There are a number of considerations for creating learning experiences, perhaps the most obvious being whether it will be an individual or collaborative activity. In active approaches to learning, students are required to participate in thinking and processing information in some way. For example, problem-based and inquiry activities work well for integrating knowledge sources with collaboration and communication skills. However, it is wise to consider whether some students will find this sort of task too challenging.

Students need to be persistent in the face of developing iterations (or potentially failures, in the case of generating devices, prototypes or system solutions). Activities for connecting with professionals or people who work in government agencies, related industries and businesses may be important for solving the problem. Students may need to be reminded about appropriately managing any connections with community groups. Connections should be respectful, timely and relevant.

Identify resources and sources of information

There are many tools and resources that students could use. Try to predict these and therefore guide students to key sources, software and technical resources, ensuring equitable access to them. People can serve as resources, so students should be encouraged to contact people as further resources, such as librarians, who are well trained in appropriate data base searches. Students may need to be aware of protocols, such as respecting work timelines of others and ethical procedures, if they are seeking opinions or expertise. Students will need clear guidelines and instructions, as well as digital links to resources and "how tos" for specific tasks. Frequently asked questions (FAQ) sections located on learning management systems can circumvent many student queries, especially by those uncertain about how to proceed.

86 *Designing integrated STEM curriculum*

Support students to integrate knowledge and skills

It is important for students to experience steps in success and to receive appropriate and ongoing feedback about what they have achieved so far: what they are good at and what they need to work on. Of prime importance when integrating STEM is providing support for students to integrate knowledge sources, skills and capabilities. Students can identify these aspects for themselves as well, using self-reflection on quality and progress statements and peer review protocols based on rubrics (with levels for indication of expectations and high-quality outcomes). However, educators can also support students with a range of levels of guidance to achieve acceptable outcomes. This can easily be achieved through prompting students to *think*, by using questions, cues and prompts (Conner, 2014). It is worth considering how check points could be built in to identify student progress achievements. Timelines and the frequency of feedback also need to be considered carefully, depending on the complexity of tasks, and expectations should be made explicit to students. Managing student expectations is a core part of effective teaching.

Including active learning opportunities

As emphasised in Chapter 3, active learning requires cognitive engagement of some kind in relation to set tasks. It is the role of the educator to inspire students through questions and to provide clear instructions in writing. Actively engaging with content; questioning validity and reliability of claims; questioning analysis protocols and consequences; and tinkering and adjusting prototypes are important in STEM and provide a means to advance active engagement. In the next sections, critical thinking, creative thinking and design thinking (through challenge activities) are discussed in more detail to show how they can support active thinking and learning.

Critical thinking

Using critical thinking presupposes that not everything is known and that not everything known is based on verifiable evidence. The capability to critique and evaluate sources of information, interrogate facts, check veracity of alternative views and derive a considered position based on evidence have all been identified as incredibly important skills for the future (Goldsprink & Kay, 2018). In STEM, it is very important for students to develop dispositions that question the validity of competing claims and interpretations, especially as information is ubiquitously available. With the power of social media, we are being bombarded with citizens' opinions, which are increasingly displacing public and peer-reviewed sources. Historically, science has been based on facts and empirical evidence, as this leads to objectivity. The facts seemingly speak for themselves, when in reality the facts have been chosen to support a biased standpoint. There may be conditional elements for applicability, context dependencies, competing perspectives and so on. A critical interpretivist approach uncovers the motives, interests and ethical (or unethical) standpoints of those who contributed to information (Cope & Kalantzis, 2015).

Criticality can refer to either analysing functions or to applying an evaluation mindset. In mathematics, for example, Kotsopoulos et al. (2017) suggested that critical thinking about conceptual, digital and mathematical objects can use four overlapping types of activities:

- Unplugging – not using computers.
- Tinkering – taking objects apart and changing or modifying their component parts.
- Making – constructing new objects.
- Remixing – appropriating objects and components to make new ones.

Some examples in which these activities would be useful are sorting mathematical expressions, changing the content of a spreadsheet, creating an interactive mathematical presentation and modifying existing reports to visualise data by using a digital dashboard.

Further, taking a critical stance does not necessarily involve resolving conflict or contested claims, but rather ensures students value being engaged in trying to understand that there may be contextual or contingent factors that influence outcomes. Question-asking and getting students to develop their own questions (and to seek answers) helps with this. Another way taking a critical stance has been translated to pedagogy in the schooling sector is to provide provoking exit questions for students to ponder until the next session (Flannagan, 2019). As part of promoting critical thinking, then, it is very important for educators to take the view that knowledge is tentative and limited by the technology that has enabled us to understand. Knowledge may only be partial, be contestable, have an emerging efficiency and be bounded by specific contexts. Educators can support students to critique information when they model relentless curiosity by continually asking questions.

Creative thinking

Creative thinking is where multiple or alternative possibilities and provocations are considered, developed and generated. De Bono (1995) elaborated on the concept of *serious creativity* by stressing its importance in problem-solving and indicating how serious creativity can be marshalled through lateral thinking processes and specific techniques. He stated:

> The normal behavior of the brain in perception is to set up routine patterns and to follow these. In order to cut across patterns we can use deliberate techniques (provocation, movement, random entry). These techniques can be learned, practiced and used deliberately.
>
> (p. 12)

88 *Designing integrated STEM curriculum*

Creative thinking was positioned by De Bono as being at the heart of generating new knowledge.

In STEM, creative thinking provides a mindset for innovation and for generating solutions that might not have been thought of previously. Innovation is advanced through the collective capacity to work alongside others for inspiring and imagining new ideas. Creative thinking is integral to design thinking but also accommodates attributes of risk-taking, seeking alternatives, being seriously playful and self-criticality, as these can support problem-solving with an evaluation flair in design contexts. Therefore, creative thinking is important for the generation of new knowledge in STEM, especially if the aim is to generate knowledge and techniques as innovative solutions for addressing local and global issues.

Use of high-end digital tools adds value and a whole new dimension to the possibilities for representing information, visualising information, investigating possible connections, creating new frames of reference and systems models and viewing simulations in multiple dimensions. All of these can enhance and augment learning experiences and assist in creating new knowledge and solutions. Use of digital tools for inquiry and problem-solving in STEM contexts is discussed more fully in Chapter 2.

Design thinking within challenge activities

Challenges are types of activities that actively engage student design thinking. They may be set up as a competition for students to derive solutions for issues or problems and can be sequentially structured and even extremely open-ended. Challenges can be enabled through hackathons to ideate solutions using a design process for solving a local or regional issue and may include industry partners as guides and mentors. Benefits are that challenges usually involve "sprints" – fast, concentrated ways to come up with as many possible ideas and choose one or more to trial as part of a design thinking process. This can be used to enable transformation or solutions at scale. For example, in an Empathy Jam held at the National University of Galway (Hogan, 2020, p. 305), the driving questions for the hackathon were:

- How might technology ease the issue of traffic congestion in Galway City?
- How might elderly people engage with technology to prevent loneliness and social exclusion?

The first question relates to a specific local issue, for which students were able to design a preferred solution. The second question is one that applies locally but could be scaled up nationally and globally.

The process for running a hackathon involves icebreakers and guidelines for team building; collective discussions; checkpoints for progress; developing a prototype; evaluating a prototype or potential process solution; and developing a future-oriented proposal, product or service pitch. Hackathons provide opportunities for blending practical skills, contextual and social factors simultaneously. In the case of the Empathy Jam, assessment was mediated through student journals and videos of them undertaking the process (Hogan, 2020). Students on winning teams in hackathons may be invited to become mentors and are guided to support future teams. Mentors (industry participants or previously successful students) are often rewarded for enabling the generation of ideas (Gibson et al., 2018).

In collaborative challenges, any member of a group can contribute ideas and feedback to create possible solutions. Feedback on structured problems can be pre-empted and therefore can potentially be automated in online systems. In contrast, feedback or support given to students on more open-ended challenges may require quite detailed responses and use of peer scoring rubrics to assist students in providing peer feedback (Kelsey, 2001).

Peer review builds students' capability to provide constructive feedback, exposes them to more perspectives and helps to reduce errors (Gaynor, 2019). Therefore, the amount and type of feedback will vary, depending on content, skills students have and the complexity of the challenge. For example, in the Curtin University Balance of the Planet challenge, there were multiple topics to choose from (Gibson et al., 2018). Each topic had its own associated rubric that included solution elements to help guide team decisions. Each team had to create a compelling pitch and present this as a seven-minute video. Members of teams decided what components were included in the video to meet performance indicators or criteria. In developing student support for this challenge, members of Curtin University's online development team worked with the Curtin University Sustainability Policy Institute, UNESCO Bangkok and the Australian Sustainable Development Institute to design the challenge process. Setting up challenges in this way can be considered innovative education, in which external agencies and businesses work with learning designers and technical teams (Grummon, 2010).

Two further examples of themes and challenges that connect with big issues for communities and provide opportunities for students to think deeply and act for better humanistic futures are Resilience in the Face of Natural Disasters and the Silver Lining Challenge (The Challenge Institute, 2018). Even when the titles of challenges indicate the desired outcomes, students still require effective support.

Supporting effective learning environments

Specific educator actions can support learners to progress, including, for example, scaffolding the steps in the learning process, providing prompts, cues and questions at the right time, which is important for enabling specific progress. Saye and Brush (2006) distinguish between static scaffolds prepared as part of task instructions (because often educators can predict what information and difficulties students might encounter) and adaptive scaffolds contingent on student progress through a task. Adaptive scaffolding requires continuous checking: on

90 *Designing integrated STEM curriculum*

how students understand (through questioning), on their progressive thinking, on how they are applying this thinking to tasks and on their levels of procedural knowledge (including where to find information or how to critique methods). According to Saye and Brush (2006), this kind of student support is crucial for creative inquiry and for developing experts. Grouping students so they can provide each other with support (asking and answering questions) is also useful for advancing group outcomes. Jadallah et al. (2011) found that it was very useful to provide constructive feedback to groups, especially during group discussions. Additional pedagogical considerations and challenges are profiled in Chapter 6.

Conclusion

Designing integrated STEM curriculum in higher education should use instructional models and frameworks that apply backwards design principles, that is, starting with an authentic situation and then developing the outcomes, assessments and learning experiences. Using themes, contexts, issues or challenges as the basis of integration helps to build capability and capacity among graduates to solve local and global issues. The resources, technologies and pedagogies chosen must be appropriate and link to and support the development of the desired outcomes. Through student-centred interdisciplinary inquiry, problem-solving and design-based innovation activities, students can integrate different types of knowledge, skills and capabilities (especially thinking skills). Students benefit from collaborating as emerging, creative, enquiring experts who are ever-curious about alternative possibilities and can effectively communicate to appropriate audiences. By using contexts for integrating learning experiences that incorporate relevant technologies, educators can focus on creativity, connections with real applications in practice and the potential for social and economic development. Effective curriculum design takes account of students' knowledge and needs, is inspiring, leverages interactions between people, places and resources and is situated within real-world contexts for developing multiple humanistic solutions.

Designing activities, courses and programmes that integrate STEM will become more comprehensive with experience, research and evaluation of what works. Guides for backwards alignment, as described in this chapter, are probably most useful for new courses. Backwards design enables learning in STEM to call on patterns, connections, actions and applications from real-world examples and situate learning in current issues and problems that need to be addressed.

Much more research is needed on the wide range of ways for implementing integrated STEM. Further ideas for research are given in Chapter 7.

References

Bell, F. (2011). Connectivism: Its place in theory-informed research and innovation in technology-enabled learning. *International Review of Research in Open and Distance Learning*, *12*(3), 98–118.

Biggs, J. (2003). *Teaching for quality learning at university* (2nd ed.). SRHE and Open University Press.

Branch, R. M., & Kopcha, T. J. (2014). Instructional design models. In J. M. Spector, M. D. Merrill, J. Elen, & M. J. Bishop (Eds.), *Handbook of research on educational communications and technology* (pp. 77–87). Springer.

The Challenge Institute. (2018). *Challenge-based learning.* www.challengebasedlearning.org

Conner, L. (2014). Students' use of evaluative constructivism: Comparative degrees of intentional learning. *International Journal of Qualitative Studies in Education, 27*(4), 472–489. http://doi.org/10.1080/09518398.2013.771228

Conner, L. (2020). *Integrating STEMM in higher education: A proposed curriculum development framework.* Paper published in the proceedings of 6th International Conference on Higher Education Advances (HEAd'20). Universitat Politècnica de València. http://doi.org/10.4995/HEAd20.2020.11058

Conner, L., & Kolajo, Y. (2020). The chemistry of critical thinking: The pursuit to do both better. In E. P. Blessinger & M. Makhanya (Eds.), *Improving classroom engagement and international development programs: International perspectives on humanizing higher education* (Vol. 27, pp. 93–110). Innovations in Higher Education Teaching and Learning. Emerald Publishing Limited. https://doi.org/10.1108/S2055-364120200000027009

Cope, B., & Kalantzis, M. (2015). The things you do to know: An introduction to the pedagogy of multiliteracies. In B. Cope & M. Kalantzis (Eds.), *A pedagogy of multiliteracies: Learning by design* (pp. 1–36). Palgrave Macmillan.

De Bono, E. (1995). Serious creativity. *The Journal for Quality and Participation, 18*(5), 12.

Easa, S. M. (2013). Framework and guidelines for graduate attribute assessment in engineering education. *Canadian Journal of Civil Engineering, 40*(6), 547–556. http://doi.org/10.1139/cjce-2012-0485

Fink, L. D. (2013). *Creating significant learning experiences: An integrated approach to designing college courses.* Jossey-Bass.

Flannagan, J. S. (2019). Designing a tiered science lesson. *Science and Children, 57*(2), 42–48.

Gaynor, J. (2019). Peer review in the classroom: Student perceptions, peer feedback quality and the role of assessment. *Assessment & Evaluation in Higher Education, 45*(5), 758–775. https://doi.org/10.1080/02602938.2019.1697424

Gibson, D., Irving, L., & Scott, K. (2018). Technology-enabled challenge-based learning in a global context. In M. Shonfeld & D. Gibson (Eds.), *Collaborative learning and a global world* (pp. 32–42). Information Age Publishers.

Glasser, W. (1998). *Choice theory.* HarperCollins.

Goldsprink, C., & Kay, R. (2018). *Towards education 3.0: The changing goalposts for education.* Corwin.

Grummon, P. T. H. (2010). Trends in higher education. *Planning for Higher Education.* http://doi.org/10.2307/1974977

Hogan, M. (2020). *From Times Square to Eyre Square: Hackathons as authentic learning for information systems students.* Paper published in the proceedings of 6th International Conference on Higher Education Advances (HEAd'20). Universitat Politècnica de València. http://dxdoi.org/10.4995/HEAd20:2020.11046

Hussain, W., Spady, W. G., Naqash, T., Khan, S. Z., Khawaja, B. A., & Conner, L. (2020). ABET accreditation during and after COVID19-navigating the digital age. *IEEE Access, 8*, 218997–219046. http://doi.org/10.1109/ACCESS.2020.3041736

International Baccalaureate Organization. (2017). *Fostering interdisciplinary teaching and learning in the MYP.* International Baccalaureate Organization.

92 Designing integrated STEM curriculum

Istance, D., & Paniagua, A. (2019). *Learning to leapfrog: Innovative pedagogies to transform education*. Brookings Institute.

Jadallah, M., Anderson, R., Nguyen-Jahiel, K., Miller, B., Kim, I., & Kuo, I. (2011). Influence of a teacher's scaffolding moves during child-led small-group discussions. *American Educational Research Journal, 48*, 194–230.

Kaminski, K., Johnson, P., Otis, S., Perry, D., Schmidt, T., Whetsel, M., & Williams, H. (2018). Personal tales of instructional design from the facilitator's perspective. In B. Hokanson, G. Clinton, & K. Kaminski (Eds.), *Educational technology and narrative story and instructional design* (pp. 87–101). Springer.

Kelley, T. R., & Knowles, J. G. (2016). A conceptual framework for integrated STEM education. *Journal of STEM Education, 3*(1), 1–11.

Kelsey, K. D. (2001). Overcoming standardized testing with authentic assessment strategies in the classroom. *The Agricultural Education Magazine, 73*(5), 4.

Koedinger, K. R., Booth, J. L., & Klarh, D. (2013). Instructional complexity and the science to constrain it. *Science, 342*, 935–937.

Koh, J. H., & Chai, C. S. (2016). Seven design frames that teachers use when considering technological pedagogical content knowledge (TPACK). *Computers and Education, 102*, 244–257.

Kotsopoulos, D., Floyd, L., Khan, S., Namukasa, I., Somanath, S., Weber, J., & Yiu, C. (2017). A pedagogical framework for computational thinking. *Digital Experiences in Mathematics Education, 3*, 154–171. http://doi.org/10.1007/s40751-017-0031-2

Leisman, G., Mualem, R., & Mughrabi, S. K. (2018). *How people learn II: The science and practice of learning*. The National Academies Press.

Lim, W. Y., & Cheah, H. M. (2015). Experiencing desire outcomes of adult education through participatory practice design. In The International Academic Forum (Ed.), *Proceedings of the European conference on education* (pp. 169–183). The International Academic Forum.

Marton, F., & Saljö, R. (1976). On qualitative differences in learning: I – outcome and process. *British Journal of Educational Psychology, 46*, 4–11. https://doi.org/10.1111/j.2044-8279.1976.tb02980.x

National Academies of Sciences, Engineering and Medicine. (2018). *The integration of the humanities and arts with sciences, engineering, and medicine in higher education: Branches from the same tree*. The National Academies Press. https://doi.org/10.17226/24988

Paniagua, A., & Istance, D. (2018). *Teachers as designers of learning environments: The importance of innovative pedagogies*. OECD Publishing. http://doi.org/10.1787/9789264085374-en

Park Rogers, M., & Abell, S. K. (2008). The design, enactment, and experience of inquiry-based instruction in undergraduate science education: A case study. *Science Education, 92*(4), 591–607. https://doi.org/10.1002/sce.20247

Phelps, R., Hase, S., & Elis, A. (2005). Competency, capability, complexity and computers: Exploring a new model for conceptualising end-user computer education. *British Journal of Educational Technology, 36*(1), 67–85.

Rios, J. A., Ling, G., Pugh, R., Becker, D., & Bacall, A. (2020). Identifying critical 21st-century skills for workplace success: A content analysis of job advertisements. *Educational Researcher, 49*(2), 80–89.

Saye, J. W., & Brush, T. (2006). Comparing teachers' strategies for supporting student inquiry in a problem-based multimedia-enhanced history unit. *Theory & Research in Social Education, 34*(2), 183–212.

Schmidt, J. A., Rosenberg, J. M., & Bayner, P. N. (2018). A person-in-context approach to student engagement in science: Examining learning activities and choice. *Journal of Research in Science Teaching, 55*(1), 19–43.

Seel, N. M., Lehmann, T., Blumschein, P., & Podolskiy, O. A. (2017). *Instructional design for learning theoretical foundations*. Sense Publishers.

Siemens, G. (2005). A learning theory for the digital age. *Instructional Technology and Distance Education, 2*(1), 3–10.

Sniedze-Gregory, S. (2018). *Enhancing interdisciplinary teaching and learning through guided assessment design* [Unpublished PhD thesis]. Flinders University.

Stenhouse, L. (1975). *Introduction to curriculum research and development*. Heineman.

Stohlmann, M., Moore, T. J., & Roehrig, G. H. (2012). Considerations for teaching integrated STEM education. *Journal of Pre-College Engineering Education Research, 2*(1), 27–34.

Tomlinson, C. A., & McTighe, J. (2006). *Integrating differentiated instruction and understanding by design*. Association for Supervision and Curriculum Development.

Treacy, P., & O'Donoghue, J. (2014). Authentic integration: A model for integrating mathematics and science in the classroom. *International Journal of Mathematical Education in Science and Technology, 45*(5), 703–718.

Vasquez, J. A., Sneider, C., & Comer, M. (2013). *STEM lesson essentials, grades 3–8*. Heinemann.

Zemelman, S., Daniels, H., & Hyde, A. (2005). *Best practice: New standards for teaching and learning in America's schools* (3rd ed.). Heinemann.

5   Assessment

Introduction

Traditionally, the purpose of formal education has been to acquire information, understand concepts, master skills and apply all of these appropriately. Information was treated as a commodity and learners simultaneously as both consumers and products of knowledge. Higher education institutions (HEIs) typically assessed knowledge and skills because there was usually a right or wrong answer and achievements were based on practical skill outcomes that could be measured easily. Historically, curriculum planning in higher education involved organising knowledge and skills into manageable topics or subtopics, i.e. organised by content. Unless the components were integrated or linked, the tendency was to treat these components as separate chunks that could be assessed in chunks. However, research on learning has indicated that, to the contrary, people can demonstrate understanding (and especially creativity) in a wide variety of ways (National Research Council, 2005). Educators have been advocating for more integration and connected ways of viewing knowledge, processes and transferable thinking skills for some time now (Boix Mansilla & Gardner, 2003; Klein, 2005; Martin-Kniep et al., 1995; Schleicher, 2018). Central to the reform of integrating curriculum and therefore to integrated models for STEM education is a redesign of assessment to be outcomes-focussed and contextualised according to the issue or problem being addressed (Yanez et al., 2019).

For most of the 20th century, education focussed on set assessments that provided a common (normative) way of evaluating student knowledge and skills that was designed to compare individuals for ranking and, ultimately, employment purposes. As a result, learners were given very little choice about what they learned or how they demonstrated learning through assessment. This perpetuated the idea that student ability can be measured through their mental recall (cognitive) abilities. Education and learning, when viewed from a commodification model (as opposed to a developmental one), do not necessarily develop a sense of wonderment, empowerment or curiosity that would lead to multiple learning experiences for in-depth understanding and application to world issues. It certainly doesn't encourage innovation, because there are preconceived, correct answers that enable students to gain credit for qualifications.

In contrast, authentic assessment, because of its situatedness in real issues, does not come with preconceived answers.

Assessment is a key part of constructive alignment in curriculum design, as evidence of knowledge, skills and capabilities must be gathered if they are to be valued by students and educators. Assessment of learning must measure and collect evidence of outcomes, provide judgements on a range of levels of attainment and focus on competencies (Milligan et al., 2020). As such, teachers need to plan explicitly to support student development of the skills needed for demonstrating outcomes (O'Malley et al., 2017). Constructive alignment means that there is a direct connection between the experiences with which students are provided and how students use these experiences to contribute to the learning outcomes.

In a study by Hussain et al. (2020), learning outcomes were further elaborated on as being culminating, enabling or discrete outcomes. Each type of outcome helps to determine the kinds of activities included within curriculum design (see Chapter 4) and how these are evaluated, either informally (to provide learning progress feedback or formative assessment for learning) or formally (thereby contributing to credit for qualifications). It can be challenging for educators to reconsider which learning experiences need to be assessed, choosing those that truly contribute to student progress or enable outcomes.

Even with clarity for assessment in courses, assessment *tasks* must be suitable for learners at a level appropriate for the course and qualification outcomes. Assessment criteria must match and measure the learning outcomes and include judgements of those outcomes in terms of the proficiency and sufficiency required. Assessment tasks need to be manageable ("doable") by learners and should ideally be easily assessable by the marker or assessor. Constructive alignment also means that the outcomes for qualifications align with and contribute to the overarching graduate attributes for an institution.

In Chapter 4, it was recommended that curriculum design start with the desired outcomes in mind and then move to considering the learning experiences (activities) and learning environment that supports students. Assessment matters in that it has a great deal to do with driving what kind of learning occurs (Biggs, 2003) and is particularly crucial for integrated design, in which interdisciplinary knowledge and skills need to be developed and assessed simultaneously. This is shown in Figure 3.1 (Chapter 3).

Students in higher education tend to be quite strategic in terms of effort; often they will not work on what is not assessed, as their focus is on completing assessments to pass a course, and they are not prepared to expend effort if it does not result in a significant change to their grade (Conner, 2014). Learning and assessment are therefore interdependent (Ketelhut & Tutwiler, 2018), which means that assessment methods strongly determine what students expend effort on and what kind of effort or learning is invoked. For example, a heavy reliance on examinations is likely to lead to surface recall approaches to study and an emphasis on memorisation (Prosser & Trigwell, 1999). Knowing this, it is important to take a very considered approach to assessment design, to

96 *Assessment*

create situations that more aptly assess the range of knowledge, skills and capabilities aligned with desired learning outcomes.

The luxury, or perhaps a confounding issue that educators face, is that there are many possible forms that assessment could take that equally provide information about student learning progress and outcomes. However, some types of assessment are more suited to some contexts than others. Therefore, the next section discusses the purposes and associated types of assessments to support integration in STEM in more detail.

Purposes and outcomes of assessment

Assessment provides a range of purposes (Crisp, 2020) that include:

- Providing feedback to learners about progress in their learning as well as reasons for their grade (Gunn, 2015).
- Demonstrating achievement, skills and capabilities.
- Providing focus or purpose for the learning.
- Motivating students and providing guidance about the desired outcomes.
- Providing feedback about learning to the teacher: what was easy or difficult to inform teaching modifications or indicate if mediation is needed.
- Demonstrating transfer of knowledge, skills or capabilities to further contexts.
- Gaining credentials and qualifications.
- Indicating readiness for more advanced study.
- Providing a quality assurance mechanism for institutions and professional bodies.

As evident in this list, there is a strong connection between assessment and demonstration of quality of learning that has meaning beyond a grade for a qualification. Assessments should provide intellectual challenge for students and provide motivation for continued learning (Crisp, 2020). This means it is important to communicate to students how each type of assessment contributes to the broader goals and outcomes for a qualification, so they clearly understand why an assessment task is important in enabling them to demonstrate their learning gains.

Due to the high-stakes nature of assessment for meeting outcomes and standards, educators and students have shown an unwillingness to take risks with changing assessments and with building in developmental sequences to support students to advance the skills and capabilities they need. A deep understanding of how students make connections across ideas is needed to redesign assessment types to accommodate outcomes in STEM.

The importance of shifting to more open-ended assessments through inquiry and problem-solving tasks (as explained in Chapters 3 and 4) provides students with the flexibility to derive multiple solutions and to work collaboratively. Educators must therefore deliberately value assessment tasks that help students demonstrate how they have evaluated sources of knowledge and connected disparate ideas, potentially generating new knowledge and innovation.

The shift in thinking about assessment also needs to accommodate and value collective contributions (Zhao, 2016). This means that rather than assessment tasks capturing only individual talent, collaboration and collective contribution should also be assessed. Assessment tasks for integrated STEM should value student collaboration, as this is how the real world works – to produce better outcomes than what could be produced by individuals alone. Tasks that deliberately value collaboration also enable students to develop communication skills, as applied to their learning and real-life contexts, finding their own solutions rather than replicating a predetermined answer (Härtig et al., 2020; You et al., 2018; Zhao, 2016). In this approach, there is much more emphasis on the performativity of knowledge (Gilbert, 2005), its application to real problems (Krajcik et al., 2008) and the development of skills and capabilities. This trend is occurring across education sectors more generally.

The purpose of this chapter, therefore, is to provide insights into some key questions related to assessment when integrating STEM. They are:

- What is authentic assessment?
- Why is it important to assess capabilities?
- How do we design assessments for integrated STEM?
- What are some promising examples of assessment methods that can be transferred to multiple learning contexts?

Authentic assessment

Authentic assessment of student knowledge, skills and capabilities is situated in real-world examples and can support student development for either continuing studies or future careers (Ashford-Rowe et al., 2014; Boud & Falchikov, 2006). An inquiry or problem, that is, the focus of the assessment, must come from a real example, scenario or issue and must be relevant to students (Bulte et al., 2005) personally, as groups, as communities more generally (Bybee et al., 2009) or to broader people–planet issues (Conner, 2020).

In the same way that STEM education should be designed for integrating knowledge, authentic assessments should be designed with integration of knowledge, skills and capabilities in mind. Authentic assessments combine more than one discipline's knowledge, as well as specific processes that are relevant to the learning context, issue or problem. Students must have opportunities through assessment to demonstrate how they have connected ideas, how they can use intersubjective dialogue to evaluate and compare ideas and how they must base their responses and justifications on findings and evidence claims.

Part of the shift from more traditional content-based assessments to authentic assessment is the move away from knowledge per se as being the most important thing for students to understand. Instead, the utility of knowledge, how it is applied to settings and is connected may be more important,

98   *Assessment*

described by Gilbert (2005) as the *performativity* of knowledge, and by Krajcik et al. (2008) as *knowledge-in-use*. To account for cognitive and non-cognitive skill development simultaneously, Zhao (2016) recommended using product-based assessments, such as the creation of physical products (including presentations, services or models of processes) that meet a genuine need, since these types of assessments can provide more comprehensive information about the levels of a student's development. Assessments in a chemistry course at Monash University were altered to accommodate industrial applications (for example, traditional titration of acetic acid was changed to developing an appropriate level of acid for sauces that Mars Food® produces; George-Williams et al., 2018). In the same chemistry course, a partnership was established with Rationale®, a personal care company, to evaluate and design molecules for inclusion in sunscreens. Other modified assessments required students to develop their own synthetic protocols based on peer-reviewed publications. As tangible outcomes of these shifts in assessment focus, students recognised they developed transferable skills such as time management, experimental design and critical thinking.

Assessment activities in integrated STEM overall should provide opportunities for students to demonstrate how they integrate knowledge (Härtig et al., 2020) and skills simultaneously. The choice of context or scenario makes a difference, as some contexts are more amenable to particular assessments. However, using authentic contexts for assessment is not without challenges, as inappropriate contexts, those to which students do not relate, can block use of prior knowledge or create a positive bias towards those who are more familiar with the context. As Fortus and Krajcik (2020) have stated:

> Using different contexts to assess the same ideas can lead to dramatically different results. We need to recognize that students' performance on assessments is dependent on multiple factors, not just the understanding of the ideas underlying a specific assessment item.
>
> (p. 179)

In most HEIs, students in every class and qualification come with different sets of prior knowledge and levels of proficiency that are related to their previous experiences. A constructivist approach would seek information about student capabilities and accommodate these as part of the ongoing support and changes to the types of formative assessment so that assessment and feedback contribute significantly to student learning experiences.

One way that this is being circumvented in some institutions is to take a deliberate focus on outcomes. For example, Schneider and colleagues (2019) provided convincing examples in chemistry and physics classes in Finland and the USA that when students learn in meaningful contexts, they are more likely to be innovative and creative. The learning experiences and associated assessments for these courses are experiential and immersive, using contexts, themes, issues or challenges and make use of advanced new technologies. At Flinders

University, South Australia (www.flinders.edu.au), there are undergraduate courses in integrated STEM for each year level in bachelor's qualifications:

1   Nature of STEM (STEM1001) – principles of STEM, investigations that include evaluating valid scientific endeavours. Outcomes relate to developing critical reasoning, teamwork and oral and written communication skills.
2   Innovation in STEM (STEM2005) – range of innovation for developing new products, social innovation and policy change, developing problem-solving, design thinking and developing pitches, innovation management, commercial viability and partnering.
3   Science Connect (STEM3001) – students undertake an internship or project with a business or industry.

Faculty at the university reflect continuously on these outcomes when designing new or adjusting assessment tasks in these courses.

Another example comes from the Universitat Politechnica de Valencia (2020). In this course, data science is used as an integrator because the ideas and processes can be applied to a range of disciplines. At this institution, the bachelor's degree in data science is described as follows:

> Data is the basis of our knowledge of the world: from vehicle movements to temperatures in a hospital.
> Data Science graduates are capable of creating knowledge extracted from data. Those professionals trained in Data Science will be able to design data collection in any environment (industrial, sociological, economic, political, business, etc.), they will be able to process, analyse and combine data from different sources, as well as extract knowledge and communicate effectively how to manage the strategic decision making.
> (Universitat Politechnica de Valencia, 2020, paras. 1–2)

In the previous examples, the descriptions of outcomes for these courses and qualifications include the skills students are expected to develop and implications related to how graduates are expected to connect ideas and apply their understanding and skills to potential careers. These outcomes clearly communicate to students that authentic contexts and therefore authentic assessments that include capability, are inherent to these courses.

Assessing capability

Capability refers to the ability to acquire knowledge and to demonstrate skills (for example, specific practical techniques and application of ICT, communication and collaborative skills), as well as to the development of critical and creative thinking, as shown in Figure 3.1 (Chapter 3). Since learners come to higher education with differing levels of prior knowledge, experience, ability

100 *Assessment*

and capacity (Biggs, 2003), it is important to build in opportunities for students to get feedback on their developing capabilities. Such feedback may include self and peer assessment as part of formative assessment practices, that is, those that inform learning.

In a study seeking student preferences for types of assessments, Fook and Sidhu (2016) found that students preferred assignments, projects and presentations ahead of tests or exams. This was because students perceived they got better feedback than from tests or exams which, once completed, could not be improved on. Many other students across multiple synthesised research studies (for example, National Research Council, 2005) valued having multiple opportunities to provide evidence of their progress in learning, especially when there were opportunities to improve.

In integrated STEM learning contexts, students need to demonstrate how they can combine and synthesise knowledge from different domains, using a range of disparate sources of information, in interesting ways (Griffin & Care, 2015; Griffin, 2018). Assessment of the application of knowledge, skills and capabilities to solve a problem within a context is of prime importance to integrated STEM. This has implications for the design of STEM assessment tasks for evaluating student application of knowledge, skills and capabilities. Not only do instructions matter (to cue integration), but the types of tasks created for assessments tend to determine the ability of students to demonstrate their learning, especially depth and application of knowledge and skills to a specific issue or problem. For example, when assessing the integration of knowledge, it is not enough simply to embed assessment in a real-world situation or scenario. As You et al. (2018) point out, application of disciplinary knowledge may be thwarted from two directions: first by student inability to solve a problem because they lack fundamental understanding of the discipline knowledge sources contributing to a context, and second by student inability to apply this knowledge in a novel context. Therefore, when designing learning tasks, educators should carefully consider what discipline knowledge students might need (or where they can find it).

Developing the capabilities of critical and creative thinking may involve helping students to consider systems thinking, modelling of causal mechanisms, explanations and justifications, as well as communication and collaboration (which are core to the success of integrating and synthesising, as shown in Figure 3.1). Students can also be exposed to situations and activities or assessments where they can demonstrate their ability to work with ambiguity and uncertainty and to build in processes to produce the most likely viable solutions. Students can analyse, build and modify (tinker) with many different kinds of dynamic systems before coming up with a solution. This may involve planning, collecting data, identifying relevant theories or concepts, creating theories, testing results, trialling, evaluating iterations and documenting and communicating the outcomes. They can be asked to evaluate their ideas and solutions based on evidence and trials with built-in reflection on processes and exploration of how interactions within systems influence the potential for these solutions to be viable through structured, evaluative (critically reflective) processes (Conner, 2014). Therefore, when assessing STEM knowledge, skills and capabilities simultaneously, methods for designing, collecting, interpreting and communicating cross-cutting concepts and systems analysis should be included (Quellmaiz & Silberglitt, 2018). In this frame, assessments need to be designed for specific learning contexts. For this reason, this chapter provides a wide range of examples that may be able to be adapted to other contexts.

Often assessments are sequenced or tiered to require students to demonstrate knowledge and skills built on previous outcomes. In other words, students are required to pass the first part before moving onto the next part. Many learning management systems have the capacity to set up adaptive protocols so that resources for sections are not released before a previous section has been completed. This is useful for gradually revealing learning materials according to the stage of individual progress with tasks. A specific example is from the simulation-based assessments designed as part of the SimScientists project (Quellmaiz & Silberglitt, 2018), in which concepts from life sciences, physical sciences and earth science were integrated within interactive technologies designed to provide feedback to learners and teachers as students progressed through tasks to improve their capability (http://simscientists.org).

Examples of assessing capability

There have been many innovations using different types of assessments, especially in science education, at various levels throughout the education system (Fensham & Rennie, 2013). A variety of assessment tasks can be used to target knowledge and capability simultaneously while students solve problems (Delandshere, 2002) or produce artefacts (Zhao, 2016). Assessment of student artefacts can take a variety of forms, including concept maps, online contributions and using a wide range of apps, portfolios, literature reviews and journals that document experimental processes, presentations and project plans, to name a few. These examples help to inform what could be done (or is currently being developed) in higher education and demonstrate alternative ways to personalise learning outcomes and how more open-ended assessment within a context that is relevant for students can be accommodated (Härtig et al., 2020).

The examples of assessing capability provided in this subsection relate to the capabilities of inquiry and PBL, communication, ICT, analytical thinking, critical thinking, WIL, collaboration and peer review.

Inquiry and problem-based learning

A significant way to make assessment authentic and embedded in real issues is to create learning experiences that call on PBL and inquiry approaches (Diffily & Sassman, 2002). Inquiry and PBL have the purpose of actively engaging learners to find information or solutions and, potentially, to generate new knowledge, as opposed to students merely being the receivers of previously

102 *Assessment*

known knowledge (Thomas, 2000). In PBL, assessment requires learners to solve a problem related to application of knowledge. In inquiry, students have to find the required knowledge sources and integrate and evaluate those sources, potentially synthesising ideas and possibilities.

Often, group and collaborative processes support both PBL and inquiry, especially when tasks are allocated and accountability is built in. In these cases, it may be more appropriate to provide a group assessment rather than an individual one. Self and peer assessment of contributions to the project/group can be included as part of individual student grades. Note that joint interdependence and accountability need to be built into a task if a group submission is required. This helps to develop the skills of collaboration, which is valued by being included as part of what is assessed.

Discussions and comments are useful for receiving and giving formative feedback (including forum posts for an online course) concerning the focus of the inquiry, issues or problem. However, rather than the frequency of posts (which can produce unintended behaviours), it may be better to measure how well other students responded to each post or incited others to respond as part of a measure of collaboration. Other ideas for promoting student responses, in a formative sense to each other or to promote dialogue and questioning, include:

- Inserting a regular question time slot in sessions or a question space on a learning management system (could be a forum).
- Getting students to post questions that are tagged to their group. The group is required to respond.
- Setting up a question wall where students choose which questions they answer.
- Getting students to evaluate each other's questions for relevance or as important to consider for viable investigations or problem-based projects.
- Creating online polls on ranking specific questions they'd like help with during a session. This provides educators with an indication of what students mostly would like help with.
- Getting students to design their own assignments, including criteria for achievement in the assignment and how these criteria link to course outcomes.

Discussions that arise within groups undertaking inquiry or PBL can lead to more general considerations of the broader issues of justice and human dilemmas (the people–planet imperatives) (Conner, 2020). If the intention is to engage students in socially relevant and just issues, then students should be undertaking discussions about these and should be assessed on becoming aware of multiple perspectives. This is because when students identify and compare meanings or understandings, opinions and assumptions with others, they learn that multiple views are possible (Conner, 2014). Although we can deliberately use experiences to expand student consciousness, doing this for every experience is time consuming, with students constantly reflecting and having very little mind space for anything else. The point here is that students are more likely to appreciate that there may be alternative possibilities or solutions to problems when they undertake activities and assessments that require them to demonstrate alternative solutions.

Everyone is entitled to their opinion, of course, but the strength of acknowledging multiple perspectives is increased when there are regular invitations to contribute to the collection of ideas and to substantiate claims with evidence. Inquiry and PBL opportunities help students to move from ideas based just on opinion to those based on considered (evidence-based) judgement. In this way, ideas can gain depth, subtlety and refinement and can reveal instances where ideas might be relevant to some contexts but not others.

An example of a rubric for inquiry or problem-solving that requires integration in STEM is given in the section on rubrics later in this chapter.

Communication

There are many activities and associated assessments that can provide indicators of student communication capability. For example, synthesising data and then writing an evaluative report has been used as a key communication tool in STEM for probably the last century or more. Some specific examples of how communication skills can be embedded as part of assessments have been highlighted by Miles and Foggett (2019), including:

- News rebuttals.
  Students use an item from the news, seek evidence from the peer-reviewed literature and complete an annotated bibliography related to the evidence or a short rebuttal to the news item, based on the evidence from the articles.
- Letter to the editor or online platform post.
  Students choose a news item that has been commented on in either a newspaper or an online forum post on a specific topic. They filter (evaluate) evidence to compile a compelling argument for a point of view that is based on this evidence.
- Famous person's diary entry.
  Students choose a famous scientist, inventor, engineer or technologist and write a diary entry that they might have written related to their activities and discoveries.
- Nominate a person for a Nobel prize.
  Students create a blog post or short article about a person who deserves to win a Nobel prize, justifying the nomination persuasively.
- Taking alternative perspectives.
  Students write an article about a social or ethical issue related to the implications of a new scientific discovery, technological process or invention from a perspective that is different from their own.
- Create a presentation/video production.

104   *Assessment*

Students create and present relevant outcomes of an inquiry or project or pitch and include evidence of scholarly research that may include data visualisations and data analysis to emphasise key aspects.

- Create a visual representation, diagram or chart.
  Students construct a visual representation (infographic) of connected ideas, processes or theories and justify the way they have been linked.
- Lead a discussion.
  Students take on a leadership role for a peer discussion about an industrial or design process, scientific method or models or theory explanations indicating multiple views.
- Television interview.
  Students take on the role of interviewer and interviewee in a videoed mock television interview on an issue relevant to their study.

In many courses around the world on the history and theory of science (nature of science), and in public perceptions of and communication in science, students focus on current issues and events. Assessment often involves sharing ideas through forums, blogs, interviews with scientists, technologists, engineers and medics and critiques of each other's interviews. Students may identify topics that may be more difficult to communicate, in which case students may be required to develop artefacts for communicating with different audiences about the topic (for example, government briefing versus newspaper article) in order to develop nuanced communication skills in relation to the audience. In a course on environmental science at the University of Canberra (Australian Council of Deans of Science, 2013), each student created a critical review of the scientific methods and results in provided articles. In a separate assessment, students were required to critically review ethical aspects in a short, published study.

With the increased use of digital media and networked approaches to working in STEM, it is important that communication skills are developed alongside ICT technical capabilities.

ICT

Along with the usual assessment practices using ICT tools for writing, co-curation of reports and presentations and analysing data in STEM disciplines, additional authentic and situated assessments may be included. These assessments may involve simulations of processes and procedures, immersive technological experiences (augmented reality, virtual reality, extended reality), gaming, remote internships using video conferences, synthesising and applying knowledge and skills gained through reflection on WIL, capstone portfolios (including specific project outcomes or solutions that have drawn on people, places, systems and the world through the internet) and demonstrations of an ability to evaluate resources for accuracy, bias, validity and scholarly integrity.

Assessment 105

Therefore, as well as the convenience of providing assessments digitally, students may simultaneously be assisted to develop ICT capabilities, especially when the demonstration of use of the technologies is an inherent part of an assessment. The use of ICT is so strongly embedded in STEM that students ought to be demonstrating skills in using digital technologies as part of the coherent set of capabilities included in their qualifications.

Analytical thinking

A critical evaluation of ideas and consequences of actions requires a deeper examination of pertinent evidence. Analytical thinking is the ability to argue a logical point of view while taking different perspectives on data (information) into account. Enabling students to manipulate data and to view results of these manipulations is a form of simulation. Applying and evaluating the consequences of these manipulations can help students to make decisions about problems or issues. This approach was reported as being advanced most quickly in engineering courses (Goodhew, 2020). Multi-structural and relational manipulations can inform learning about decision-making, especially when interactive and automated responses are inherent to the task. Java applets, Flash files, and QuickTime VR using 3+D images can enable students to explore, trial and test out ideas and changes to variables.

There are many programmes designed to provide automatic feedback to students about their developing mathematical understanding. Often, these are developed for supporting students who do not have the required pre-entry requirements (math index scores). For example, self-paced, online math-skills prep courses are provided to students at Augustina College, Illinois, USA. The course automatically identifies areas of math strength and where students need development. An AI system then provides tutorials and activities to advance student knowledge and skills, with student self-monitoring checkpoints built in.

At Alverno College in Milwaukee, Wisconsin, USA, students undertake assessments related to mathematical connections: representing data, predicting data and measurement concepts. Each section of these assessments consists of word problems as applied to real-world contexts. In one example, a context about growing and marketing cranberries is extended to the sale of other farming products. Students are required to represent and interpret data visually in various ways and to make predictions based on probability and statistics.

In some engineering courses, for example, the New Model for Technology and Engineering (NMiTE) in Hereford, England, and Singapore University of Technology and Design (SUTD), A-level equivalencies in mathematics are not required for entry into their engineering programmes. Instead, the mathematics components are embedded within student projects and students receive guidance on an as-needed basis (Goodhew, 2020). Therefore, the development and assessment of analytical thinking, in these instances, is customised.

106 *Assessment*

Critical thinking

Assessment of critical thinking can take multiple forms, as critical thinking seeks to answer questions such as "what if . . .", "what else . . .", "how accurate . . .", "does the evidence justify the claims", "what assumptions . . ."? Critical thinking can help students to focus on reflecting on and evaluating sources of information and outcomes from their investigations (resource- and practical-based) and to help students question dominant narratives and assumptions.

Identifying significant discoveries and inventions and evaluating the role technology and data played in these discoveries, can enable students to integrate their thinking about the intersections of technology with science, engineering and mathematics. Students can identify public resistance to new ideas and devices and challenges to adoption of their use and can indicate what might need to happen to change perception and acceptance. Changing people's opinions calls on the ability to communicate effectively on the purpose and application of the ideas, which students can demonstrate as part of assessments. Embedding assessments in real-world examples can be supported by connecting with professionals who work in STEM occupations, representing some of the most authentic assessment contexts of all, as discussed in the next section.

Work-integrated learning (WIL)

There are very promising examples of authentic assessments provided in the *Good Practice Guide* (Australian Council of Deans of Science, 2013), including where groups of students interview scientists and technologists or participate in technology-centred or work-based teams. By engaging with professionals, students find out specifically on what the scientist, technologist or engineer focusses, and especially the implications of their work for society.

Additional resources related to this approach, where scientists provided snapshots of their work and evaluated its applications, can be found as enduring online resources through the Science Learning Hub (www.sciencelearn. org.nz), a New Zealand website designed to support context learning in integrated ways.

Increasingly, higher education students are gaining work-related experiences as part of their qualification. A challenge with workplace assessments is to make them achievable, feasible, valid and targeted to assess the desired capabilities (Ajjawi et al., 2019). Good practice for on-the-job assessment includes collecting evidence about what students have done, produced or demonstrated in order to show their levels of attainment, progress on a continuum and competence (Alkema & McDonald, 2014, 2016). These practices include:

- Collaboration and partnership between qualification provider and workplace, so that assessments are aligned to workplace needs and to national or accreditation requirements of professional standards. Many companies have their own training, so there is an opportunity to align organisational-based training with assessments for qualifications.

- Clear communication between stakeholders to develop a shared understanding about why, where, when and how assessment is taking place in order to generate evidence.
- Celebration of success through events, stories and congratulatory messages.
- Use of naturally occurring evidence of actual work and projects undertaken. These can be captured through photos, diaries, any artefacts (real or virtual) and so on. Assessment should happen as part of the learning-through-work experiences and should be more than a one-off event.
- Appropriate recruitment, training and professional development of people who are making judgements. Assessment for qualifications is high stakes, so people who are undertaking or contributing to assessment must be suitable.
- Moderation, for both constructing tasks and following allocation of marks, in order to attest to the validity and reliability of assessment tasks and marking schedules across a range of assessors and students. This is important because assessments must be fair and fit for purpose.

The power of using meaningful, authentic contexts is that students can provide divergent responses to assessment tasks because they are given some choice about the focus to take and the processes to be used for solving an issue or problem. Building in aspects of complexity, with students determining (with guidance) how to proceed, helps students learn how to deal with intersections of ideas and complexities (Crisp, 2020). This approach also provides motivation for students, as it enables them to make connections to their previous experiences and to see that their choices work because they have real consequences with humanistic applications (Draper, 2009). Students may come up with new connections and solutions that may not have been thought about previously. When this occurs, students are more likely to see the significance of reaching and potentially exceeding course outcomes, including engaging in collaboration and communication, because their skills are valued by being assessed.

A word of caution about assessing collaboration, though. Tensions can occur among groups when there appear to be choices between seemingly equal alternatives. There will also be situations when consensus among individuals may be difficult. Students may need to be given opportunities to raise any concerns about group dynamics and be guided to work through these tensions.

Collaboration – peer and self-assessment

Being a professional requires self-reflection and collaborative work with peers. Continuous self-reflection and improvement are expected of professionals and para-professionals. For example, to solve technical problems, it is not unusual to seek advice from a peer or colleague, or to expect peer

108   *Assessment*

review as part of what it means to undertake research. This collaborative form of problem-solving and feedback should be captured as a core attribute for STEM graduates.

In contrast to apprenticeship models that emphasise mimicry and performance of novices (with progression towards expert performance), peer-assisted models can extend learning beyond what a single supervisor can provide. Peer responses can provide expansive forms of reflection that use multiple inputs, rather than the one-to-one relationship that is traditionally the case in apprenticeship and mentoring models of learning on the job. Peer-assisted models can help align what students do in relation to assessment standards and can lead to higher grades (Yalch et al., 2019). Self and peer reflection should therefore be natural components and expectations of assessing building collaboration in team-focussed activities.

Reflection on feedback received from peers can help students to identify their own strengths, capabilities and areas that need work (Black & Wiliam, 2010; Earl, 2006; Hattie & Timperley, 2007). The use of peer feedback and peer-assisted learning (PAL) is increasing (Rivers & Willans, 2013), as it includes students mentoring others, often leading to improved outcomes. Creating peer feedback as formative tasks during class time (usually through group work) is useful as it requires students to engage with the content and assessment criteria and is more likely to ensure that students undertake the thinking required for the task, consider more carefully what was required and learn from others. When students get practice in articulating concepts and consolidating examples, they are embedding ideas and potentially creating better connections that will enable them to demonstrate their capabilities in more formal assessment tasks.

Often, it is not until students are given an opportunity to assess either their own work or that of peers that they align what was required with the criteria of the assessment. Students can also take an active role in designing assessments that they think are relevant to the learning outcomes, especially capabilities (Crisp, 2020). For example, students can create questions to generate quizzes for their peers (for example, http://peerwise.cs.auckland.ac.nz). In order to generate questions, students need to process information and reflect on possible misconceptions in order to come up with possible answers. When students have to explain answers in their own words through this process of generating assessment questions, it reinforces their understanding.

Peer review

Students may not realise that when using peer assessment, they are developing a core skill required in STEM fields, that of peer review. Through evaluating their own work and comparing it with that of their peers, students can become constructively critical and more adept at determining the level at which their contribution has met requirements. In STEM contexts, this is particularly important because peer review is an inherent part of being a professional or successful entrepreneur.

Peer review in a biochemistry class at Flinders University included the following steps:

1 Students practised reviewing and using the assessment rubric prior to the formal process.
2 Students provided online feedback to two other students using a supplied assessment rubric. Each student receives two peer reviews.
3 Students submitted and reviewed each other's work using the digital self-assessment and feedback tool on the learning management system.
4 Students scored their reviewer on the quality of their feedback.
5 Students reflected (400 words) on how they will apply the feedback received.
6 University employed markers graded all components of the process.

The key outcomes for the students of peer review as documented by student feedback were that students:

- Gained skills and experience in peer review.
- Were exposed to diverse writing styles, levels of inquiry and project approaches.
- Developed critical appraisal of information (fact-checking and evaluation of appropriate application of knowledge and biochemical processes).
- Applied suggestions to improve their own work.

A word of caution, though, about using peer and self-assessment. Sometimes students will judge their own work to be adequate when in fact it lacks coverage, depth and critical elements. This can arise if the criteria do not clearly indicate the scope or depth of what is required or what success looks like (proficiency or sufficiency). In addition, in a study of 18-year-olds who knew each other reasonably well, students reported that when giving peer feedback, they did not want to be mean to their friends (Conner, 2004). Given this, when introducing peer assessment, there needs to be an explicit indication that feedback given to peers should be constructive and informative, as specific feedback leads to enhancements of their work. Another issue regarding peers assessing content knowledge is that often students reported not knowing enough to be able to say whether or not the information they were peer assessing was accurate (Conner, 2004).

Culminating, enabling and discrete outcomes

As mentioned in Chapter 4, student outcomes should drive the kinds of learning experiences created. There are multiple types of outcomes for assessments

110   *Assessment*

in any qualification in higher education. These have been described by Hussain et al. (2020) as:

- Culminating outcomes are those at the programme or graduating exit level.
- Enabling outcomes are the processes and skills that help students to demonstrate progress in learning.
- Discrete outcomes are quite specific to a discipline or practical skill, and/ or are "nice to have".

Culminating outcomes can be considered as the exit or programme level outcomes and are usually assessed in a summative form of assessment (for example, project paper, portfolio of experiments, production and evaluation of a product). Development of skills (including cognitive, affective and psychomotor skills) can involve students demonstrating an understanding of specific discipline processes and learning strategies that contribute to overall outcomes and are therefore termed enabling outcomes. These are essential for students to eventually succeed in the culminating outcomes and could be thought of as subskills or enabling knowledge (knowing what, how and when knowledge could be applied).

Discrete outcomes may be discipline-specific concepts, cross-cutting interdisciplinary concepts or technical details related to practical procedures and skill development or technical knowledge and appropriate application. Discrete outcomes are nice to know but are not essential to a student's culminating outcomes. Educators may need to eliminate outcomes and their associated activities if they are not truly enabling. As mentioned in Chapters 3 and 4 in this book, the process of designing integrated STEM should start with the outcomes in mind. This is followed by designing assessment tasks, especially identifying which learning components to be assessed are crucial and which components will contribute to learning (enabling outcomes), to assist students in their progress towards the culminating outcomes.

Designing assessment tasks

This section outlines the process for designing assessments that integrate knowledge and capabilities simultaneously. Figure 5.1 outlines a process for designing assessment tasks. The process starts with identifying and clarifying the aims and outcomes for the course. These become the headings for focus areas within the assessment. It is important to ask *what are the intentions for learning?* as this determines the assessment types possible and the levels related to outcomes that students are expected to demonstrate. Checking involves going backwards and forwards, as shown by the arrows in Figure 5.1, so that the learning experiences can be planned alongside developing the assessment task(s). For example, there is no point assessing collaboration or communication if there are no opportunities provided for students to practise and demonstrate capabilities in these areas.

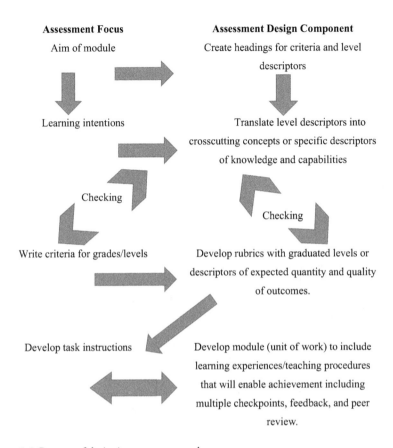

Figure 5.1 Process of designing assessment tasks

There will need to be assessment tasks and criteria developed for each course outcome. It is always wise to build in multiple points for providing feedback to students so there is alignment between learning experiences, assessment and their development towards the desired outcomes. The assessment task instructions must include descriptions that indicate the depth of knowledge, critical and creative components and scope (length, scale, any trialling required, timelines and type of collaboration), as well as specific indications of how connections between STEM ideas and processes could be demonstrated.

Embedding assessments to inform learning can lead to increased engagement (Dunne & Owen, 2013; Quellmaiz & Silberglitt, 2018), although such assessments require careful planning and thought. The rich feedback that such assessments provide tends to foster student confidence through telling students how well they have done and what can be improved (Crisp, 2020). For educators, evidence of student progress helps them to redesign instructions if they were

112 *Assessment*

not clear enough, identify what students most need help with and evaluate the effectiveness of specific learning experiences. Anything missing can be added into the next iteration of the course as part of continuous improvement.

Increasingly, ICT tools are supporting formative assessment as online tools can support dialogue, collaboration and interaction between students, and between teachers and students, asynchronously. In a large literature review on technology-enhanced assessment, Sweeney et al. (2017) found that technology affords opportunities for feedback in a timely and constructive way. Some digital assessment models have built-in feedback that provides immediate responses for students to evaluate their progress, especially when multiple attempts are permitted, because then students are encouraged to have another attempt. These online, self-paced, immediate feedback tools help students to identify their prior knowledge, skills and progress.

Using rubrics

A key to assisting authentic learning is development of assessment tools that target transferrable skills alongside interdiscipline-specific knowledge and processes. This is especially important for integrated STEM, in which interdisciplinary understanding, technical and practical skills and more general capabilities can be assessed simultaneously.

Development and use of assessment rubrics can support feedback and overall assessment in multiple ways. Rubrics provide guidance for students to drive their progress, enabling them to evaluate the quality of their outcomes (and potentially improve them) prior to submission of an assessment. Rubrics specify (describe) levels of knowledge, connections, technical skills and transferable capabilities at different levels of proficiency. The precise language of a rubric provides a scoring "rule" (descriptor) that indicates outcomes expected for a particular level or score. These help students to identify what to put effort into and how they will be judged. The described levels of outcomes increase in complexity with higher levels of proficiency.

Rubrics assist educators in assessing the quality of the processes and content outcomes and in providing feedback to learners accordingly (Biggs & Collis, 1982). Quality definitions explain what students must demonstrate (on a scale) in terms of a practical skill, connecting ideas and processes or other thinking or collaborative capabilities.

Some advice for educators on designing and using rubrics has been given by Reddy and Andrade (2010), including:

- Use clear and appropriate language (content and construct validity).
- Identify the critical components in an assignment (criterion validity).
- Include evaluation criteria, quality dimensions and a scoring strategy.
- Teach students how to use rubrics actively to enhance their outcomes, especially if rubrics are used in peer and self-assessments.
- Train raters (assessors) sufficiently in order to achieve reliability in marking of assessments.

These aspects can support educators to design and develop rubrics that can be quite generic for integrated assessment. Alternatively, they can be more specific and target particular content, concepts, connections, processes and viable solutions that have undergone ideation and evaluation of prototypes, or processes where solutions have been trialled experimentally.

Hybrid rubrics can assist in assessing several descriptors or outcomes simultaneously. Table 5.1 shows an example of assessing interdisciplinary concepts and integration of ideas and skills at the same time for an integrated inquiry or problem-solving activity. Table 5.2 provides a multi-layered rubric for assessing levels of transferable capabilities within group work and shows possible indicators for levels of achievement. These are written to be quite generic and therefore could be applied across a wide range of assessment activities. They could be used as is, or adapted to be more specifically aligned with content, processes or tasks as well.

Examples of assessment

This section provides some specific examples of assessment in integrated STEM contexts. These are useful because they highlight how educators in higher education have integrated content, skills and capabilities and, in some cases, used novel ways to assess student learning outcomes. Assessment examples include case studies, using gaming to develop a solution and project-based sprints that are profiled in capstone portfolios.

Case studies

Case studies as a teaching tool can be very useful in STEM contexts because they provide examples that are situated in real problems. Cases can be communicated through many channels (podcasts, streamed videos, student–stakeholder conferences, public events or written examples). Cases (scenarios) can therefore be posted for students to read ahead of discussions and assessment.

For case studies to be effective for advancing outcomes in STEM, they need to have an element of challenge or novelty, as these tend to invoke an enduring curiosity for dimensions of the problem that contribute to or influence the case, or towards alternatives that might be reasonable (rather than single specific, right answers). Case studies can provide rich descriptions of the nature of science, of the role of technology and data and for evaluations of engineering projects in terms of validity, reliability and the tentative or relative nature of findings. Cases are best developed and analysed in groups or through collaborative discussion, especially if the case focusses on ethical or sustainable practices.

Assessment of case studies may take the form of written reflections on group discussions (with students leading the discussion), which are then synthesised and summarised in terms of what surprised participants or what has changed in terms of their views about the particular case. Students could also make inferences about how integration of concepts, processes and transferable skills were

114 *Assessment*

Table 5.1 Rubric for authentic inquiry

Category	Excellent (4)	Good (3)	Some aspects (2)	Limited (1)
Knowledge, connections and application to real-world issues	Thorough and detailed explanations and evaluations of the connections and interplay between several disciplinary knowledge types and processes. Analysis, synthesis and application was highly evident and contributed significantly to the claims or solution.	Good connections between disciplinary knowledge types. Explanations, analysis and application were appropriate and linked to claims or solution.	Some understanding and connections made between disciplinary knowledge types and application, but not directly linked to claims or solution.	Limited understanding of how disciplinary knowledge and processes integrate; limited analysis and application. Claims or solution could not be derived from the evidence.
Inquiry or problem-solving processes	Demonstrated outstanding process skills: derived suitable questions, used a wide range of resources and showed high levels of evaluation of how the ideas and processes may have limitations or bias; high levels of collaboration that may include leading a group or supporting others.	Demonstrated good processing skills: derived questions, used a range of resources; clear evidence of collaboration and reflection.	Demonstrated some processing skills: derived question(s), some resources used and integrated; collaboration evident, but minimal.	Demonstrated little or no understanding of how several discipline ideas could be used to solve an issue/ problem/ challenge. Lack of integration of knowledge sources; little evidence of collaboration.
Communication (oral or written)	Explanations or arguments were clear, well-structured (logically sequenced), convincing and accurate; makes suggestions to counter any challenges to the solution, with no significant errors.	Explanations or arguments were clear and accurate, but not convincing.	Explanations, arguments or representations used discipline-specific language, but were not complete or may have errors.	Limited use of discipline-specific concepts, processes or explanations, but were not complete or may have errors.

Assessment 115

Table 5.2 Multi-layered rubric for assessing transferable capabilities in group work

Criteria	Excellent	Good	Some	Limited
Participation	Participated consistently well and supported others to participate.	Participated and contributed to the group most of the time.	Participated satisfactorily, but not effectively or was rarely on task.	Did not contribute well to the group, wasted time or worked on unrelated material.
Leadership	Leadership demonstrated by monitoring progress of others and the group, posing possibilities and showing a positive attitude.	Some leadership evident that supported the group to progress.	Mostly allowed others to assume leadership, or often dominated the group, or did not value the contributions of others.	No leadership of others in the group. Passive.
Listening	Valued and listened carefully to ideas of others.	Usually valued and listened to ideas of others.	At times did not listen to ideas of others or dismissed them as irrelevant.	Did not listen to others or often talked over or interrupted them.
Feedback	Offered detailed, constructive and appropriate feedback.	Offered constructive feedback when asked.	Occasionally offered constructive feedback, but sometimes comments were inappropriate or not useful.	Did not offer constructive feedback.
Cooperation	Respected others and shared workload fairly and appropriately.	Usually respected others and shared workload fairly.	Sometimes treated others with disrespect or did not share workload fairly.	Often treated others with disrespect or did not take on their share of workload.
Time management	Completed individually assigned tasks on time and actively helped the group to manage timely completion, through sequencing or editing processes.	Usually completed individually assigned tasks on time and supported the group to meet timelines.	Often did not complete individually assigned tasks on time.	Did not complete most of the assigned tasks on time.

116 *Assessment*

important. Some specific examples of where cases have been used for novel assessment are provided in the following subsections.

Pollution of university ground water

As part of the Massachusetts Institute of Technology's education arcade, students became environmental detectives using a digital game (Klopfer, 2008). In order to investigate and contribute solutions for this case, undergraduate students became environmental engineers, with the project brief for the game being to advise the university about appropriate actions to take regarding a pollutant in groundwater from recent building construction. Students integrated primary data (measurements, statistics, patterns, trends and factual information) with secondary data (interviews with experts). Students played the game on mobile devices, with multiple inputs from multiple players, who fed back responses to each other. Accountability for learning and participation was built in, including accountability to peers within each group to complete their part of the task in a timely way.

This is an example of how gaming was used to teach the importance of integrating ideas with other thinking skills, such as strategic thinking and tentative analysis problem-solving, planning and providing recommendations, through an iterative, evaluative and collaborative process. The activity was situated in the very real context of a problem that was occurring at MIT, as recommended for solving problems as part of assessments by the Federation of American Scientists (2006).

It also tapped into gaming as a motivational tool to gain and sustain the attention of undergraduates. In such highly immersive, rich, multimedia-driven, interactive environments, learners can be supported through multimodal means. When specific cases are a real issue, it is also likely that learners have a greater emotional connection with the outcome because they have had a hand in generating a solution for a local problem.

There are many emerging examples of problem-solving assessments of this kind using video games, created by game developers who include many of the axioms found in research in the learning sciences for developing thinking, reasoning, decision-making and some technical skills that employers want (Jiao & Lissitz, 2018). Gaming can support formative assessment for practical skills training (e.g. titrations), training for high technical performance and reinforcing skills. At the same time, cases can be used (with or without the use of technology) to assess enabling outcomes, especially if they emulate how experts use and approach problem-solving and team building.

Mosquito-borne diseases

The next example compares two different approaches to assessing student understanding of transmission of mosquito-borne disease. This example was provided by the Australian Council of Deans of Science (2013) to show how assessment processes could be changed to accommodate more authentic cases, as a means to assess integrated problem-solving. The more traditional assignment is outlined first and can be contrasted with the more authentic case approach to assessment.

The following is the more traditional instructions for a video presentation:

> In your video presentation, discuss how mosquitoes transmit a variety of bacterial and viral diseases. Explain the efficiency of disease transmission using examples of the persistence of the disease within mosquito populations and how it relates to mosquito habitats, their lifecycles and general ecology. Present your findings as a video presentation highlighting the differences between the diseases.

The case notes and instructions were designed for a problem-solving approach with the consequent shift to student-driven problem-solving, where students are required to develop evidence to support possible solutions:

> Ahn has returned home from a holiday in Samoa where she has been bitten by mosquitos three times. She has headaches, some muscle pain and is developing a fever. Her blood tests indicate that she has a mosquito-transmitted infection. Over 1 million people die each year from malaria, which is a mosquito transmitted disease. Although malaria has been eradicated from many countries, other diseases such as Dengue, Zika and Chikungunya could also be indicated, as these are also transmitted by mosquitos. Currently, there are no vaccines or treatments for these diseases. Therefore, prevention is the only way people can protect themselves against them. International health organisations are aware of this issue and are trying to reduce these diseases through managing mosquito populations.
>
> You are a member of a disease control group, assigned to identify Ahn's disease. Your group is also required to minimise other people becoming infected. Prepare a presentation for the Minister of Health and Human Services on your findings and recommendations. A range of issues will need to be considered, such as the habitat of the mosquito, lifecycles, population frequencies, transmission, existence and prevalence within mosquito populations, possible technological solutions for reducing mosquito populations, the ecological effects of any proposed solutions, social and economic implications and the likelihood of and predictions for increases in cases of the disease. Use data as much as possible to back up your claims and recommendations as being the best possible solution for people in the area.

These two approaches to assessment of the same case are very different! The second approach requires students to undertake an inquiry approach, where they seek information and data to support their claims. In contrast to the first set of instructions, it includes a very real situation and the need to present

118   *Assessment*

information related to minimising spread of the disease. Such problem-solving assignments that require considering humanistic solutions invoke a range of capabilities, including connecting ideas, evaluating claims, making recommendations and situating the case as a personal and population-related issue. The latter was not apparent in the traditional assessment activity because it was not directed to the issues that directly affected people.

Other ways have also been devised to assess the development of student thinking about socio-scientific issues. These include continuous assessment of student understanding that scientific knowledge is contestable and testable; that data does not necessarily speak for itself but needs to be interpreted; and that socio-scientific issues may not have an obvious solution because of their frequent complexity (Conner, 2004). Teachers may develop fictional cases, with extreme cases of positioning, as taken by the media. As part of an assessment, students can identify factual inaccuracies and provide details related to any scientific misconceptions (which are deliberately inserted in the cases). Students may need to create a presentation, documentary or video reporting on the issue. Reflection on how such assessments have influenced student thinking has been reported (Australian Council of Deans of Science, 2013).

Challenges as assessments at NMiTE

The New Model for Technology and Engineering (NMiTE) in Hereford has implemented a project-based model in which about a third of all student work is non-technical and integrated into projects. There is no requirement for maths or physics at A-level (the UK equivalent of final year high-school assessments) for entry because the pertinent content is addressed as needed. There are no lectures and no exams. Teaching units are organised into sprints lasting three and a half weeks and are connected to employer-inspired or community projects. In these sprints, groups of five students work with industries to address specific challenges.

Learning outcomes are collated using a map to the Quality Assurance Agency benchmark and UK-Standard for Professional Engineering Competence (Marshall, 2020). Specific skills needed in several sprints, for example, computer assisted design, are provided through specific digital toolkits. Capstone topics use group-based industrial internships requiring collaboration across a team to share technical know-how; participation in seminars and presentations by experts; evaluation of the project process; and, for the team, creation of deliverables, such as evaluating the cost and impact of the proposed solutions. Since each student will complete about 20 sprints, there are opportunities to consolidate and practise reflection in action and develop skills in a progressive way. In this model, assessments are competency-based, with the quality reflected by items in student portfolios (for example, designs, software analyses, prototypes and products). Marshall (2020) reported that an overall issue for curriculum in this model is balancing core, enduring, fundamental knowledge (e.g. Newton's laws) with contemporaneous issues (use of drones, privacy, data security, reducing carbon footprints and so on).

Collating assessment data across outcomes

Technology-enhanced assessment is potentially useful for supporting and managing learning outcomes that integrate content, skills and graduate attributes simultaneously (Sweeney et al., 2017). Of importance to institutions and to accreditation bodies (for example, ABET) is how learning data is reported for cohorts of students. While digital solutions are able to contribute substantively to the capability and capacity to collate large amounts of variable data across a large number of assessment activities, these activities may contribute to multiple outcomes. This represents a complex mapping exercise (Hussain et al. 2020).

The Faculty of Engineering at the Islamic University of Saudi Arabia has developed all of their engineering programmes as outcomes-based education (OBE), in which levels of skills align with course outcomes and are collated in levels within a specific data base. In the framework for a qualification, all assessments are weighted prior to collation of outcome data. Research on this approach to assessment (Hussain et al., 2020) has shown benefits in generating specific performance indicators (levels of outcomes) and collating them. The indicators also supported authentic OBE principles, including being able to identify where students were not achieving as well as they should be. Engineering educators have been able to use the collated data to inform students about their progress and for continuous improvement of both courses and assessment design.

For accreditation (with ABET) of engineering programmes at the Islamic University of Saudi Arabia, a web-based automated system incorporates Eval-Tools® for assessing the massive amounts of outcomes data from the engineering courses (Hussain et al., 2020). To enable this digital data collection system for all domains of engineering, it was important to align all curriculum design components (especially learning outcomes) with assessment activities and learning experiences that supported the development of student knowledge, understanding of engineering processes and practical and transferable skills (Hussain et al., 2020). This is an example of a complex assessment system designed to collate multiple integrated outcomes simultaneously.

Summary of assessing integrated STEM

There has been much debate about assessment and higher education (Boud & Falchikov, 2007), and its application to designing curriculum in STEM is no exception. There is no doubt that assessment has a huge influence on student learning (Biggs, 2003), especially in determining what students focus on. The bottom line is that what is assessed is deemed to be what is important, by both students and faculty.

120 *Assessment*

The intentions and scope of curriculum and, by implication, innovation in curriculum design are often constrained by assessment (Fensham & Rennie, 2013). There is little point in designing for integrated STEM unless there are also changes made to assessment. Integrating STEM must therefore be driven by changes to assessment. Good practitioners tend to start with the end (assessment) in mind when designing courses and work backwards to identify what learning experiences will enable students to develop and demonstrate the desired outcomes.

This chapter has provided multiple examples of alternatives to tests and exams for assessing content knowledge, skills and capabilities, as deemed important for the future of students. In an integrated approach to STEM, assessment approaches and tasks should provide opportunities for students to demonstrate how they can connect ideas; critically evaluate claims based on evidence; use their awareness of multiple points of view or contingencies; be adaptable and flexible; and create new ideas and solutions (be innovative) within collaborative teams. Assessment rubrics should provide descriptions of the judgements used for assessing levels of attainment. These rubrics can support students in focussing on what matters as they demonstrate how they integrate knowledge sources from different domains, their understanding of appropriate processes important for problem-solving and their development of transferable skills that have been situated within authentic problems.

References

Ajjawi, R., Tai, J., Le Huu Nghia, T., Boud, D., Johnson, L., & Patrick, C. J. (2019). Aligning assessment with the needs of work-integrated learning: The challenges of authentic assessment in a complex context. *Assessment & Evaluation in Higher Education, 45*(2), 304–316. https://doi.org/10.1080/02602938.2019.1639613

Alkema, A., & McDonald, H. (2014). *Learning in and for work: Highlights from Ako Aotearoa research.* Ako Aotearoa.

Alkema, A., & McDonald, H. (2016). *Principles of on-job assessment for industry training.* Ako Aotearoa.

Ashford-Rowe, K., Herrington, J., & Brown, C. (2014). Establishing the critical elements that determine authentic assessment. *Assessment & Evaluation in Higher Education, 39*(2), 205–222. http://doi.org/10.1080/02602938.2013.819566

Australian Council of Deans of Science. (2013). *Good practice guide – understanding science.* www.acds-tlcc.edu.au/wp-content/uploads/sites/14/2013/01/Science-Good-Practice-Guide-2013-TLO1.pdf

Biggs, J. B. (2003). *Teaching for quality learning at university: What the student does* (2nd ed.). Open University Press.

Biggs, J. B., & Collis, J. F. (1982). *Educating the quality of learning: The SOLO taxonomy.* Academic Press.

Black, P., & Wiliam, D. (2010). Inside the black box: Raising standards through classroom assessment. *Kappan, 92*(1), 81–90.

Boix Mansilla, V., & Gardner, H. (2003). *Assessing interdisciplinary work at the frontier: An empirical exploration of "symptoms of quality".* https://static1.squarespace.com/static/5c5b

569c01232cccdc227b9c/t/5e90baabd7b18d59e3af41db/1586543275795/26-Assessing-ID-Work-2_04.pdf

Boud, D., & Falchikov, N. (2006). Aligning assessment with long-term learning. *Assessment & Evaluation in Higher Education, 31*(4), 399–413. http://doi.org/10.1080/026029 30600679050

Boud, D., & Falchikov, N. (2007). *Rethinking assessment for higher education: Learning for the longer term*. Routledge.

Bulte, A., Klaassen, K., Westbroek, H., Stolk, M., Prins, G., Genseberger, R., Jong, O., & Pilot, A. (2005). Modules for a new chemistry curriculum: Research on a meaningful relation between contexts and concepts. In P. Nentwig & D. Waddington (Eds.), *Making it relevant: Context-based learning of science* (pp. 273–299). Waxmann Verlag.

Bybee, R., McCrae, B., & Laurie, R. (2009). PISA 2006: An assessment of scientific literacy. *Journal of Research in Science Teaching, 46*(8), 865–883.

Conner, L. (2004). Assessing learning about social and ethical issues in a biology class. *School Science Review, 85*(314), 1–7.

Conner, L. (2014). Students' use of evaluative constructivism: Comparative degrees of intentional learning. *International Journal of Qualitative Studies in Education, 27*(4), 472–489. http://doi.org/10.1080/09518398.2013.771228

Conner, L. (2020). *Integrating STEMM in higher education: A proposed curriculum development framework*. Paper published in the proceedings of 6th International Conference on Higher Education Advances (HEAd'20). Universitat Politècnica de València. http://doi.org/10.4995/HEAd20.2020.11058

Crisp, G. (2020). Assessment: New developments in design, marking and feedback. In S. Marshall (Ed.), *A handbook for teaching and learning in higher education: Enhancing academic practice* (5th ed., pp. 61–71). Routledge.

Delandshere, G. (2002). Assessment as inquiry. *Teachers College Record, 104*(7), 1461–1484. http://doi.org/10.1111/1467-9620.00210

Diffily, D., & Sassman, C. (2002). *Project-based learning with young children*. Heinemann.

Draper, S. (2009). Catalytic assessment: Understanding how MCQs and EVS can foster deep learning. *British Journal of Educational Technology, 40*(2), 285–293.

Dunne, E., & Owen, D. (2013). Students taking responsibility for their learning. In E. Dunne & D. Owen (Eds.), *The student engagement handbook: Practice in higher education* (pp. 271–290). Emerald.

Earl, L. M. (2006). Assessment – a powerful lever for learning. *Brock Education, 16*(1), 1–15.

Federation of American Scientists. (2006). *Harnessing the power of video games for learning: Summit on education*. www.informalscience.org/sites/default/files/Summit_on_Educational_Games.pdf

Fensham, P. J., & Rennie, L. J. (2013). Towards an authentically assessed science curriculum. In D. Corrigan, R. Gunstone, & A. Jones (Eds.), *Valuing assessment in science education: Pedagogy, curriculum, policy* (pp. 69–100). Springer.

Fook, C. Y., & Sidhu, G. K. (2016). Assessment strategies to enhance learning in higher education. In C. Y. Fook, G. K. Sidhu, S. Narasuman, L. L. Fong, & S. B. Raman (Eds.), *7th international conference on university learning and teaching (InCULT 2014) proceedings: Educate to innovate* (pp. 117–130). Springer.

Fortus, D., & Krajcik, J. (2020). Supporting contextualization: Lessons learned from throughout the globe. In I. Sánchez Tapia (Ed.), *International perspectives on the contextualization of science education* (pp. 175–183). Springer.

122 *Assessment*

George-Williams, S. R., Soo, J. T., Ziebell, A. L., Thompson, C. D., & Overton, T. L. (2018). Inquiry and industry-inspired laboratories: The impact on students' perceptions of skill development and engagements. *Chemistry Education Research and Practice, 19,* 583–596.

Gilbert, J. (2005). *Catching the knowledge wave: The knowledge society and the future of education.* NZCER Press.

Goodhew, P. (2020). The new engineering. In S. Marshall (Ed.), *A handbook for teaching and learning in higher education: Enhancing academic practice* (5th ed., pp. 218–231). Routledge.

Griffin, P. (2018). *Assessment for teaching* (2nd ed.). Cambridge University Press.

Griffin, P., & Care, E. (2015). *Assessment and teaching of 21st-century skills: Methods and approach.* Springer.

Gunn, C. (2015). Online assessment and learner motivation in the twenty-first century. In C. Koh (Ed.), *Motivation, leadership and curriculum design: Engaging the net generation and twenty-first century learners* (pp. 53–62). Springer.

Härtig, H., Nordine, J. C., & Neumann, K. (2020). Contextualization in the assessment of students' learning about science. In I. Sánchez Tapia (Ed.), *International perspectives on the contextualization of science education* (pp. 113–144). Springer.

Hattie, J., & Timperley, H. (2007). The power of feedback. *Review of Educational Research, 77*(1), 81–112.

Hussain, W., Spady, W. G., Naqash, T., Khan, S. Z., Khawaja, B. A., & Conner, L. (2020). ABET accreditation during and after COVID19-navigating the digital age. *IEEE Access, 8,* 218997–219046. http://doi.org/10.1109/ACCESS.2020.3041736

Jiao, H., & Lissitz, R. W. (2018). *Technology enhanced innovative assessment: Development, modelling, and scoring from an interdisciplinary perspective.* Information Age Publishing.

Ketelhut, D. J., & Tutwiler, M. S. (2018). *Science learning and inquiry with technology.* Routledge.

Klein, J. T. (2005). Integrative learning and interdisciplinary studies. *Peer Review, 7*(4), 8–10.

Klopfer, E. (2008). *Augmented learning: Research and design of mobile educational games.* MIT Press.

Krajcik, J., McNeill, K. L., & Reiser, B. J. (2008). Learning-goals-driven design model: Developing curriculum materials that align with national standards and incorporate project-based pedagogy. *Science Education, 92*(1), 1–32.

Marshall, S. (2020). *A handbook for teaching and learning in higher education: Enhancing academic practice* (5th ed.). Routledge.

Martin-Kniep, G., Feige, D., & Soodak, L. (1995). Curriculum integration: An expanded view of an abused idea. *Journal of Curriculum and Supervision, 10*(3), 227–249.

Miles, C., & Foggett, K. (2019). *A shift from discouraging academic dishonesty to authentic assessment.* Presentation on Transforming Assessment Webinar. https://transformingassessment.com/events_7_august_2019.php

Milligan, S., Luo, R., Hassim, E., & Johnston, J. (2020). *Future-proofing students: What they need to know and how educators can assess and credential them.* Report #2. Melbourne Graduate School of Education Industry Reports. https://education.unimelb.edu.au/mgse-industry-reports/report-2-future-proofing-students

National Research Council. (2005). *How students learn: History, mathematics and science in the classroom.* The National Academies Press.

O'Malley, C., McLaughlin, P., & Pocaro, P. (2017). Inclusive STEM: Closing the learning loop. In C. Reidsema, L. Kavanagh, R. Hadgraft, & N. Smith (Eds.), *The flipped classroom* (pp. 151–161). Springer. https://doi.org/10.1007/978-981-10-3413-8_9

Prosser, M., & Trigwell, K. (1999). *Understanding learning and teaching: The experience in higher education.* SRHE, Open University Press.

Quellmaiz, E. S., & Silberglitt, M. D. (2018). SimScientists: Affordances of science simulations for formative and summative assessment. In H. Jiao & R. W. Lissitz (Eds.), *Technology enhanced innovative assessment: Development, modelling, and scoring from an interdisciplinary perspective* (pp. 71–94). Information Age Publishing.

Reddy, Y., & Andrade, H. (2010). A review of rubric use in higher education. *Assessment & Evaluation in Higher Education, 35*(4), 435–448. https://doi.org/10.1080/02602930902862859

Rivers, S., & Willans, T. (2013). Student engagement in private sector higher education. In E. Dunne & D. Owen (Eds.), *The student engagement handbook: Practice in higher education* (pp. 111–132). Emerald.

Schleicher, A. (2018). Educating learners for their future, not our past. *East China Normal University Review of Education, 1*(1), 58–75. https://doi.org/10.30926/ecnuroe2018010104

Schneider, B., Krajcik, J., Lavonen, J., & Salmela-Aro, K. (2019). *Learning science – crafting engaging science environments.* Yale University Press.

Sweeney, T., West, D., Groessler, A., Haynie, A., Higgs, B., M., Macaulay, J., Mercer-Mapstone, L., & Yeo, M. (2017). Where's the transformation? Unlocking the potential of technology-enhanced assessment. *Teaching and Learning Inquiry, 5*(1), 41–56. http://doi.org/10.20343/teachlearninqu.5.1.5

Thomas, J. W. (2000). *A review of research on project-based learning (PjBL) environment.* Autodesk Foundation.

Universitat Politechnica de Valencia. (2020). *Bachelor's degree in data science.* www.upv.es/titulaciones/GCD/indexi.html

Yalch, M., Vitale, E., & Ford, J. (2019). Benefits of peer review on students' writing. *Psychology, Learning & Teaching, 18*(3), 317–325. http://doi.org/10.1177/1475725719835070

Yanez, G. A., Thumlert, L. K., de Castell, S., & Jenson, J. (2019). Pathways to sustainable futures: A "production pedagogy" model for STEM education. *Futures, 108*, 27–36. https://doi.org/10.1016/j.futures.2019.02.021

You, H., Marshall, J., & Delgado, C. (2018). Assessing students' disciplinary and interdisciplinary understanding of global carbon cycling. *Journal of Research in Science Teaching, 55*(3), 377–398.

Zhao, Y. (2016). *Counting what counts: Reframing education outcomes.* Solution Tree Press.

6 Challenges and professional learning for integrating STEM

Introduction

While the promise of integrating STEM disciplines has been realised in some schooling systems, many educators in higher education institutions (HEIs) have been reticent about applying an integrated approach to the design and implementation of coursework. Of course, there are exceptions. The reasons given for this reticence relate to deeply held views about the value of separate disciplines; the discipline constraints (including language, resources and technical issues, faculty backgrounds and previous teaching experience); faculty willingness to change; time to plan and reconceptualise learning experiences that are inclusive of capabilities (rather than "deliver" content); and the competitive forces of the need to stay productively researching. Even the word "deliver" connotes the view that the teacher is the knower. While this view may still prevail in many HEIs, there is much research evidence and specific examples that support integration of disciplines and integration of content knowledge, skills and capabilities, especially in STEM (Corrigan, 2020), in which active and generative learning approaches are used to foster problem-solving.

Integrating STEM requires educators to shift from thinking about themselves as "knowers" (and therefore conveyers and keepers of content knowledge) to "enablers" of understanding, by providing a wide range of learning experiences. Associated with this are shifts in expectations about roles (educator and student roles in the learning process) that represent the greatest challenges to integrating STEM.

The form of assessment, course sequence, learning environment, type of student support and student self-efficacy have an effect on student engagement, progression and outcomes (National Academies of Sciences, Engineering and Medicine, 2018). Institutional strategies for improved instruction and co-curricular support have yielded improvements in student outcomes (Malcolm & Feder, 2016), although there is still much more that can be done for implementing integrated STEM curriculum. For instance, identifying the knowledge to be learned is particularly challenging in integrated models, especially when educators highly value their own expert knowledge. The assumptions educators have about what needs to be learned and how people learn tend

Challenges and professional learning   125

to drive their interpretations of the value of particular content, their design of learning experiences and consequent assessment practices.

In addition, students come to higher education with expectations about what and how they will be taught, often based on reputation and traditional expectations. Focussing on content knowledge has dominated higher education for centuries and has been reinforced through valuing recall in assessment. If we are really serious about developing critical and creative thinkers who can solve problems through innovation, then student learning must be based on more expansive considerations about what supports the development of learning, as provided in Figure 3.1 (Chapter 3). What turns most people on to learning is when they can demonstrate they are effective at something that is personally meaningful and potentially makes a contribution to others (Fullan, 2011). Intrinsic motivation also grows when people are part of a team contributing to an outcome. Coursework in STEM should, therefore, leverage these social motivators, while at the same time widening and enhancing student capabilities.

For some students, the greatest change is an expectation that they will be given agency (choice and power) over their own learning. This requires a shift in thinking from educators and students, as students will not be "told" the information they need, but rather will be supported in how to find out what they need and even how to co-create new knowledge. The ownership of knowledge and capabilities, in this view, shifts from teacher to student. Self-directed learners are those who deliberately strategise what they think and do in order to optimise their time and energy to achieve what they want (intention) (Conner, 2014). For students who do not do this naturally, what makes the difference is being aware of the multiple possible ways of thinking and acting, knowing what specific strategies are useful and knowing how and when it is appropriate to choose and use them. When people deliberately reflect on what they think and do, they are using their experiences as a resource for action. Asking questions is a key strategy to drive changes in thinking for optimising effort. So, if students want to change the way they learn, they may need support to ask deliberate questions about what would help them to be more effective.

As well, the expectations of students as *producers* rather than *consumers* of knowledge (McMillan & Cheney, 1996) will be a significant paradigm shift for all. A more likely middle ground would be to think of students as *co-producers* of knowledge (Rivers & Willans, 2013). In this sense, students are viewed as essential partners in meaning-making and the generation of new knowledge, which are core purposes of universities (Werder & Skogsberg, 2013) and are absolutely fundamental to innovation in STEM.

Given the challenges detailed earlier, in order to enact and embed integrated STEM in higher education, there needs to be a change in educator beliefs about what content knowledge, skills and capabilities are important for students. This means educators should have a deep understanding of how people learn, particularly the students they teach so they can reconsider how to

126 *Challenges and professional learning*

appropriate pedagogies for guiding and supporting ongoing student development. Educator perceptions of their roles influence their effectiveness in teaching (Darling-Hammond & Bransford, 2005).

There are many examples of how HEIs use evidence-based research and apply this to creating high-quality learning experiences (for evolving examples, see Association of American Universities, 2018). The uptake of integrated STEM approaches will become more widespread when the assumptions and perceptions of educators are recognised and adjusted to accommodate student-centred, generative approaches for problem-solving, as discussed in previous chapters.

Assumptions may arise because educators in higher education may not have had training in learning design, let alone integrating curriculum elements that promote skills and capabilities. Even when they have been made aware of evidence-based good practices for enhancing learning, they may not be aware of new designs for integrating STEM curriculum (e.g. Smith et al., 2015; Chapter 4 in this book), or of teaching that fosters interactive and student-centred generative activities. Another issue is that real-world problems are not necessarily packaged in a way that can be resolved by one approach from one discipline. Instead, they are messy and complex, requiring multiple approaches, which is exactly what students need to gain: experience in solving the sort of problems that tackle people–planet issues.

Integrated approaches require careful planning and changes to teaching and learning approaches. For example, at the African Leadership University in Rwanda, a new qualification has been designed called "Global Challenges", which is a project-based degree requiring students to design their own projects to find solutions for the challenges facing Africa (Staab, 2020). Students choose to focus on one of the seven grand challenges facing Africa: education, urbanisation, health care, climate change, governance, job creation and infrastructure. The shift from a highly structured didactic (educator–knowledge centred) approach to one that features a high level of student choice and autonomy, including students managing their time effectively to undertake inquiry and work in teams (Staab, 2020), has been challenging because of the shifts needed in perceptions of the roles of educators and students to make this successful.

In applied subjects, such as agricultural science, concepts from abstract science and mathematics can be highlighted by situating learning in relevant contexts. When researching the integration of STEM within agricultural education, Smith et al. (2015) found that educators ($n = 280$) had higher confidence in incorporating mathematics and science, but lower levels of confidence for integrating technology and engineering. This study concluded that stakeholder evaluation of the pedagogies most effective for integrating STEM was needed and that educators needed ongoing support to become effective in designing and choosing appropriate learning experiences (Smith et al., 2015). Integrating STEM takes time and persistence, experimentation and evaluation, combined with reflection on what works in particular learning contexts. Because these all involve investments of time and effort, the purpose for this

Challenges and professional learning 127

effort needs reiterating: it is to expand the boundaries of students' possible futures by supporting more effective learning of knowledge, skills and capabilities simultaneously.

There is also a need to change the expectations of students, particularly about what learning involves, including the importance of developing capabilities of filtering, framing and taking responsibility for learning. The shift towards more self-directed and self-regulated learning is occurring in many countries in the compulsory education sector, but teachers in higher education have not generally been aware of this trend and have not extended it and its implications into their teaching.

We are therefore still at an emergent stage of understanding questions such as:

- What do these shifts mean for the type of support educators need to design and plan for integrating STEM?
- What happens when you empower students to drive the way they engage with problem-solving and inquiry?
- What knowledge and skills do teachers need in order to implement problem-solving, inquiry and generative pedagogies?

There are competing calls on time and effort for educators in HEIs (research, teaching and service/administration). Preparing effective *learning* experiences and using evidence to inform ongoing development for learners should be highly valued. Incentivising and valuing effective (or innovative) outcomes can motivate educators to undertake cycles of continuous improvement in teaching.

However, the shift worldwide in education to focus on *student learning* – whether specific content, specific skills and processes, ways of working in a discipline, values, attitudes, how to learn effectively or how the context for learning matters (OECD, 2013) – needs to be taken up in HEIs. Historically, teaching has focussed on the first four of these. The latter three have taken a back seat, particularly in universities. Because of the changing ways knowledge is being used and created, there is a need to reconsider the processes of teaching more carefully, so that values (ITEA, 2000, 2002, 2007), attitudes and capabilities are developed through learning in real-world contexts.

This chapter proposes that ongoing professional learning is needed to strengthen STEM through integrated course design and that ongoing critical reflective practice includes the scholarship of teaching and research on effective teaching and learning.

Blending discipline and capability

Three factors obviate against integrating STEM teaching and learning: student expectations ("why are we learning this?"), competitive demands on educators ("you must do more research") and, most pernicious of all, deeply embedded discipline practices to teaching in higher education. When integrating STEM,

128   *Challenges and professional learning*

therefore, whether at the level of activity, course or qualification, content areas can be blended and the approaches to teaching and learning themselves can include student capability alongside knowledge development. There are also perceived issues related to assessing content and capabilities simultaneously. Some examples of how these can be assessed were provided in Chapter 5 in this book.

In this section, key strategies for overcoming the challenges to implementing integrated STEM are discussed. These challenges relate to long-standing beliefs about what teaching and learning involve in these disciplines, specifically:

- Educators have *knowledge* authority and therefore believe they need to *impart* that knowledge to students.
- Students have *expectations*, including how technologies will be used.
- Educators may not know how to adapt pedagogies based on variations in levels of student *development*.
- Educators view students as *consumers* rather than *producers* of knowledge.
- Educators may lack knowledge of *evidence-based research* on how people learn.
- HEIs and their staff do not value *professional learning* as much as they could.

Each of these challenges is discussed in the following subsections.

Challenge: educators have knowledge authority

The first challenge is the belief that educators have *"knowledge" authority* and are therefore required to impart that knowledge to students. Calls for change to how STEM is taught have taken on greater urgency as more information from the learning sciences reveals that conveying information through lectures (that is, imparting knowledge) is no longer appropriate (National Academies of Sciences, Engineering and Medicine, 2018). Often the excuse for giving information through lectures is that students need to be told the information on which they can base future learning. This is outdated for many reasons. Information is ubiquitous.

Educators *telling* students information is not efficient, nor is it an effective means for students to gain understanding of that information. There is also margin for error in the transfer of information from the original source, through educator preparation, then presentation, student notes and finally (hopefully) to student understanding (Cannon & Knapper, 2011). It should be no surprise that students are likely to assimilate only a small fraction of what has been conveyed (Bligh, 2000).

Despite this, there is still a place for presenting information and focussing ideas and insights, as well as using a range of questioning techniques to stimulate thinking. A good presenter challenges evidence and asks how we have come to know. In STEM contexts, this is especially important, as there is a strong reliance on empirical evidence to substantiate claims. So, how *do* we

Challenges and professional learning 129

know? How do we imbue validity, reliability and tolerance limits? Educators who deliberately use such questioning can model evaluative (critical) thinking (Conner & Kolajo, 2020).

In contrast to learning through listening to lectures, learning through active engagement requires active thinking about real problems, using previous personal experiences, concrete examples, cases, scenarios and exposure to evidence, sorting facts and evaluating data. Students need to be provided with learning experiences that enable them to synthesise, connect, integrate and evaluate knowledge and techniques from a range of sources (Conner, 2014; Paniagua & Istance, 2018). Previous chapters have provided examples of how this is being done through themes, contexts and the use of specific activities, such as challenges, that help students to solve problems and generate new knowledge.

Historically, it has been the educators who have the power, as it is they who make decisions about content and how learning takes place. We are currently seeing a power swing in the cognitive pendulum, away from educators making all the decisions to a continuum of staged activities, in which students take charge of their own learning through opportunities to make decisions about what and how they learn (Fink, 2013). This approach encourages interdependency, with the educator being more of a guide or coach who provides feedback on progress. Of course, power still resides in the educator, as they are the person determining the assessments. Despite this, providing more open-ended tasks that allow students to choose what they focus on moves us towards empowering students.

Challenge: accommodate student expectations

The ability to exchange and co-create information is growing rapidly, due to the seemingly ubiquitous nature of information technologies and associated capacity to enable rapid and networked communication with large numbers of people. This aspect was discussed in Chapter 2 in this book, as digitisation and accessibility of knowledge influence how people expect to and already receive information. Higher education is facing a reality check about accessibility and authority of knowledge. This is changing our learning culture and, consequently, student expectations. No longer are university lecturers considered *the* source of knowledge. Students can access content freely and openly from any number of open sources and consequently expect to gain something through their educational experience beyond gaining content and skills. HEIs are considering this issue very carefully during the pivot online due to COVID-19 restrictions.

Students bring *expectations* and previous experiences grown and learned in a culture influenced by their previous education. The secret to engaging students is to tap into and leverage these prior experiences and interests. Educators need to find ways to enable students to *share* their previous knowledge and skills. Self-assessment processes can really help with this. Being clear about what is

130   *Challenges and professional learning*

expected of students as they *learn* in a particular course sets the scene by including possibilities for actions they will need to take.

Nowadays, students entering higher education tend to be more familiar with using technology for learning and consequently have been termed *digital natives* (Prensky, 2001), the *net generation* (Tapscott, 2009) and *new millennials* (Howe & Strauss, 2000). Despite such labels, it is likely that students have a range of technological competencies, thus implying that their prior skills need to be checked and adjustments made to instructions to accommodate these existing skills and needs, which lead to variations in how people learn, what they remember and the skills they develop. In general, teaching and learning in HEIs has not taken individual differences into account, especially at scale in large classes. Enabling students to act more as partners, in order to determine what they are good at and what they need help with, should be included as part of curriculum design (Conner, 2014).

Knowing how to appropriate technologies within learning experiences will require continuous professional learning for all teachers. The UNESCO ICT competency framework for teachers (ICT-CFT) helps to develop educators' use of technology along a continuum from knowledge acquisition, through knowledge deepening, to knowledge creation (UNESCO, 2020). The goal of the framework is to support the professional education of educators.

The ICT-CFT framework also helps to identify the level of capability educators have and can therefore be used to support and build capacity so that experts are those who develop their students' communication skills through using technologies in interesting and novel ways. While this framework has primarily been applied for initial and continuing teacher education in the compulsory sector, it can be applied to educator development in higher education.

Open educational resources (OER) are available to support professional learning for learning design and reside in the public domain to permit no-cost access (see oercommons.org/hubs/UNESCO). These resources can be used to:

- Develop and improve courses and quality of learning materials.
- Redesign activities and courses, including contextualising, personalising and localising for high levels of relevance.
- Increase interactivity between students, helping students to select and adapt resources.
- Create assessment tools that provide indicators for how judgements of sufficiency and proficiency will be measured (see the section on rubrics in Chapter 5).
- Connect with the world of work and authentic problems or issues.

Currently there are projects being undertaken by UNESCO (e.g. at the Jozef Stefan Institute in Slovenia) to increase access to OER substantially through using AI bots and search engines in combination. It is likely that within the next few years, OER will actively disrupt current models of education in HEIs.

Challenge: adapting pedagogies based on student development

There is a tension for educators between wanting to ensure the well-being and educational *development* of their students and yet, at the same time, provide students with skills for being self-directed learners. Knowing how much guidance to give is a constant dilemma for educators (Conner, 2004). In a study with 18-year-olds, some students became very frustrated because they felt the teacher was not telling them what to do, whereas he was deliberately letting them choose their own approaches and strategies to support their self-directed development as learners (Conner, 2014). If we only use directed instruction, students do not need to think for themselves. In this case (Conner, 2014), the teacher was a "guide on the side", but there was a gap in understanding from the students because this was not how they had experienced learning previously, and this change in culture was difficult for them. The highest achievers were the most frustrated of all, because they wanted to be told what they needed to know, as they were very capable of memorising. Unfortunately, the teacher had not been explicit about his approach or how he was identifying what skills students already had and what he could assist with or that students were responsible for developing. Being clear about expectations and responsibilities is a very important part of teaching for more effective learning.

Most universities select students based on the expectation they will succeed. It is likely that students who have already succeeded in education prior to entering an HEI already know how to learn, or at least how to memorise, information (depending on emphasis in previous assessments). But what if these students could work alongside those who did not have as highly developed skills? Could this increase the capacity of students to be more effective learners? The social nature of learning has not yet been utilised in HEIs anywhere near to the extent it could be in order to enhance learning.

Considerations for advancing student development of collaboration include:

- Students take time to build relationships for working in trusting communities of learners. This can be built into coursework.
- Variable quality of relationships make it complicated to work in groups for equitable outcomes (that is, equitable input into contributions and products).
- Students bring different knowledge, expertise and skills sets (including comfort with using technologies) that need to be accommodated.

There is huge potential for students to support development of other students. Unfortunately, the cultural capital agenda of building group capability is not strong in many Western universities (Zhou, 2014). Instead, we have created and celebrated individual achievement, as if that is the only way. In contrast, educational agendas in China are very strongly grounded in building collective human capital (Zhou, 2014).

132 *Challenges and professional learning*

Challenge: students as consumers and producers of knowledge

In STEM education, there is a huge opportunity to build students as curators and creators of knowledge. As previously mentioned (*challenge: educators have knowledge authority*), this is fundamental to innovation and to the creation of new knowledge more generally. The shift in power to student-centred pedagogy is aligned with a shift in thinking that students can be both *consumers* and *producers* of knowledge, not just in research contexts but also as part of their participation in coursework.

For example, STEM practical and laboratory experiences can be directed towards problem-solving and knowledge (or artefact) generation, rather than recipe-following or confirmatory experiments. Inquiry, in which students genuinely contribute to new knowledge through undertaking practical experimentation, should be highly valued. The modern laboratory is changing significantly as new technologies are introduced (see Chapter 2), and there is therefore an ongoing need for students to become familiar with using new technologies to prepare them for future workplaces. Students may be able to refine and generate new methods as part of a creative quest to solve problems related to real-world issues.

Student-centred course design has been in focus for some time, yet engaging students in co-creating curricula is much more recent, and the inclusion of students as partners in designing courses is emergent (Bovill & Felten, 2016). Partnership does not necessarily fit with existing structures in higher education, especially where there are standards and accreditation requirements to meet, or where students have little knowledge about a subject (Bovill & Felten, 2016) and consequently do not know what they need to know or how to be able to do something. Despite this, students are already designing their own learning experiences and determining their own outcomes (albeit aligned with assessment frameworks) in some jurisdictions in the compulsory sector (for example, in Australia and New Zealand).

Challenge: application of evidence-based research

Active approaches to learning (including supporting student thinking), as discussed in Chapters 3 and 4, tend to increase students' engagement (Davis et al., 2008). From a broad study across a range of disciplines (Conner, 2015), it was clear that educators needed to consider additional, multiple affective (such as student sense of identity and belonging) as well as cognitive influences as to why students choose (or choose not) to engage with tasks. What is "okay" to do in a situation will be part of the "culture" of each educational setting. Educators are struggling to come to grips with such influences, as they may be slightly different for different individuals. There is a reluctance to use the somewhat under-rated power of celebrating and making use of student diversity, especially in higher educational contexts. Educators can extend their awareness of research on factors influencing learning (for example, National Academies of Sciences, Engineering and Medicine, 2018) and how approaches, pedagogies and supports within a learning environment can make a huge difference to student outcomes. Above all, educators can benefit if they have opportunities to apply this research to their practice (Guskey, 1986).

Much evidence on creating effective learning environments points to educators using strategies to support learner motivation (Leisman et al., 2018), which may involve:

- Helping students to establish appropriately challenging learning goals.
- Creating learning experiences that have value for students.
- Supporting student autonomy and providing choice.
- Enabling students to recognise, monitor and strategise their learning progress through effective and frequent feedback.
- Creating a positive, supportive and non-threatening learning environment in which learners feel safe and valued through mutual respect.

Setting up the conditions to support learning is therefore a crucial part of planning and implementing integrated STEM. This was highlighted in Figure 3.1, Chapter 3, and also in Chapter 4 of this book.

Challenge: valuing ongoing professional learning

One of the difficulties of teaching within a knowledge society is that knowledge is always changing and growing. Therefore, educators need continual updating as to what is current, not only from a discipline or interdisciplinary perspective, but also with regard to what can be done to teach skills and how to learn more effectively. Guskey (1986) indicated that changes to professional learning for teaching can be targeted in three ways:

- Changes to practices of educators.
- Changes to learning outcomes for students.
- Changes to the beliefs and attitudes of educators about teaching and learning.

Multiple studies have indicated that when teachers see that changes they have made in their practice have resulted in better outcomes for students, then their beliefs and attitudes have changed (Guskey, 2002; Conner, 2015). Finding new ways to teach and become proficient with them takes time, action and reflection. Given that there are multiple benefits for students when educators enhance their teaching, *professional learning* must be prioritised and incentivised. Structured professional learning, as well as other forms of professional learning, such as action research and the scholarship of teaching (SoTL), are essential to driving the changes to teaching needed for integrating STEM. Because of this, the following section in this chapter is dedicated to professional learning.

Professional learning

It could be argued that some educators in HEIs do not need to be updated with current theories of learning because they already teach well. Others contend that it is through experience, not theory, that good teaching is developed. Often, educators in HEIs consider that if their students are achieving well, there is no need for them to change what they do (Conner & Kolajo, 2020). Good teaching is much more complex than technical competence, as nuances and multiple contingencies can enhance or hinder learning, and changes might bring about new affordances for students (National Academies of Sciences, Engineering and Medicine, 2018). Educators in higher education cannot possibly know all there is about teaching for effective learning. There is always more everyone can learn. For many university academics, teaching takes second place to research. Teaching in HEIs has also historically been an individual rather than a collaborative venture and especially lacks collaboration with students.

Carvalho (2020) summarised in general terms what great educators know and how they create the conditions conducive for effective learning. These included that great educators:

- Are open to learning and improvement (for excellence and for benefit of students).
- Provide respectful, structured learning environments (with effective learning relationships based on trust, expertise, fairness and reliability, offering structure and consistency).
- Have (expert) subject knowledge and passion (show commitment to intellectual and personal learning).
- Ask inspiring questions and fan the flames of wonder (so that students have enduring curiosity).
- Understand the wider emphasis of education (such as knowing yourself).

Carvalho (2020) stated that:

> When teachers do these things well, their conversations with their students about knowledge and the world under construction will flourish from the creative and critical thinking of a new generation of lifelong learners who understand that they have minds, and that they can use them responsibly for the common good.
>
> (para. 20)

These noble aims are worth pursuing.

Kelley and Knowles (2016) suggested that professional learning is key to preparing STEM educators for integrating curriculum. They suggested that as part of this process, educators benefit from understanding how to apply appropriate learning theories and how to adapt and change approaches to meet the needs of students. Of particular interest to integrating STEM is the ability of educators to blend discipline knowledge, skills and capabilities by providing appropriate learning experiences. Prosser and Trigwell (1999) advised that pedagogy in universities should expand the capabilities of educators in the following areas:

- Increase their awareness of effective teaching and learning within their subjects.
- Take account of how context relates to and affects how they teach.
- Understand ways in which students perceive learning situations.
- Appreciate the value of continual improvement, revision, adjustment and adaptation to teaching.

Professional learning for integrating STEM, as part of cycles of continuous improvement, should also expand educator capability for designing assessments. This is especially so for assessment dimension descriptors that indicate levels of proficiency for content, processes and skills outcomes to be assessed simultaneously. These considerations were discussed in Chapter 5 in this book. This is because if the assessment is designed well, it can drive integration of STEM disciplines and enable the demonstration of capabilities.

Proposing and implementing an integrated STEM programme renewal agenda provides an opportunity to drive systematic evaluation studies of improvements in teaching and learning, including assessment practices (Hines, 2009). Evaluation needs to move beyond satisfaction surveys to consider how specific changes have impact on the dimensions that are assessed. For example, in project work with teaching specialists, Ross (2019) described a framework for professional learning that focussed on knowledge, practice, scholarship and students. More broadly, key enablers for professional learning were found to focus on student-centred learning, developing expertise and research on teaching, as well as developing connections and collaborations (with stakeholders in government agencies, industries or businesses), communication, influence and impact, personal effectiveness and reflective practices (Ross, 2019). In combination, these strategies are likely to have impact on effective teaching more widely throughout HEIs. Institutions can nurture effective teaching capacities, especially through collaborative efforts to increase the spread throughout institutions and share good practices and ideas throughout the sector more generally. Educators can be entrusted and given time to direct their own educative efforts but will need support and guidance with this.

This section considers approaches for professional learning under the following subheadings:

- Scholarship of teaching and learning (SoTL).
- Reflective practice.
- Competencies for using technologies.
- Collaborating and mentoring.

136 *Challenges and professional learning*

Scholarship of teaching and learning (SoTL)

Of importance for professional learning is how to apply theoretical knowledge of the learning sciences to STEM (National Academies of Sciences, Engineering and Medicine, 2018). This includes how to plan and evaluate integrated teaching and learning, student outcomes and characteristics of learning environments that promote thinking skills (for example, infusing student support structures such as questions, prompts, cues and so on).

Pedagogical research, or the scholarship of teaching and learning (SoTL) undertaken by educators, should be valued because it can continually contribute to changes in teaching (Boyer, 1990). SoTL pulls together knowledge of what works for a specific discipline, with the latest ideas gleaned from research on teaching and learning. Usually SoTL involves teachers sharing their reflections on evidence of the effects of their teaching with wider communities (Murray, 2008) by means of publications and scholarly discussions.

As a form of SoTL, action research can focus on any aspect of the teaching and learning process (Mills, 2003), using data to support decisions educators make. Curriculum decisions should be based on informed knowledge of the literature, on teaching and learning in higher education, as well as evidence from student responses and outcomes. High-quality professional learning that enables educators to appropriate pedagogies must be based on evidence of what works. Research on teaching approaches can help institutions to confront issues they face and to develop policies and practices for providing more effective learning experiences. It is therefore strategic for institutions to invest in such research.

Several comprehensive texts have given specific examples of effective teaching practices in higher education (Entwistle, 2007; Biggs, 2003; Trigwell & Prosser, 1997). Although many of these take account of the need to pay attention to student perceptions and expectations of their academic contexts (as student learning behaviours tend to align with what is valued), they do not necessarily take account of more contemporary theories of learning, such as sociocultural theory, motivational theory, complexity thinking and connectivism. This is unfortunate, as these theories help to explain why particular pedagogies might be more useful than others, especially in relation to a specific learning context that may include social and technological dimensions. Even when educators have teaching methods, strategies and ways to enable students to connect in meaningful ways with their learning, greater effectiveness may arise through an increased understanding of why particular approaches can promote learning and help students to adjust their learning behaviours.

Changes in outcomes for students will only occur when changes are made to the pedagogy or assessments employed. Such changes are best made when based on empirical research about learning, factors influencing student engagement and effective teaching. Yet, evaluating any changes made and the resulting outcomes for students is challenging for a number of reasons, including:

*   Most educators have their own discipline field of research, they tend not to research aspects of learning or even consider teaching (or enabling

learning) as a means of generating new knowledge. That is, most higher education academics do not research their own teaching or have time or a wish to do so.

- Many educators in higher education may be anxious about their teaching. They may have been employed because of their research reputation or may be quite new to teaching. Therefore, while expert in other areas, they may not feel expert in teaching.
- Educators may be unaware of contemporary research on learning (especially on appropriating digital technologies) and how this research can be applied to enhancing learning. As a result, there needs to be a revision of the translation of dominant theories about how people learn to teach.
- Educators may not know how to undertake research or evaluative methods in order to examine their teaching effectiveness. This is despite the fact that all HEIs have, as part of their quality assurance processes, student evaluation and other sources of feedback, such as peer observations, peer evaluations of teaching and so on.

There are exceptions, of course, in which tertiary educators continually engage in progressive developments of their teaching. Despite this, Young (1998) indicated that a lack of research on teaching represents a crisis in higher education generally, one that needed to be addressed urgently. It is unlikely that this situation has improved today. Good teaching needs to be founded on a strong intellectual base and should refer to the emerging scholarship of effective teaching. A growing number of teaching specialist staff have been employed because they have demonstrated effective teaching and leadership skills and are not required to undertake academic research. However, they could contribute significantly in the field of SoTL.

Discipline-based networks and associations are doing a lot to promote effective teaching and learning, especially in STEM disciplines. In Australia, the Science and Mathematics Network of Australian University Educators (SaMnet) aims to provide acknowledgement of achievement of educators, as described by Fullan (2005). SaMnet supports a network of educators so there is:

- Coherency of effort for action-learning projects in teaching science and mathematics.
- Incentives for effective teaching supported by government.
- Support from university administrators in terms of alignment with school and college key performance indicators.

In addition, SaMnet encourages former teaching award winners to act as mentors, particularly for new staff. Networks such as SaMnet enable a more cohesive effort to share good practices by improving the rigor of SoTL and the benefits of peer support. Palmer (1992) argues that it is important to have a rewards structure for educators to help them continue the surge of change. Networks and associations can actively support organisational rewards, such as teaching awards and promotions for excellent teachers.

138   *Challenges and professional learning*

Reflective practice

The relationship between teaching as a professional competence and reflection on action has been conceptualised by Schön (1987), who distinguishes between "theories-in-use" (containing assumptions about the professional situation) and "espoused theories" (used to describe and justify behaviour). Often educators do not recognise the difference between their "theories-in-use" and "espoused theories", because they do not make their theories explicit nor do they even interrogate these theories (McLean, 2006) to check whether their assumptions, especially about students, are founded. For example, in universities, an espoused theory is that teaching is designed to develop critical thinking and questioning in students, while a theory-in-use encourages students to reproduce information that has been "given" in lectures. Effective teaching requires a congruence between learning intentions and the methods for enabling them and is achieved when educators reflect on what the learning intentions are and how well the teaching behaviours enable these to be fulfilled. Reflective practice, then, is about not just what was done but also the *effectiveness* of what was done.

Adaptations to practice can be informed from many sources, such as one's own experiences of success and failure, discussions with others and ideas about pedagogy based on research and theory. Brookfield (1995) advocated for the use of critical frameworks to reflect on adaptations made in teaching to reduce reinforcement of ill-founded views about teaching and learning. Such frameworks are very useful.

Open discussions among colleagues can reduce the climate of anxiety that new teachers often have by acknowledging difficulties and leveraging issues that arise. Discussion is especially helpful in professional training courses, in which shared issues can be problem-solved by a small group of supportive peers. McLean (2006) described how beginning university educators participated in critical reflection, using collaborative inquiry as part of a certificated programme. Educators in this programme were required to develop teaching portfolios, in which they were encouraged to reflect on what they could improve and discuss this with the group. Because each educator worked with a mentor in her/his department, there were additional reciprocal opportunities for collaborative ways to improve teaching programmes and showcase improvements in their portfolios. Not only did the mentors suggest other ways of approaching teaching but beginning teachers also contributed to mentor understanding and departmental course development. What impressed experienced educators was the willingness of the beginning teachers to change and adapt to the needs of their students. Some even wondered whether assessing portfolios of the new teachers was a covert way of getting experienced educators to change as well!

Competencies for using technologies

Given continuing advances in technologies, professional learning is essential for teachers to adopt their use of technologies as learning tools (see Chapter 2).

Along with developing flexible learning environments, the educational software and apps industry has burgeoned in the last five years, with its own need for developers and implementers. The use of augmented reality (AR), virtual reality (VR) and mixed realty (XR) is just beginning. Educators in higher education are therefore potential neophytes who need support. These tools represent changes to learning environments that require response and application within teaching programmes. Educators need time to consider how to adopt and adapt new tools in order to enhance learning.

Systematic change requires that a majority of educators participate in pedagogical changes. Stein and Coburn (2008) commented on how successful systematic uplift requires multiple channels of influence, including leadership and groups of educators who collaboratively support each other through communities of practice. In other words, people learn from each other as well as from other sources. Therefore encouraging educators to collaborate as they design new experiences for students through using technologies (including hardware and digital technologies) is important for systematic uplift. When these changes are evaluated through critical reflective practice (Brookfield, 1995) and the scholarship of teaching, it is more likely that these changes will lead to better outcomes for students. Collaborative co-design within HEIs using technology can be an effective form of professional learning. Taking this further, networked communities have the power to scale up significant change (Istance & Paniagua, 2019) and therefore can provide valuable connections for professional learning.

As part of the changing world of work, students must appreciate the importance of using applications related to Industry 4.0 that will affect their need for specific knowledge and technical skills. Educators may also need to refresh their understanding about Industry 4.0, advancing their use of communication channels and responding by incorporating technologies as part of learning experiences and assessments. Further, economic shifts seen around the world recently mean that increasingly we need to make use of connected ways of communicating and networking at a global level. The challenges of these shifts reflect the increasing demand for improved effectiveness and productivity in online education. If educators can build in emerging technologies as part of teaching and integrating STEM content skills and capabilities, qualifications are more likely to prepare students for future work.

There are multiple digital sources to check on learner interactions with course materials and with each other (Lu & Law, 2012). For example, learning management systems, such as Blackboard, Moodle and Canvas, provide analytics in the form of learner IDs, time stamps and activity clicks. Data can be scanned for completion of activities, grades, grade distributions and cohort reporting. These types of data analytics (GISMO, MOCLog, and Learning LAe-R Analytics Enhanced Rubric) can provide powerful information about student progress and achievement (Mwalumbwe & Mtebe, 2017; Yassine et al., 2016). There is a need for much more systematic use of available data for improving practice and specific pedagogies when integrating STEM (National Academies of Sciences, Engineering and Medicine, 2018).

140 *Challenges and professional learning*

Collaborating and mentoring

It takes considerable confidence to question what you're doing, and why and how you might teach differently. When teachers are supported by colleagues and their institution more generally, they are more likely to ask questions and to systematically evaluate what they are doing. Pairs of educators can support each other to evaluate their teaching (including peer review of online delivery), helping each other to think about creative options for student-centred activities and moderating assessments for integration of content and skills within the same assessment task. Passion and energy generated through collaborative commitments can fuel the fire that is needed to complete complex goals. Fullan (1999) reminded us that change can be a roller coaster managed through collaboration and support:

> The true value of collaborative cultures is that they simultaneously encourage passion and provide emotional support as people work through the roller coaster of change.
>
> (p. 38)

McLean (2006) indicated that it is very important for new university educators, including part-time and post-graduate students who might be teaching, to have a mentor within their department. Good mentoring is compassionate and affirmative and enables informal, open and honest discussion. Whatever the professional learning mechanism, theoretical ideas about teaching for effective learning can inform reflective practices.

When collaborative approaches are used for action research, thereby establishing communities of practice (Wenger, 1998), there is potential to solve similar pedagogical issues in multiple contexts, thus building teaching expertise and enabling faster uplift of capability. These types of collaboration will be very important to building educator capabilities to integrate STEM.

Addressing challenges for integrating STEM

Integration of STEM within coursework will require shifts in perceptions of educators and students about which content, skills and capabilities are important and how new knowledge can be co-generated through coursework. Learning in higher education must prepare students for the future. This implies that educators really need to ask whether what they currently provide, in terms of learning experiences, will meet future needs of their students.

Effective changes in design and implementation of integrated STEM curriculum, including assessing student outcomes, requires ongoing professional learning. This involves educators making changes to their practice and evaluating the effects these changes have on student outcomes. Often, it is not until teachers see the benefits for students that their belief and attitudes about teaching change (Guskey, 1986). The question for educators

Challenges and professional learning 141

should be: what needs to change, especially when integrating content, skills and capabilities in STEM?

Professional learning could focus on taking on new roles, such as a facilitator, guide and coach, rather than being a keeper and conveyor of content knowledge. Being more of a guide requires an educator to navigate the nuances of using multiple sources of information, assisting students to work collaboratively and working with the ambiguity, tensions and complexity inherent in investigating issues and problem-solving, in which there may be potentially unknown outcomes (Henriksen et al., 2020). Guiding roles are necessary for effectively supporting students through inquiry and problem-solving and for implementing challenges and design thinking approaches. These roles may be new for many educators in higher education but can be supported through collaborative approaches and systematic research on innovations in teaching.

Student expectations can be fostered to revolve around *developing* their knowledge and skills to find solutions through collaborative efforts to cope, manage and be innovative as students forge new knowledge. As part of this agenda, learning programmes could emphasise:

- The importance of collaborating to coalesce STEM ideas.
- Providing opportunities for students to co-generate new knowledge and solutions to global issues.
- Building communication skills through virtual tools and networking.
- The ability to work with ambiguity and uncertainty.
- The value of trying out ideas through ideation processes, problem-solving tasks (including mapping the risks of possible outcomes) and trialling ideas.

An emphasis on these agendas can support the integration of STEM through professional learning for refocussing and evaluating teaching and learning. This would support the quest for ensuring students have the knowledge, technical skills and capabilities they will need to contribute to their own (humanistic) futures.

It is also important for educators to work collaboratively in strategic ways to discuss possibilities for promoting *learning* in STEM contexts. There is a need to manage divergent views about appropriate pedagogies for particular contexts based on educational sciences (Bransford et al., 2000; National Academies of Sciences, Engineering and Medicine, 2018), as such considerations become even more important when there is a change from transmissive (didactic) teaching to student-centred, active and generative learning approaches.

These are exciting times as we consider multiple possibilities for pedagogies that leverage these new ways of sharing and creating new knowledge through student engagement in coursework. There is a huge opportunity for HEIs to treat teaching and learning as an academic endeavour to produce the new knowledge needed to transform communities and to enhance human experience. For effective integration of STEM, educators can foster the development of knowledge, skills and capabilities and at the same time build in

142 *Challenges and professional learning*

student agency, respect for others and empowerment to contribute to making the world a better place. The question remains as to how HEIs will find ways to include collaborative, critical perspectives in which educators and students are empowered to question how they can co-contribute to new knowledge generation.

References

Association of American Universities. (2018). *Framework for systematic change in undergraduate STEM teaching and learning.* www.aau.edu/sites/default/files/STEM%20Scholarship/AAU_Framework.pdf

Biggs, J. (2003). *Teaching for quality learning at university* (2nd ed.). The Society for Research into Higher Education and Open University Press.

Bligh, D. A. (2000). *What's the use of lectures?* Jossey-Bass.

Bovill, C., & Felten, P. (2016). Cultivating student-staff partnerships through research and practice. *International Journal for Academic Development, 21*(1), 1–3. https://doi.org/10.108 0/1360144X.2016.1124965

Boyer, E. L. (1990). *Scholarship reconsidered: Priorities of the professoriate.* The Carnegie Foundation for the Advancement of Teaching. www.umces.edu/sites/default/files/al/pdfs/BoyerScholarshipReconsidered.pdf

Bransford, J., Brown, A., & Cocking, R. (2000). *How people learn: Brain, mind, experience and school.* National Research Council.

Brookfield, S. (1995). *Becoming a critically reflective teacher.* Jossey-Bass.

Cannon, R., & Knapper, C. (2011). *Lecturing for better learning* (3rd ed.). Higher Education Research and Development Society of Australasia.

Carvalho, D. (2020). Five qualities of great teachers. *Teacher: Evidence + Insight + Action.* www.teachermagazine.com.au/articles/five-qualities-of-great-teachers

Conner, L. (2004). Teaching values through the process of facilitation. *Pacific Asian Education, 16*(2), 65–80.

Conner, L. (2014). Students' use of evaluative constructivism: Comparative degrees of intentional learning. *International Journal of Qualitative Studies in Education, 27*(4), 472–489. http://doi.org/10.1080/09518398.2013.771228

Conner, L. (2015). *Teaching as inquiry with a focus on priority learners.* New Zealand Council for Educational Research.

Conner, L., & Kolajo, Y. (2020). The chemistry of critical thinking: The pursuit to do both better. In E. P. Blessinger & M. Makhanya (Eds.), *Improving classroom engagement and international development programs: International perspectives on humanizing higher education* (Vol. 27, pp. 93–110). Innovations in Higher Education Teaching and Learning. Emerald Publishing Limited. https://doi.org/10.1108/S2055-364120200000027009

Corrigan, D. (2020). *Implementing an integrated STEM education in schools – five key questions answered.* Education Futures Spotlight Report 2. Monash Education Futures.

Darling-Hammond, L., & Bransford, J. (2005). *Preparing teachers for a changing world.* Jossey-Bass.

Davis, B., Sumara, D., & Luce-Kapler, R. (2008). *Engaging minds: Changing teaching in complex times* (2nd ed.). Routledge.

Entwistle, N. (2007). Research into student learning and university teaching. *BJEP Monograph Series II, Number 4 – Student Learning and University Teaching, 1,* 1–18. www.researchgate.net/publication/233637014_1_-_Research_into_student_learning_and_university_teaching

Challenges and professional learning   143

Fink, L. D. (2013). *Creating significant learning experiences: An integrated approach to designing college courses*. Jossey-Bass.

Fullan, M. (1999). *Change forces: The sequel*. Falmer Press.

Fullan, M. (2005). *Leadership and sustainability: System thinkers in action*. Corwin Press.

Fullan, M. (2011). *Choosing the wrong drivers for whole system reform*. Centre for Strategic Education.

Guskey, T. (1986). Staff development and the process of teacher change. *Educational Researcher, 15*(5), 5–12.

Guskey, T. (2002). Does it make a difference? Evaluating professional development. *Educational Leadership, 59*, 45–51.

Henriksen, D., Jordan, M., Foulger, T. S., Zuiker, S., & Mishra, P. (2020). Essential tensions in facilitating design thinking: Collective reflections. *Journal of Formative Design in Learning, 4*, 5–16. https://doi.org/10.1007/s41686-020-00045-3

Hines, S. R. (2009). Investigating faculty development program assessment practices: What's being done and how can it be improved? *The Journal of Faculty Development, 23*(3), 5–19.

Howe, N., & Strauss, W. (2000). *Millennials rising: The next great generation*. Vintage Books.

Istance, D., & Paniagua, A. (2019). *Learning to leapfrog: Innovative pedagogies to transform education*. Brookings Institute.

ITEA. (2000). *Standards for technological literacy: Content for the study of technology*. International Technology Education Association.

ITEA. (2002). *Standards for technological literacy: Content for the study of technology*. International Technology Education Association.

ITEA. (2007). *Standards for technological literacy: Content for the study of technology*. International Technology Education Association.

Kelley, T. R., & Knowles, J. G. (2016). A conceptual framework for integrated STEM education. *Journal of STEM Education, 3*(1), 1–11.

Leisman, G., Mualem, R., & Mughrabi, S. K. (2018). *How people learn II: The science and practice of learning*. The National Academies Press.

Lu, J., & Law, N. W. Y. (2012). Understanding collaborative learning behavior from Moodle log data. *Interactive Learning Environments, 20*(5), 451–466.

Malcolm, S., & Feder, M. (2016). *Barriers and opportunities for 2-year and 4-year STEM degrees: Systemic change to support students' diverse pathways*. The National Academies Press. http://doi.org/10.17226/21739

McLean, G. N. (2006). *Organizational development: Principles, processes performance*. Berrett-Koehler Publishers.

McMillan, J., & Cheney, G. (1996). The student as consumer: The implications and limitations of a metaphor. *Communication Education, 45*, 1–15.

Mills, G. (2003). *Action research: A guide for the teacher researcher* (2nd ed.). Merrill, Prentice Hall.

Murray, R. (2008). *The scholarship of teaching and learning in higher education*. McGraw-Hill Education.

Mwalumbwe, I., & Mtebe, J. S. (2017). Using learning analytics to predict students' performance in Moodle learning management system: A case of Mbeya University of Science and Technology. *Electronic Journal of Information Systems in Developing Countries, 79*(1), 1–13.

National Academies of Sciences, Engineering and Medicine. (2018). *How people learn II: Learners, contexts and cultures*. The National Academies Press.

OECD. (2013). *Innovative learning environments*. OECD Publishing. https://doi.org/10.1787/9789264203488-en

144 Challenges and professional learning

Palmer, P. (1992). Divided no more. *Change Magazine, 24*(2), 10–17.

Paniagua, A., & Istance, D. (2018). *Teachers as designers of learning environments: The importance of innovative pedagogies.* OECD Publishing.

Prensky, M. (2001). Digital natives, digital immigrants. *On the Horizon, 9*(5), 1–12.

Prosser, M., & Trigwell, K. (1999). *Understanding learning and teaching: The experience in higher education.* SRHE and Open University Press.

Rivers, S., & Willans, T. (2013). Student engagement in private sector higher education. In E. Dunne & D. Owen (Eds.), *The student engagement handbook: Practice in higher education* (pp. 111–132). Emerald.

Ross, P. (2019). *The changing nature of the academic role in science.* Australian Council of Deans Teaching and Learning Centre. www.acds-tlcc.edu.au/wp-content/uploads/sites/14/2019/08/FS14-0232_Ross_AchievementsStatement_2019.pdf

Schön, D. A. (1987). *Educating the reflective practitioner toward a new design for teaching and learning in the professions.* Jossey-Bass.

Smith, K. L., Rayfield, J., & McKim, B. R. (2015). Effective practices in STEM integration: Describing teacher perceptions and instructional method use. *Journal of Agricultural Education, 56*(4), 182–201.

Staab, L. (2020). *Creating a project-based degree at a new university in Africa.* Paper presented at the 6th International Conference on Higher Education Advances (HEAd'20). Universitat Politècnica de València. http://doi.org/10.4995/HEAd20.2020.11180

Stein, M. K., & Coburn, C. E. (2008). Architectures for learning: A comparative analysis of two urban school districts. *American Journal of Education, 114*(4), 583–626.

Tapscott, D. (2009). *Grown up digital: How the net generation is changing your world.* McGraw-Hill.

Trigwell, K., & Prosser, M. (1997). Towards an understanding of individual acts of teaching and learning. *Higher Education Research and Development, 16*, 341–352.

UNESCO. (2020). *ICT competency framework for teachers harnessing open educational resources.* https://en.unesco.org/themes/ict-education/competency-framework-teachers

Wenger, E. (1998). *Communities of practice: Learning, meaning, and identity.* Cambridge University Press.

Werder, C., & Skogsberg, E. (2013). Trusting dialogue for engaging students. In E. Dunne & D. Owen (Eds.), *The student engagement handbook: Practice in higher education* (pp. 133–144). Emerald.

Yassine, S., Kadry, S., & Sicilia, M. A. (2016). A framework for learning analytics in Moodle for assessing course outcomes. In S. Yassine (Ed.), *Proceedings of the 2016 IEEE global engineering education conference 10–13 April* (pp. 261–266). IEEE.

Young, M. F. D. (1998). *The curriculum of the future: From the "new sociology of education" to a critical theory of learning.* Falmer Press.

Zhou, Y. (2014). *Who's afraid of the big bad dragon? Why China has the best (and worst) education system in the world.* Jossey-Bass.

7 Future directions for integrating STEM in higher education

Introduction

The first chapter of this book posed questions relating to whether integrated approaches in STEM clusters of disciplines enable graduates to solve problems and address global issues. Many examples have been provided in previous chapters to illustrate how this is manifesting in both the compulsory sector and higher education institutions (HEIs). Usually, changes have been driven by a belief that integrating STEM will lead to improved educational, social and career outcomes (National Academies of Sciences, Engineering and Medicine, 2018). Integrating STEM within coursework will require rethinking educational opportunities and experiences that embrace learning through purposefully designed active learning approaches (Chapters 3 and 4). While the integration of content combined with developing transferable skills can confer benefits for students (particularly their development of critical and creative thinking, collaboration and communication skills), it can also assist developmental agendas for societies, economies and people's chances in life, through confronting global issues such as climate change, sufficient nutritious food, poverty and global pandemics.

Despite these identified outcomes and needs, integrating STEM in higher education is still in its infancy. There has not been enough time or uptake (in my opinion) to establish clear benefits. After all, it makes sense intuitively, and as shown in the preceding chapters, there is research evidence to support integration, especially when we know that skills required for active problem-solving, creativity and innovation can be developed through activities that simultaneously integrate multiple content domains with transferable capabilities. In addition, collective human reasoning is going to become increasingly important as a human capacity, especially for mitigating global crises; yet, higher education, as currently constituted, focusses almost exclusively on individual achievement. Therefore, building collective capability through STEM coursework will assist problem-solving and can promote innovative solutions.

The levers for integrating STEM were outlined in Chapter 1 and are elaborated here in this chapter in terms of both disrupting and enabling trends in higher education more generally. The extent of uptake (discussed more fully in

146 *Future directions for integrating STEM*

Chapter 6) depends on the willingness of educators to use these levers within a range of curriculum levels and within projects, courses and qualifications.

Systems thinking is useful as it is inherent in natural phenomena; it is one of the dimensions to consider within the framework for integrating STEM, as presented in Figure 3.1 (Chapter 3). This chapter develops the idea of systems thinking, as applied to STEM integration, even further.

While there are many examples from research to support STEM integration in higher education provided throughout this book, much more research is needed to identify the affordances of different types of integration, effectiveness of various teaching and learning approaches, use of technology as an integrator and the teaching innovations that enhance learning and assessment. Research is desperately needed on how all of these contribute to positive outcomes for students (Henriksen et al., 2020), including more longitudinal studies about how curriculum reform has resulted in graduates with the transferable skills needed for generating new knowledge, innovation and future employment.

Changing agendas and trends

The future directions for integrating STEM are closely aligned with the enablers and disruptors that are affecting higher education across the world. HEIs have significant impact on economies and social enterprise in the way that they build human capital (skills) and create new knowledge, including innovations that provide solutions to global issues. These institutions will be vital for helping national economies recover from downturns that resulted due to COVID-19 restrictions.

Drivers in higher education

According to PwC (2020), the top five drivers for higher education include:

- Industrial expectations: drive inclusion of both specific and transferable capabilities (problem-solving, critical thinking, creative thinking, emotional intelligence and digital literacy) in qualifications. This implies a greater need for collaboration between industry and higher education.
- Technological change: greater use of emerging technologies and the impact of new technologies, as well as digitisation of learning experiences. We are at the beginning of a technology revolution that is changing the nature of work, making it imperative for HEIs to increase information and technology transfer for commercialisation and relevancy.
- Competition: students can choose where they learn, domestically and globally, with an online presence driving institutions to be even more distinctive, to capitalise on and to reduce barriers to the free flow of ideas.
- Student expectations: more customised, just-in-time opportunities to upskill or reskill through shorter courses, allowing for a greater diversity of

levels of skills. There is an increasing blurring of research, innovation and educational outcomes.

- Policy and funding: governments are promoting and funding education that leads to employment or graduates being job-ready, with potentially less funding for research.

There are strong economic pressures on students to choose qualifications, aligning these with previous work experience or reskilling opportunities. The cost, time and effort involved in completing qualifications means that students choose very carefully, a choice that acts as a driver in the trend towards micro-credential provision and more stackable qualifications. Potentially, there is a huge incentive for students to reduce the time and expense of gaining a qualification, such as enrolling in summer school or enrolling in double qualification tracks. Students are also presented with a wide array of choices in terms of courses and institutions that offer them. In response, HEIs strategise how they can improve their messaging, marketing and reputational rankings. This includes developing job readiness skills and publicising the employability outcomes of graduates.

Changes in HEIs

Other competing agendas and drivers, such as status hierarchy and unbundling (McCowan, 2019), are also influencing what institutions offer. Competitive forces for gaining student enrolments contribute to status hierarchies in the form of international rankings, mostly based on research metrics. Also, HEIs are increasingly participating in and prioritising revenue-generating activities, funded by states or industries, to the near exclusion of other forms of community engagement – a potential conflict for education as an intrinsic value and public good (McCowan, 2019). *Unbundling* refers to the separation of activities (for example, packaging tuition along with other services, such as on-campus accommodation) to drive down costs and to manage financial constraints. This was linked to the rise of digital access to learning (Williamson, 2018) and accelerated by COVID-19 considerations.

Increasingly, students are patching courses together from several different organisations (for example, Open Universities). Millions of students are doing this through the Allama Iqbal Open University in Pakistan and the Indira Gandhi National Open University in India. While traditional tertiary institutions have been competitors and rivals, this trend almost necessitates that tertiary institutions work collaboratively at multiple levels or that there is significant government regulation.

Internationally, there is a strong trend for multiple institutions to partner in offering qualifications co-jointly or at least (cross-credit) transfer courses through mutual agreements. This trend will increase in the future, as there are huge advantages for students to obtain qualifications from multiple institutions.

148　*Future directions for integrating STEM*

This trend is especially the case for qualifications taught in English, as English is highly valued in academia and international business. Such co-joint offerings assist institutions in maximising efficiency of curriculum development to meet the needs of students and to act as attractors in the competition for student enrolments. Connecting with other universities for providing qualifications (as well as research), having international students on campus and adjusting curriculum to include globalisation agendas help institutional international benchmarking and rankings. Worldwide demand for higher learning has never been greater.

HEIs and future education

Qualifications are likely to be more narrowly focussed on skills for a job or sets of discrete capabilities rather than educating rounded graduates with a comprehensive or a professional set of competencies. Higher education must provide experiences for graduates that build capability to be open to new ways of thinking; to be adaptable, flexible and comfortable taking some risks; and to cope with perturbations and global changes to the world of work. This has started. There has been a relatively recent change in emphasis in higher education and by employers in relation to developing capabilities, often called graduate attributes or transversal skills (Milligan et al., 2020). This means that for graduates to be successful in an increasingly complex world, they need opportunities to develop and learn capabilities as part of their qualifications, including:

- Literacy, numeracy, computational and ICT skills.
- Ability to communicate effectively through multiple channels.
- Capacity to work in teams: collaboration and cooperation.
- Critical thinking as applied in STEM contexts, such as the ability to evaluate evidence, claims, trustworthiness, interpretations, reliability and validity.
- Creative thinking as core to innovation.
- Problem-solving using multiple perspectives, resources and disciplinary approaches.
- Ethical behaviours to guide humanitarian approaches: to do no harm.
- Flexibility and ability to work in agile ways and adapt to changes and shifts in emphasis.
- Enterprise skills.
- Citizenship and community service experiences.

Claims of value-added components specific to an institution are often linked to international ranking metrics, such as the staff to student ratio or the opportunity for service learning, internships and international student exchanges. Instead, HEIs could promote the kinds of learning experiences the institution values that could not be gained by simply accessing content online. Those institutions offering programmes that matter, that are engaging and relevant to

Future directions for integrating STEM   149

employment and society more generally, will be the ones that thrive. This may require staff to undertake some professional learning to make these experiences a reality (see Chapter 6 in this book).

Education, now and in the future, is very different for different individuals and groups of people, especially as students entering universities from a reformed school learning environment have become accustomed to choosing what they learn and do as part of their learning. They have been encouraged to experience more autonomous ways of learning (Bissaker, 2014). According to Davis et al. (2015), what is certain is that:

- What teachers do makes a difference to student experiences.
- Prior experiences are very important in how students engage with their learning.

An evolving trend in higher education is to design and provide micro-learning with connected experiences. Instead of one-hour lectures, we will probably be asking: "how can we make learning experiences meaningful in 15-minute segments?" This trend is evidenced most recently through other domains as well, such as "Duolingo" (learning a language by listening to small segments online) and a new trend for entertainment called "clipping", in which feature length movies are shown in ten-minute chunks.

Future of STEM integration

What do these trends and changes mean for integrating STEM? World experts provided their views on the future of STEM education (Akpan, 2019), with forecasts including:

- Ever-increasing development of knowledge and techniques in science, technology, engineering and mathematics will continue to provide the world with tools, services and innovations needed to improve quality of life and vocations.
- Coverage of huge science content will be dwarfed by a need for authentic learning (in real and applied contexts), in which knowledge, skills and values are applied to new situations.
- Emphasis on separate disciplines will dip steadily, but significantly, in favour of interdisciplinary approaches.
- Global issues and problems will require people to collaborate (communicate) and evaluate processes, and this must be reflected in education.
- Sustainability, as well as effective use and management of the world's precious resources, will become more and more important.
- A wide range of choices for students as to what to learn, how and when learning takes place will result in a change in approach to *learning* and changes to the role of teachers and learners, that is, a change in *learning* culture.

150 *Future directions for integrating STEM*

The implication of these ideas is that STEM integration in higher education will require much more focus and deliberation about what is offered and how learning occurs. Simply increasing accessibility and the number of HEIs is not going to produce sufficient human talent to synthesise knowledge and apply skills and capabilities to address the issues facing humanity. There needs to be a significant shift to providing serious learning experiences that use multiple sources of knowledge and multiple approaches for problem-solving, using appropriate technologies and systems that support the development of what graduates need.

As part of the changing world of work in response to changing technology (see Chapter 2), the range of technological tools for learning in STEM has come into focus, highlighted by the COVID-19 pandemic. This has led to a reconsideration of practical work, a rise in use of online labs, simulations, video recordings of complex experiments and procedures and the wide use of video conferencing. The question is, how do we make better use of emerging technologies to teach aspects of STEM and to generate new technological solutions, as industry is doing, through the infusion of video materials for training purposes, developing robotics, artificial intelligence and 3D visual objects? Technology can help us envision, collaborate, create and take action, socially, environmentally and economically – a triple bottom line for sustainable futures (Sachs, 2012).

Levers for integrating STEM

Content contexts and learning environments conducive for making interdisciplinary connections are important because they provide the rationale, purpose and, indeed, ability for students to see the relevance of their learning by applying it to real-world situations. Contexts that focus on people–planet imperatives and issues are naturally amenable to integration of STEM disciplines (Conner, 2020). It is likely the world will be in a state of instability and change for some time. The need to solve complex problems offers incentives to combine multiple perspectives that may have been separated previously across disciplinary boundaries. Using integrated approaches to address global issues enables people to bring ideas together from different sources. Development of experts, who deeply understand content and processes associated with a discipline, and connectors, who have the ability to transfer ideas and processes to novel situations, can occur simultaneously (Zhao, 2016). However, the development of connectors is more likely to occur through a range of active learning and open-ended problem-solving and assessment approaches.

Based on the research reviewed and ideas proposed in previous chapters in this book, the main levers for integrating STEM in higher education will be:

- Enabling students to demonstrate newly acquired knowledge and skills, as applied to issues and problems of significance to people, using guided, authentic activities and assessments (Figure 3.1). Capstone assessments (for example, creating portfolios) may relate to WIL opportunities or projects applied to the jobs they already have. People–planet imperatives and innovation will be in focus.

- Setting up opportunities for multidimensional interactions for active learning among ideas, processes, applications, use of technology and communities of practice. Learning activities will include a blend of information source provision and acquisition (possibly through co-curation and co-creation), simulations, collaboration, case evaluation, inquiry and problem- and project-based opportunities, including connections with industries, businesses and communities.
- Creating flexibility in learning environments by using a blend of synchronous and asynchronous activities in which students demonstrate desired outcomes. Students will increasingly demand the ability to complete activities in their own time and at a convenient pace and place that simultaneously leverages the advantages of working collaboratively with appropriate technologies for supporting progress. For example, there may be deadlines for the end of a week, but there will be flexibility of activities undertaken within that week, with the creation of (their own) videos and other artefacts that are also shared.
- Providing customised experiences using discipline-specific technologies, because some technologies have a specific purpose and are embedded within practical inquiry or project work.
- Valuing student time and intelligence much more than previously. This requires using diagnostic assessment practices and encouraging students to use what they already know and can do, within an environment that raises expectations to enhance future outcomes. Undertaking a qualification is a huge commitment in time, financially and emotionally. Greater relevance leads to greater engagement and likelihood of success.
- Enabling students to contribute to new knowledge as part of their coursework by integrating STEM. Providing students with opportunities to be creative within real-world contexts, in which they are given choices to create open-ended solutions, is crucial for new knowledge creation and innovation. The world needs innovative processes, products and new technologies to solve both local and global issues.

For students to have rich experiences, they need to be given opportunities to connect ideas and reflect on content (and its application) and on their own learning trajectory to reach the desired outcomes. The implication is that to do this, students need to be involved in tasks that require them to process information as part of their learning. This requires providing students with problems to solve and challenging questions that need answering.

What is clear is that students cannot learn the skills they need if they are dependent on carefully directed instruction, set texts and assessments that rely on memory recall (Milligan et al., 2020). While many HEIs espouse critical thinking as a graduate attribute, students cannot develop critical thinking

152 *Future directions for integrating STEM*

unless they are given opportunities to do so (Conner & Kolajo, 2020). Rich experiences need to be valued through authentic assessments (Chapter 5) that target both cognitive and non-cognitive skills concurrently (Zhao, 2016). This not only tends to drive what students and educators focus on but also helps to develop motivational aspects, such as willingness to engage in activities, relentless curiosity and a level of challenge.

A range of methods and technologies was highlighted in the chapter on assessment, showing how reliable assessment can be constructed to recognise levels of attainment and capability when undertaking problem-solving (Sweeney et al., 2017). What is *valued* by students is what they need to demonstrate in *assessment*. Careful assessment design must focus on key concepts, connecting ideas and competencies within and across disciplines. Appropriate developmental feedback can build student capability to transfer their skills to novel situations and to enhance these skills through ongoing use.

In order to drive change, demand and appetite for integrated STEM, it is not enough to tinker around the edges of current offerings. Deeper, connected frames for implementation and incentives for advancing STEM will be needed. Some already exist and have been indicated previously as being situated within projects, courses, qualifications and even at whole institutional levels (for example, the University of Newcastle). Additional incentives, such as scholarships, may be needed as well.

The notion of interdisciplinary course design is still emergent in HEIs and is much more advanced in the compulsory education sector (Akpan, 2019). Many secondary schools, for example the Australian Science Maths School (ASMS), developed integrated STEM more than ten years ago (Bissaker, 2014). Students who have experienced these types of integrated STEM learning environments, where they are put in charge of their own learning, expect an extension of this approach in higher education.

When overarching social agendas are included, such as social justice, addressing the use of the Earth's resources, innovation and creation of new solutions with ever-mindfulness of environmental sustainability, transformative education is more likely. Design models essentially revolve around problem-solving and use a backwards mapping process that begins with desired learning outcomes and assessment (Chapter 5 in this book). The challenges in design are discussed in the next section.

Challenges in designing courses for STEM

The importance of choosing authentic contexts, themes, issues and challenges for integrating STEM was emphasised previously (in Chapters 3 and 4). Choosing which context can be a challenge. Only a few HEIs have significantly redeveloped their courses to ensure they contribute to the UN Sustainable Development Goals (SDGs). There are still many questions around how seriously institutions take their role of supporting the SDGs (Franco & McCowan, 2020).

Future directions for integrating STEM   153

In choosing contexts, themes, issues or challenges, it is important to ask:

- How can the knowledge deemed important be redirected towards that which is most needed by society?
- How can knowledge created through coursework contribute to new understandings that can be taken up by communities, industries and professionals?
- How can redevelopment ensure a focus in coursework on public good (for example, SDGs), rather than simply maximising private returns for graduates?

In proposing a unified introductory (combined) science programme in universities, Bialek and Botstein (2004) indicated a need for some form of curriculum integration when they wrote:

> The emergence of new frontiers of research in functional genomics, molecular evolution, intracellular and dynamic imaging, systems neuroscience, complex diseases, and the system level integration of signal transduction and regulatory mechanisms require an ever-larger fraction of biologists to confront deeply quantitation issues that connect to ideas from the more mathematical sciences. At the same time, increasing numbers of physical scientists and engineers are recognising that exciting frontiers of their own disciplines lie in the study of biological phenomena. Characteristics of this new intellectual landscape is the need for strong interaction across traditional disciplinary boundaries.
>
> (p. 788)

Given this statement, universities should seriously consider structures that support the future learning of sciences that are highly relevant to future pathways and careers for students. In many instances, students undertake a range of courses in mathematics, chemistry, biology and physics to gain entry into medicine (or engineering). As educators who teach these courses are usually service teaching from their own discipline, educators are, not surprisingly, prepared to provide courses explicitly relevant to medicine or engineering students. There are often different tracks (separate courses) for students wishing to major in mathematics, physics and chemistry. This may mean that those wishing to major in biology or become physicians undertake courses that have less sophistication in terms of quantitative content and consequent levels of perceived difficulty. These traditions have led to differences in competency and culture between the physical science (and engineering) students and those studying biological-based sciences. Those undertaking the physical science track generally gain a high level of quantitative expertise, including calculus and differential equations, Fourier analysis, linear algebra, probability and statistics (Bialek & Botstein, 2004). Graduates in this track are generally able to use computational skills and apply these skills to projects using customised software to analyse data or to use simulation technologies. However, what is becoming

154 *Future directions for integrating STEM*

apparent is that integrating aspects of the data sciences is becoming increasingly more important for STEM, as many systems rely much more on data and systems of analysis. The biological sciences have become much more attuned to the use of pattern seeking, data manipulation and identifying factors of influence. Course design can take these trends and needs into account.

Findings related to integrating curriculum, as reported by the National Academies of Science, Engineering and Medicine (2018), were that:

- Some integrative approaches in STEM led to positive learning outcomes, such as increased critical thinking abilities, higher-order thinking, reasoning and analysis, problem-solving, communication and teamwork.
- Integrating STEM content and pedagogies into arts and humanities may improve interdisciplinary relations, scientific and technological literacy and data analysis used in humanistic inquiry.
- Medical students experiencing arts and humanities within their coursework develop increased communication skills, empathy, resilience, teamwork and tolerance for uncertainty and ambiguity.
- Around the world, there is an increase in the number of educational institutions that are integrating curriculum.
- More research is needed to determine the impact and advantages for students of integrating disciplines.

Despite these findings, the report did not capture the core of what is advocated in this book: that integrating STEM can provide students with the wherewithal to solve issues, and that new knowledge can be generated as part of STEM coursework in HEIs, especially in partnership with communities. In addition, the affordances of data sciences and technologies as integrators for STEM can be investigated in much more depth.

Educating STEM graduates to be highly specialised will remain important. Ideally, though, students in higher education will be given opportunities to develop thinking and collaborative skills by straddling and utilising knowledge, processes and practices of a range of (or at least several) disciplines during their qualifications. In this book, interdisciplinary approaches for STEM have been shown to provide a vehicle for authentic learning experiences that potentially enable students to become experts in a field and to develop capabilities desired by employers, while cultivating an enduring (lifelong) approach to learning. However, working in interdisciplinary ways requires teamwork and extended planning on the part of students and educators. Successful implementation would represent a significant shift by HEIs in thinking, professional learning, collaboration and ongoing development. The chapter on challenges and professional learning indicated that the resistance to integrating curriculum is very real and will require careful navigation on the part of implementers.

Accommodating notions of development of student self-direction is still relatively radical in higher education, as it requires reconceptualising what effective learning is, how it needs to be situated in authentic contexts and what is really important, in terms of improving learning outcomes for individuals and groups of students. Customised learning has not been the norm in universities, as it is easier to teach masses of people the same thing. However, the growing trend of using self-paced learning, analytics, megalytics and AI-based software enables sequencing and tailoring of prompts and scaffolds in response to student answers (or choice protocols). The use of technology for enabling more effective learning should not be underestimated.

According to Young (1998, p. 181), an educational theory for the future should have the following elements:

- Concept of the future and of education in relation to a vision of society for the future.
- Connection to (rather than insulation from) concepts and approaches developed by different educational disciplines.
- Primacy given to issues of learning and production of new knowledge.
- Educational purpose associated with realising the emancipatory potential of learning for all people throughout their lives.
- Critique the expansion of mass education and take into account any limits of learning in workplaces and communities.

Taking Young's list into account when designing learning experiences in higher education implies a shift from discipline knowledge as the currency towards learning for a purpose and more application of knowledge, skills and capabilities. Interconnectedness of disciplines in STEM is an opportunity to reveal both relevance and application to create innovative solutions.

Aligning STEM with purposes of HEIs

Many HEIs claim, in by-line missions, "people who make a difference" or something similar. However, such claims have not necessarily been directly translated into curriculum reform. Almost a decade ago, Delanty (2001) discussed possibilities for universities in contemporary society and reappraised upon what universities should focus. He outlined how universities should emphasise a new type of citizenship that draws on and is responsive to the changing nature of knowledge production. He believed that universities were poised to promote "self-transformation of cultures through a critical self-engagement with each other" (p. 128). Delanty considered democracy to consist of three elements: "constitutionalism", which he described as the rule of law that restrains the state; "pluralism", the representation of the interests of all groups in society; and "citizenship", in which people participate in establishing rights, duties and responsibilities. By emphasising such citizenship, HEIs can provide both technocratic (skills for serving society professionally and through providing services) and cultural capital (developing citizens who are capable of socially responsible action, including the generation of new knowledge and innovation that improves society).

One of the purposes of universities has always been to produce new knowledge through research. Universities also engage in systematic teaching and learning and have an obligation to enable their students to succeed. The success of students is incredibly important for universities as a key indicator that they are on the right track. There is an assumption that student success in coursework is linked to effective teaching. Surprisingly, when students are not successful, the reason given is often that students did not apply themselves to their studies effectively enough. While both are true to some extent, it is highly likely that there are students who succeed *despite* the quality of their lecturers, and students who fail in classes in which there is exemplary teaching. There is no doubt that effective educators make a difference to student achievement, but success is more likely a combination of teaching, learning environment and student effects.

So, while a purpose of universities is to create new knowledge, there is a move away from thinking about this as solely coming from research. What role can students play in knowledge creation through learning, as co-collaborators (with other students and faculty)? How can we make use of the idea that students can create new knowledge during coursework? In my opinion, traditional notions of excellence do not take account of changes to the nature of knowledge or to how learning processes can generate new knowledge that may contribute to solving problems or creating innovation. Further, when developing an understanding of a phenomena or contribution to solving a local or global issue, society itself has a vested interest in the knowledge generated. The knowledge (or solution or innovation) becomes a public good.

According to the Post Growth Institute (2018), post-growth involves building on existing aspects of the world in order to create sustainable, resilient futures, by acknowledging the physical limits of the Earth and seeking to strengthen social and ecological practices that are sustainable. This creates global challenges we need to solve, especially in how we use the Earth's resources, yet at the same time ensure the quality of water and air, and that land management is sustainable. The world economy has placed a huge emphasis on the growth of financial markets and populations by exploitation of resources and these populations. While a focus on growth has brought with it improved living conditions and well-being for some, it is often at the expense of others and the planet.

Global challenges, such as climate change and complex health issues, call for working across disciplines that transcend discipline silos (Honeybun-Arnolda & Obermeister, 2019). Integration of disciplines can support development and innovative solutions for a more systems-based, humanistic future. We should improve educational opportunities essential to addressing global issues, such as poverty, climate change and current health issues (Desai et al., 2018).

Further research is warranted to investigate how integration of curriculum through STEM can prepare students for dealing with complex situations that call for evidence-based and humanistic solutions, while living in the world as

Future directions for integrating STEM 157

workers and citizens. The research on uses of technology can no longer just focus on the use of "things" (digital tools, apps, games, gadgets), but must pivot to focus on how technologies can help support more effective learning (Reeves & Lin, 2020). When problem-, project- or challenge-based activities focus on global challenges, learning is aspirational. By setting goals to help save the world, by raising awareness, hope and action, there is a call to dream of possibilities, to be socially or economically entrepreneurial, that requires students to integrate the development of their competencies, self-directedness and relatedness (Ryan & Deci, 2000).

The approaches for the integration of STEM advocated here align with a more general shift in higher education from delivering facts to designing rich learning experiences that use real-world problem-solving, inquiry and challenges and require connecting ideas, conceptual mastery and capabilities including collaboration, critical and creative thinking and effective communication. Well-designed learning experiences take account of student needs and address them with timely and appropriate input (Delandshere, 2002), as well as appropriate levels of individual and collaborative ways of working.

Success is mediated by constant reflection by students, with effective guidance and support from their educators. In successful models of teaching and learning in integrated STEM, there should be an enduring focus on enhancing student potential. In this way, different levels of accountability can be built in: accountability for students to themselves, their peers, communities and industry. This shift will require institutions to support learning design more seriously. Educators in higher education will need to rethink how they provide these types of learning experiences and what might be appropriate ways to develop understanding, skills and capabilities simultaneously, rather than just what content is taught and assessed.

This implies a need for staff development that is systematic and iterative, in which reflection on progress towards effective active and generative learning occurs and is both celebrated and rewarded through HEI promotion systems. There is likely to be reticence on the part of some faculty to change, as discussed in Chapter 6. In addition, some students may have come through more contemporary learning environments in which they have experienced inquiry and cross-disciplinary approaches within senior schooling, especially using STEM approaches (for example, ASMS, Ao Tawhiti Unlimited Discovery). Despite this, many students will not have experienced context-based approaches to learning in STEM in schools. These students may need to be enculturated into new ways of thinking about and managing their own learning, especially those who expect to be taught in higher education through more traditional teaching and learning approaches.

There is an increasing recognition that we need to move away from teaching programmes that rely on the assumption that learning is largely an individualised process (rather than a collaborative one) and that is enabled by transmitting (providing) the "right" information. In a transmissive model, the teacher is the

158 *Future directions for integrating STEM*

knowledgeable expert who conveys information and students are required to demonstrate knowledge and understanding of this information in assessments. Curriculum mostly consists of predetermined content items that, once spoken about or provided in readings or online resources, have been "covered". There is usually little reflection on whether content "delivered" is of interest or whether the way it is "delivered" inspires students to want to find out more or to collaborate to help each other to learn. Nor does this approach tend to acknowledge students' prior knowledge or their contributions and ideas that might advance this knowledge. There is usually little space (time) in this approach for students to question ideas or to consider how they might connect with their previous knowledge or understanding. Fortunately, this approach is fading rapidly, and there is a growing momentum towards providing information for students to "digest" in their own time and to make more use of shared time for highlighting the important concepts, connecting key ideas and discussing the issues and problems.

Already we are seeing a trend towards increasing the value of creating knowledge through inquiry processes as part of learning that accommodates and extends how students can connect disparate ideas. This includes ways to enable students to gain social and cultural capital since the ability to work with others will be a key skill, along with the ability to communicate appropriately, using specific language at the right time to the appropriate audience. Experts in specific STEM disciplines are still needed, but the world also needs people who are integrators and connectors of disparate knowledge sets to creatively craft new solutions.

It will also become even more important for graduates to be able to demonstrate how they can think creatively for contributing to innovation, how they can transfer ideas between contexts and apply what was learned in one domain to another with alterations or adaptations and refinements. Creativity can also be used to transfer ideas into reality, whether that relates to new ideas, new devices, new materials or new procedures in STEM. Hybridised skills can be fostered through engaging in problem-solving, ideation processes, WIL, experimentation and evaluation in STEM contexts. To achieve these skills and capabilities, students need learning experiences and assessments that require then to connect disparate ideas.

Discipline challenges

Learning within authentic contexts (rather than disciplines) implies curriculum planning for interdisciplinary understanding (showing connected thinking) and leveraging what can be gained when combining discipline approaches. It is important to note that some disciplinary knowledge is essential to reach interdisciplinary understanding (Wilson et al., 2012). However, teaching, learning and assessing in single disciplines tends to hinder students from making links between disciplines (You et al., 2018) and creating new knowledge or innovations.

Future directions for integrating STEM 159

To create authentic contexts, particularly for inquiry, internships and other work-related experiences will require cooperation with governments, industries, technology developers, investors and society more generally (especially for social entrepreneurship).

The content learned when using context-based approaches may be different for different learners. This has huge implications for designing assessment because it means the focus cannot be on assessing specific content knowledge as a prescribed set of answers. Rather, there is a shift to focus on how students *use* knowledge appropriately to solve problems, connect ideas or come up with a range of potential solutions that have been evaluated, based on evidential processes.

There may be instances in which connecting relevant content knowledge from another discipline is highly relevant. For example, the use of algebra and calculus is fundamental to understanding engineering concepts and their applications in practice. What is appropriate for learning in one discipline might not be important in another. However, content knowledge in an integrated course would not depend on discipline prescriptions, but rather on what knowledge, skills and capabilities were needed for the context, issue, challenge or problem. There would be more emphasis on connecting ideas and finding solutions.

If higher education reform follows reform in the schooling sector, we are likely to see a merging of subject areas, a rise of integrated STEM, more applied and cross-domain studies that call on multiple disciplines (such as environmental studies that include aspects of biology, geography, chemistry, earth science and engineering, biosynthesis and chemical engineering) and the development of technological devices that integrate medicine, engineering, economics, entrepreneurship and design thinking.

One of the rationales for STEAM (including the arts in STEM) is that policy decisions in government and civic participation often rely on "design thinking" that leverages intra- and inter-system relationships and patterns, on which focus can be made in STEM studies. Intended and unintended consequences or the effects of local actions (perturbations or slight changes in variables) can be considered if component relationships within a system are taken into account (Institute of Design at Stanford, 2016). Therefore, if students can experience how to take levels of influence into account (systems thinking), they are more likely to apply their use of design processing to real issues as part of their contribution to informed, evidence-based citizenry, including contributing to political decisions. It has been recommended that future approaches to integrate STEM in higher education include the design thinking that is fundamental to the "T" and "E" of STEM (Chubb, 2015; Conner, 2020; Harris, 2012).

Taking account of changes in technology

Future development of integrating STEM education in higher education must also be mindful of rapid developments in technology and how it can potentially be used to integrate STEM (Chapter 2). In particular, there will be many

160 *Future directions for integrating STEM*

changes in the application of artificial intelligence (AI). These include how AI can be used for automating decision-making related to many scientific developments, engineering solutions, solving environmentally complex problems, designing and manufacturing technological innovations, digital monitoring for experimental purposes and control mechanisms for systems. There is no doubt AI will have an increasingly significant impact on how we live and on society more generally.

The burgeoning development of AI also highlights the need in STEM to consider ethical applications of the use of STEM in society. As AI becomes more commonly used and increasingly more important, we also need to consider any bias that might lead to poor decision-making and any malevolent use of AI. For example, an AI used to provide sentencing guidelines to judges across several US states embeds sentence biases against African-American males (Hao, 2019). With global apps automatically tracking who people connect with, personal data security is now a global issue. However, harnessing the potential of AI could help to create sustainable beneficial outcomes for the planet and humanity, as it can be used to support "off-grid" water and energy resources, to improve efficiency of growing food, to improve planning for preventing or overcoming natural disasters and to run smart cities.

Challenges that our graduates will be faced with and issues that they will need to grapple with are highly likely to benefit from including technical, human and multiple ethical perspectives. For example, AI can be used to run virtual war campaigns (including autonomous fighting vehicles), which have their own set of ethical implications. The *Mass Effect* series of video games, starting in 2007, featured a "race" of sentient machines (the Geth), introduced the concept of "shackled" and "unshackled" AI and invited players to consider some of the ethical and moral issues surrounding these issues. Therefore, there may be existing examples that could assist in designing and including an ethical dimension within STEM.

It is worth noting that six of the 17 UN Sustainable Development Goals apply directly to the environment and human influence over it. These include climate change; using resources wisely (water and energy, ocean and marine resources); managing forests; desertification; innovations for sustainable cities; and clean, affordable energy. Global challenges such as these call for work across disciplines in ways that transcend discipline silos (Honeybun-Arnolda & Obermeister, 2019). Approaches that integrate disciplines in STEM can advocate for solutions that enhance life experiences and the environments in which they occur, including biodiversity, excellent air and water quality, accessibility of sufficient quality and high protein foods, housing solutions and access to health care. But these world issues need to be addressed in the social and political contexts in which they occur, since context matters and human ingenuity springs from human needs.

Wheatley (2006) discusses how social scientists use data and numerical analyses for legitimising such things as assigning values to relationships or decision-making frameworks. Complexity science, which combines and interconnects

Future directions for integrating STEM 161

ideas, gives us permission to be playful about discovery and how things are connected. She states:

> One of the principles that guides scientific inquiry is that at all levels, nature seems to resemble itself. For me, the parsimony of nature's laws gives further impetus to my desire to learn from science. If nature uses certain principles to create her infinite diversity and her well-organised systems, it is highly probable that those principles apply to human life and organisations as well. . . . Nature's predisposition towards self-similarity gives me confidence that she can provide genuine guidance for the dilemmas of our time. Science can help us develop new questions and processes that have merit at a more universal level.
>
> (p. 162)

By implication from Wheatley's work, perspectives from science and systems thinking matter when describing systems. For example, thinking and understanding about quantum physics and living processes can be viewed from the perspective of relationships and relational dynamics, as applied to how subatomic particles behave and to interconnectedness of the functioning of human body systems. This might mean that a fundamental attribute for living and understanding our world is considering what relationships in any particular context matter. Taking a relationship or system perspective on what matters may also lead to creative innovations.

Taking a systems approach to STEM

Previously in this book, I discussed how systems thinking is inherent to integrating STEM (see Figure 3.1, Chapter 3). In a systems approach, understanding develops through analysing interactions of components of a system. This may involve connecting ideas (concepts) or reflecting more on how modifications could lead to better outcomes and adaptations. Genetics is foundational in biology, with nature experimenting and creating new forms which survive depending on their adaptations and "fitness" for the environments in which they live. Evolution occurs in response to perturbations in the system, including competitive forces that act on the genetics of organisms. The same idea can be applied to curriculum integration in STEM. For integrating STEM, what gets combined and survives for future iterations in learning should depend on what is successful and has outcomes of use to graduates and society. In biological systems, with time and further feedback (adaptations), organisms tend to grow in complexity, form and function. A similar analogy can again be applied to improving STEM integration. The development of contexts that use multiple disciplines will increase in complexity with time, as feedback from our understanding of what works provides multiple back loops to iterative changes. This is why research on teaching in STEM, coupled with ongoing professional learning of educators (through action research, inquiry and SoTL models), is

162 *Future directions for integrating STEM*

very important, as emphasised in Chapter 6. The curriculum in a systems frame would always be emergent, not fixed, but being this way can respond to current and authentic issues and problems as they arise. This is a very powerful idea that, if embraced, would ensure that curriculum is always improving, current, authentic and relevant to students and their worlds, rather than being static and fixed on specific content outcomes.

A second way to consider a systems approach to STEM is to use a systems perspective for developing new knowledge, products and processes that are inherent in STEM disciplines. An example from the interesting field of robotics development provides insight into how a more systematised approach, rather than linear sequencing, can advance the field. There are already robotic toys and companions available that respond according to a multitude of inputs with conditional logic and functions. These are being used in the compulsory sector to teach STEM skills, because to build them requires some understanding of basic computing, electrical systems and psychology. However, these robotic toys do not yet match the complex operations that occur in the human brain, nor can they undertake self-repair of components when they fail. However, if a biological systems approach is applied (for example, biochip processors from bioengineering), this could advance robotics to include some self-correcting functions in the near future, making them more like a biological system that can adapt and change with continued feedback adjustments. Thus, a systems approach could create a solution (if not a scary future) for the field of robotics.

Systems thinking may also involve solving problems by decomposing the sub-components (levels) of a system. Understanding how each level of the system functions can lead to understanding the system as a whole. This is despite the fact that each level may multiply both the number of interconnections and how these influence other components and other levels of the system. In a decomposed view, it is the patterns of interactions that become important (Davis et al., 2015). A pattern may develop or emerge that shows how components connect and may represent how a problem can be distributed or solved in parallel ways.

In large, complex, organised systems, there tend to be multiple replicas of the same pattern (called fractals, scaled versions of the same pattern). The interactions of these patterns to form larger shapes of specific or repeated patterns over time lead to understanding of how a complex organised system operates. Solution seekers use patterns (of evidence or behaviours of natural phenomena) to unravel or solve problems. Pattern seeking was precisely how the structure of DNA was solved.

Of extreme interest when using a systems approach in STEM, then, is how patterns are recognised as contributing and interacting within a system. This concept was demonstrated in the movie *The Matrix*, in which pattern recognition enabled the operators to identify how to enter the matrix (a complex system in a parallel world). Similar ideas have also been used to develop voice recognition software and hand-written language recognition of a name on cell phones. Rather than build a single complex smart programme, many mini programmes, called *demons*, were developed to feed information and connect to create larger patterns. With the advance of digital technologies and Industry 4.0, the trend for using systems thinking will be amplified as this idea is applied to creating new products and processes for solving problems or issues.

Future research on integrating STEM

Multiple examples from research studies have been provided in this book in which combining discipline approaches, along with developing students' cognitive and non-cognitive skills, has led to successful student outcomes. Although this is promising, further research is warranted on integrating STEM in higher education and how different approaches can better prepare students for dealing with complex situations (National Academies of Science, Engineering and Medicine, 2018). In order to successfully solve global issues (and local ones as well), there is a need to build on these insights, to help graduates gain from studying integrated STEM for their futures as workers and citizens.

A promising approach to researching STEM integration in coursework is to use design-based research, which focusses on outcomes of innovations in learning (Brown, 1992). This approach is quasi-experimental because it tests and refines educational designs by generating evidence related to learning outcomes (McKenney & Reeves, 2013; O'Toole & Beckett, 2013). Design-based research blends two types of educational research: empirical mixed-methods educational research and theory-driven design of learning and teaching (Baumgartner et al., 2003; Collins et al., 2004). As changes occur iteratively, it captures the refinements of implementation of educational change in practice and evaluates strengths and limitations that contribute to an optimal design for learning (Collins et al., 2004) and the effects on student outcomes (Reimann, 2011; Wang & Hannafin, 2005).

There is an emerging range of research agendas related to designing integrated STEM curriculum. For example, the National Academies of Science, Engineering and Medicine (2018) asked whether there were better educational and career outcomes for graduates who have been part of an integrated STEM approach to curriculum. They concluded that more longitudinal research is needed on the employment outcomes from current integrated courses and programmes, including research on designed-based curricula. There has also been a recent call for more research on the affordances of different pedagogical approaches (Cheng & So, 2020; Yanez et al., 2019). Some possible research questions for exploring this further include:

- What integration is important for addressing global issues? The "what" refers to content knowledge (concepts), domains or disciplinary approaches, practical, technical thinking, collaboration and communication skills (see Figure 3.1, Chapter 3).
- How is learning STEM through integrated approaches different from disciplinary-focussed teaching and learning?

164　*Future directions for integrating STEM*

- What is the role of discipline-specific practices and tasks in an integrated STEM model?
- What student learning outcomes can be achieved when using integrated STEM that are more difficult in traditional approaches?
- Does integrating STEM learning lead to enhanced effectiveness of student learning, and in what ways?
- How do we include critical and creative competencies for problem-solving that include choosing the best and multiple ways to solve a problem?
- How can adaptive reasoning, using logical, analytical and intuitive thought with reflection, lead to deeper engagement and alternative solutions?
- What are the implications of integrating STEM in coursework for professional learning for teachers?
- How do students who engage in integrated STEM address global issues?

There is a huge need for more critical evaluation through research of integrated STEM approaches. This will contribute to many more examples of specific affordances related to student and social outcomes. As more integration occurs within STEM, greater pedagogical sophistication will emerge through focussing on authentic, context-based approaches to curriculum design and implementation. Students who participate in critical and creative STEM activities are more likely to succeed in crossing discipline boundaries (Sadler, 2009) and become connectors of ideas and processes for creating new knowledge. The imperative to include integration is not just to promote STEM for neoliberal reasons, such as economic progress, competitive advantage and innovation, but also, as Yanez et al. (2019) argued, to address urgent global ecological, ethical and social justice issues.

Conclusion

This chapter provided an overall summary of trends, drivers and proposed questions designed to assist educators and leaders in higher education to move an integrated STEM approach forward. Collaboration between all stakeholders (government agencies, subject matter experts, learning designers in HEIs, educators and students) has the potential to extend the reach, richness and relevance of learning experiences and contribute to solving global issues (Gibson et al., 2018).

As implied multiple times throughout this book, HEIs have an obligation to provide students with multiple appropriate opportunities to develop capabilities for working with other capable people, through peer groups and multidisciplinary teams and by connecting with experts in businesses, industries and government agencies. This is what professionals do. Potentially, pedagogies and assessment methods can augment integration to build these essential capabilities in problem-solving and innovation in order to address global issues.

However, there are constraints for designing and implementing integrated STEM in higher education. These mostly relate to openness and willingness

Future directions for integrating STEM 165

of educators to take risks and to experiment with designing appropriate _learning_ experiences. In some ways, the rich collage of choice and possibilities for integrating STEM curriculum is somewhat daunting because educators may not know where to start. Evidence from the compulsory sector indicates that some integration approaches (connecting at least two disciplines within authentic contexts, themes or issues) can develop a sense of inquiry, relentless curiosity and healthy scepticism that helps students to take on an inquisitive mindset for driving creative solution-seeking (see Chapters 3 and 4). But it requires educators to move away from traditional didactic teaching to more student-directed thinking, curation and creation in collaborative settings.

In summary, there is much to do to develop integration of STEM in higher education. Much more focus needs to be given to how coursework is deliberately designed and what themes and contexts are useful for continually improving capabilities of educators and students so they can contribute to societal needs (Franco & McCowan, 2020). There is also merit in considering localised and regionalised approaches, as context is absolutely critical. Innovations as applied to coursework in higher education (especially in STEM) benefit from focussing on geographical, local and global imperatives. Approaching STEM as an integrated sociocultural opportunity within themes, contexts or challenges has huge potential benefits, especially if students are given agency to learn and take action (Yanez et al., 2019). Not integrating STEM is likely to produce "another generation of uninvolved, unengaged and uninformed citizens" (Zeidler, 2016, p. 23).

Integrated approaches for STEM can be complementary to separate discipline models (Strober, 2011). Indeed, while there is emerging evidence of the benefits of integrating STEM, as provided throughout this book, more research is needed on emerging integrated approaches to investigate further how place, students' prior knowledge, use of technology and pedagogical shifts influence student outcomes, especially students' abilities to solve problems generally and to solve world issues. There is an urgent call to take a more critical view of curriculum design in order to strengthen the capacity for human ingenuity. A new, humanistic approach to integrating STEM can support a wellspring for problem-solving, creativity and social and economic development that can bring together the needs of people and the preservation of the planet.

References

Akpan, B. (2019). Introduction – a vision of science education 50 years ahead. In B. Akpan (Ed.), _Science education: Visions of the future_ (pp. 1–16). Next Generation Education.

Baumgartner, E., Bell, P., Brophy, S., Hoadley, C., Hsi, S., Joseph, D., Orrill, C., Puntambekar, S., Sandoval, W., & Tabak, I. (2003). Design-based research: An emerging paradigm for educational inquiry. _Educational Researcher, 32_(1), 5–8. http://doi.org/10.3102/0013189X032001005

Bialek, W., & Botstein, D. S. (2004). Introductory science and mathematics education for 21st-century biologists. _Science, 303,_ 788–790.

166 Future directions for integrating STEM

Bissaker, K. (2014). Transforming STEM education in an innovative Australian school: The role of teachers' and academics' professional partnerships. *Theory Into Practice, 53*(1), 55–63. http://doi.org/10.1080/00405841.2014.862124

Brown, A. (1992). Design experiments: Theoretical and methodological challenges in creating complex interventions in classroom settings. *Journal of the Learning Sciences, 2*(2), 141–178.

Cheng, Y. C., & So, W. W. M. (2020). Managing STEM learning: A typology and four models of integration. *International Journal of Educational Management, 34*(6), 1063–1078. http://doi.org/10.1108/IJEM-01-2020-0035

Chubb, I. (2015). *Aspiring to something magnificent.* Address to the National Press Club. www.chiefscientist.gov.au/sites/default/files/Professor-Chubb-NPC-SMP-2015.pdf

Collins, A., Joseph, D., & Bielaczyc, K. (2004). Design research: Theoretical and methodological issues. *Journal of Learning Sciences, 1*(13), 15–42.

Conner, L. (2020). *Integrating STEMM in higher education: A proposed curriculum development framework.* Paper published in the proceedings of 6th International Conference on Higher Education Advances (HEAd'20). Universitat Politècnica de València. http://doi.org/10.4995/HEAd20.2020.11058

Conner, L., & Kolajo, Y. (2020). The chemistry of critical thinking: The pursuit to do both better. In E. Sengupta, P. Blessinger, & M. Makhanya (Eds.), *Improving classroom engagement and international development programs: International perspectives on humanizing higher education* (Vol. 27, pp. 93–110). Innovations in Higher Education Teaching and Learning. Emerald Publishing Limited. https://doi.org/10.1108/S2055-364120200000027009

Davis, B., Sumara, D., & Luce-Kapler, R. (2015). *Engaging minds: Changing teaching in complex times* (3rd ed.). Routledge. https://amberroweblog.files.wordpress.com/2016/11/brent-davis-dennis-sumara-rebecca-luce-kapler-engaging-minds_-cultures-of-education-and-practices-of-teaching-routledge-2015.pdf

Delandshere, G. (2002). Assessment as inquiry. *Teachers College Record, 104*(7), 1461–1484. http://doi.org/10.1111/1467-9620.00210

Delanty, G. (2001). *Challenging knowledge: The university in the knowledge society.* Society for Research into Higher Education and Open University Press.

Desai, R. M., Kato, H., Kharas, H., & McArthur, J. W. (2018). *From summits to solutions: Innovations in implementing the sustainable development goals.* Brookings Institution Press.

Franco, C. P., & McCowan, T. (2020). Rewiring higher education for the sustainable development goals: The case of the Intercultural University of Veracruz, Mexico. *Higher Education.* https://doi.org/10.1007/s10734-020-00525-2

Gibson, D., Irving, L., & Katy, S. (2018). Technology-enabled challenge-based learning in a global context. In M. Shonfeld & D. Gibson (Eds.), *Collaborative learning and a global world* (pp. 32–42). Information Age Publishers.

Hao, K. (2019). AI is sending people to jail – and getting it wrong. *MIT Technology Review.* www.technologyreview.com/2019/01/21/137783/algorithms-criminal-justice-ai/

Harris, K. L. (2012). *A background in science: What science means for Australian society.* Study from the Centre for the Study of Higher Education, University of Melbourne, Commissioned by the Australian Council of Deans of Science. https://amsi.org.au/wp-content/uploads/2014/07/30_ACDS_BackgroundInScience_Apr12.pdf

Henriksen, D., Jordan, M., Foulger, T. S., Zuiker, S., & Mishra, P. (2020). Essential tensions in facilitating design thinking: Collective reflections. *Journal of Formative Design in Learning, 4*, 5–16. https://doi.org/10.1007/s41686-020-00045-3

Honeybun-Arnolda, E., & Obermeister, N. (2019). A climate for change: Millennials, science and the humanities. *Environmental Communication, 13*(1), 1–8. http://doi.org/10.1080/17524032.2018.1500927

Future directions for integrating STEM 167

Institute of Design at Stanford. (2016). https://dschool.stanford.edu/

McCowan, T. (2019). *Higher education for and beyond the sustainable development goals*. Palgrave Macmillan. https://link.springer.com/content/pdf/10.1007%2F978-3-030-195 97-7.pdf

McKenney, S., & Reeves, H. C. (2013). Systematic review of design-based research progress: Is a little knowledge a dangerous thing? *Educational Researcher, 42*(2), 97–100. https://doi. org/10.3102/0013189X12463781

Milligan, S., Luo, R., Hassim, E., & Johnston, J. (2020). *Future-proofing students: What they need to know and how educators can assess and credential them*. Report #2. Melbourne Graduate School of Education Industry Reports. https://education.unimelb.edu.au/ mgse-industry-reports/report-2-future-proofing-students

National Academies of Sciences, Engineering and Medicine. (2018). *The integration of the humanities and arts with sciences, engineering, and medicine in higher education: Branches from the same tree*. The National Academies Press. https://doi.org/10.17226/24988

O'Toole, J., & Beckett, D. (2013). *Educational research: Creative thinking and doing* (2nd ed.). Oxford University Press.

Post Growth Institute. (2018). www.postgrowth.org/

PwC. (2020). *Transforming the higher education workforce*. PricewaterhouseCoopers and Australian Higher Education Industrial Association. www.aheia.edu.au/cms_uploads/docs/ aheia_transforming-the-higher-education-workforce_final_20200219-s.pdf

Reeves, T., & Lin, L. (2020). The research we have is not the research we need. *Educational Technology Research and Development, 68*, 1991–2001. https://doi.org/10.1007/ s11423-020-09811-3

Reimann, P. (2011). Design-based research. In L. Markauskaite, P. Freebody, & J. Irwin (Eds.), *Methodological choice and design scholarship, policy and practice in social and educational research* (pp. 37–50). Springer.

Ryan, R., & Deci, E. (2000). Self-determination theory and the facilitation of intrinsic motivation, social development, and well-being. *Contemporary Educational Psychology, 25*, 54–67.

Sachs, J. (2012). From millennium development goals to sustainable development goals. *Lancet, 379*(9832), 2206–2211. http://doi.org/10.1016/S0140-6736(12)60685-0

Sadler, T. D. (2009). Situated learning in science education: Socio-scientific issues as contexts for practice. *Studies in Science Education, 45*, 1–42. http://doi.org/10.1080/ 03057260802681839

Strober, M. H. (2011). *Interdisciplinary conversations: Challenging habits of thought*. Stanford University Press.

Sweeney, T., West, D., Groessler, A., Haynie, A., Higgs, B. M., Macaulay, J., Mercer-Mapstone, L., & Yeo, M. (2017). Where's the transformation? Unlocking the potential of technology-enhanced assessment. *Teaching and Learning Inquiry, 5*(1), 41–56. http://doi. org/10.20343/teachlearninqu.5.1.5

Wang, F., & Hannafin, M. (2005). Design-based research and technology-enhanced learning environments. *Educational Technology, Research and Development, 53*(4), 5–23.

Wheatley, M. (2006). *Leadership and the new science*. Berrett-Koehler Publishers.

Williamson, B. (2018). The hidden architecture of higher education: Building a big data infrastructure for the "smarter university". *International Journal of Educational Technology in Higher Education, 15*(1), 1–26. https://doi.org/10.1186/s41239-018-0094-1

Wilson, A., Howitt, S., Roberts, P., Åkerlind, G., & Wilson, K. (2012). Connecting expectations and experiences of student in a research-immersive degree. *Studies in Higher Education, 38*(10), 1–15. https://doi.org/10.1080/03075079.2011.633163

168 *Future directions for integrating STEM*

Yanez, G. A., Thumlert, L. K., de Castell, S., & Jenson, J. (2019). Pathways to sustainable futures: A "production pedagogy" model for STEM education. *Futures, 108,* 27–36. https://doi.org/10.1016/j.futures.2019.02.021

You, H. S., Marshall, J. A., & Delgado, C. (2018). Assessing students' disciplinary and interdisciplinary understanding of global carbon cycling. *Journal of Research in Science Teaching, 55*(3), 377–398.

Young, M. F. D. (1998). *The curriculum of the future: From the "new sociology of education" to a critical theory of learning.* Falmer Press.

Zeidler, D. L. (2016). STEM education: A deficit framework for the twenty first century? A sociocultural socioscientific response. *Cultural Studies of Science Education, 11*(1), 11–26. http://doi.org/10.1007/s11422-014-9578-z

Zhao, Y. (2016). *Counting what counts: Reframing education outcomes.* Solution Tree Press.

Index

active learning: approaches to 54;
assessment and 54; authentic 150;
opportunities 86–88
addressing challenges for integrating
STEM 140
African Leadership University in
Rwanda 126
AI *see* artificial intelligence
alignment: activities and resources for
student learning 31; assessment and
outcomes 96, 111; curriculum and
professions 45; curriculum design
and assessment 95; importance of
in curriculum 80; outcomes and
curriculum 77; STEM and purpose of
HEIs 155
Allama Iqbal Open University 147
analysis in learning 62
applications to disciplines 49
approaches to STEM: examples 16–19;
integration 16; problem-solving 57
AR *see* augmented reality
artificial intelligence 25–26, 30, 48, 160;
assessment example 105; ethical issues
160; sustainability 160
assessment 94–119: active learning and
54; alignment with outcomes 96, 111;
alternatives for 77; analytical thinking
in 105; artificial intelligence in 105;
authentic 52, 66, 97, 152; capability
99, 101; careful design 152; case study
examples 113; challenge activities 89;
collaboration 107; collating outcomes
119; communication 103; constructive
alignment in curriculum design 95;
critical thinking in 106; designing 83,
110, 159; with digital tasks 39; effect
on outcomes 124; empowering students
129; in framework 66; ICT 104, 139;

inquiry and problem-based 101; maps
81; outdated approach to 125; peer
review 108; professional development
135; promising examples 113; review
process for 77, 80; rubrics 33, 81,
109, 112, 120; simulations 33, 101;
student value 152; tasks identifying 84;
technology and 139; work-integrated
learning 106
augmented reality 24, 30, 32–33, 104, 139
authentic: activities 150; assessment 52,
66, 97, 152; creating contexts 159;
importance of 50

capability: assessing 99; blending with
discipline knowledge 127
careers: related to STEM 6; reskilling 12
challenge-based learning 55
challenges: designing courses for STEM
152; for disciplines 158; in future
education 19; in STEM integration
128–129, 131–133, 140
change: agendas and trends in HEIs 146;
due to advances in technology 9; in
HEIs 147; in the nature of learning and
teaching 14
collaboration: in learning 63;
mentoring teachers 140; in peer and
self-assessment 107
collating assessment data across outcomes 119
communication in assessment 103
competency framework for teachers 130
computer technologies 24
connections: importance for STEM 79
creative thinking 28, 45, 59, 87, 99, 100,
141, 145, 146, 148, 157, 158
critical thinking 31, 45, 59, 79, 86,
98–101, 106, 129, 134, 138, 141,
145–146, 148, 151, 154, 157

170 *Index*

culminating, enabling and discrete outcomes 109
curriculum: alignment and professions 45; constructive alignment 77, 80; create learning experiences 85; design 76; developing theme, context, issue, or challenge 81, 83; discipline aspects, skills and capabilities 84; establish learning outcomes 84; identify assessment tasks 84; identify resources and sources 85; integrating 75, 86, 126, 154; integration of STEM 164
Curtin University 89

data literacy: importance of 9
data science 9, 47, 48, 154; degree in 99; integrator for STEM 9
design: assessment tasks 110, 159; constructive alignment in curriculum 95; courses for STEM, challenges 152; of curriculum 76
design and technology curriculum area 24
design thinking 27, 45, 49, 60, 79, 88, 99, 141, 159
development of professionals 134
digital natives 130
discipline: applications 49; blending with capability 127; challenges for future integration 158; characteristics of STEM 46; cross-cutting concepts 47
discipline aspects, skills and capabilities: assessment tasks 84
drivers in higher education 146; future, and HEIs 148

environments: supporting effective learning 32, 62–64, 89
ethics: design including 60; example of exploring 103; in games 160; use of STEM 160; for use of technology 10
evidence based research 126, 132
examples: assessing capability 101; assessment 113; assessment case studies 113

Flinders University 19, 27, 32, 65, 99, 109
flipped classroom 31
fourth industrial revolution 5
framework: ICT competency 130; for integrating STEM 65, 66
future directions for integrating STEM in higher education 145, 148–149; educational challenges 19; research on integrating STEM 163

gaming 24, 56–57, 59, 61, 104, 113, 157; exploring ethics 160; in STEM 32, 35
GEN NET students 29

goals: UN, sustainable development 24
Grand Canyon University 19

Harvard University 10
health: use of STEM in 23, 25, 27, 30
HEI: addressing needs of future work 3; aligning STEM with purpose of 155; changes in 147; drivers in 146; educate students for workforce 7; and future education 148; STEM changes, importance 44; using evidence-based research for teaching and learning, 126
Herriot-Watt University 17
higher education: brink of revolution in 5; future directions for integrating STEM 145–164
higher education institution *see* HEI
hybrid rubrics 113

ICT: assessment in 104; competency framework for teachers 130; simulation and 24, 104, 153
importance: of active learning approaches 54; authenticity 50; connections to STEM 79; constructive alignment 80; innovation 13
Indira Ghandi National Open University 147
Industry 4.0 139, 163
innovation: design thinking for learning 35, 37, 56, 60, 67, 88, 90, 97, 120, 132, 141; importance of 10–14, 16, 20, 44–47, 145–149; key to advancing STEM 1, 17, 19, 23, 26–29, 39, 52–54, 99, 149, 151, 156
inquiry and problem-based learning 14, 24, 44, 46, 53, 57, 59, 67, 75–77, 79, 84–85, 90, 97, 101–103, 113–114, 117, 127, 141, 165
inquiry learning 59, 67, 132, 151, 154, 157, 165
integration: approaches to STEM 16, 23, 158–159; curriculum 75, 126, 154, 164; future of STEM 149; levers for STEM 150, 164
interdiscipline 24, 60, 112
internships 159
Islamic University of Saudi Arabia 119
issues: knowledge authority 128; solving with technology 26; students as producers rather than consumers 125, 132

learning: active approaches to 28, 54, 85–86; analysis in 62; challenge-based 55; collaboration to promote 63; design thinking for innovation in 60; effective environments for 23–24, 31–32, 35–36,

38, 46, 51, 62–66, 86–89, 133–134, 149–152, 157; including opportunities for active 86–89; peer-learning 64; support students to integrate knowledge and skills 86; systems thinking in 61; using technology to support 31
learning experiences, creating 85
learning goals: aligning with technology, pedagogy 36
learning outcomes 2, 4–6, 8, 14–15, 28, 32, 35, 38, 40, 53, 56, 62–64; developing 38, 67, 84–86, 96, 109

Massachusetts Institute of Technology 116
Monash University 98

National University of Galway 88
National University of Singapore (NUS) 12
net generation 130
NET GEN students 29
new millennials 130
New Model for Technology and Engineering (NMiTE) 105, 118
NMiTE 118

outcomes: alignment with assessment 111; collating assessment data 119; culminating, enabling and discrete 109; effect of assessment 124; *see also* learning outcomes

pedagogy 1, 31; aligning with learning goals 50, 80, 132; challenge to integration 13, 136–138; framework for STEM 44, 66; in using technology 36–38
peer learning 64
peer review 108
Peking University 18
Politecnico di Torino 52
Princeton University 10
problem-based and inquiry learning 1–4, 9, 14, 16, 19–20, 45–50, 52, 57–58, 60, 63–67, 75–76, 81–85, 88–90, 96–97, 100–103, 108, 113–114, 116–118, 124, 127, 129–130, 145, 148, 150–152, 156–160, 162–164
problem-solving with technology 23–24, 26–28, 30, 33–35, 37, 39
professional learning 124–141; aligning curriculum with 45; assessment 135; challenge to integration 133; need for 134, 136, 138, 140, 164

references 20, 40, 68, 90, 120, 142, 165
reflective practice 138

research: applying to STEM 132, 163–164; supports integration of STEM 124, 163; use for teaching and learning 126
reskilling 12
revolution: fourth industrial 5; higher education on brink of 5
robotics 26
rubric 63; assessment 33, 81, 112; design and use 112; examples 114–115; group work 115; hybrid 2, 20, 113; peer assessment in 109; peer review using 86, 89; relate to outcomes 120; team decisions using 89

scholarship of teaching and learning 136
Science and Mathematics Network of Australian University Educators (SaMnet) 137
self-assessment 33, 51, 77, 84, 88, 102, 107–109, 112, 129
simulation 49, 58–59, 67, 88, 105, 150–151; in assessment 33, 101; ICT and 24–25, 30, 104, 153; medical 32; in STEM 32–33; virtual 25, 30
Singapore University of Technology and Design 105
smart cities 27, 160
social and economic futures 1, 3–5, 7, 17, 18, 20, 24–26, 39, 54, 147, 150, 157, 164–165
STEAM: definition 4
STEM: active learning opportunities 86, 87, 88; advancing through innovation 1, 4; aligning with purpose of HEIs 155; careers 6; challenges for integrating 140–142; challenges in designing courses 152; changes in technology 159; characteristics of disciplines 46; connections, importance 79; constructive alignment 80; create learning experiences 85; data science as an integrator 9; definition 4; developing theme, context, issue challenge 81, 83; driving innovation using 52; effective learning in 89; establish learning outcomes 84; framework for integrating 65; future directions in higher education 1, 44, 145, 149, 163; future research on integrating 163; health involvement 23, 25, 27, 30; identify discipline aspects, skills and capabilities 84; identify resources 85; integrated approaches to 16, 23; integration of curriculum 164; levers for integrating 150; pedagogical approaches to support 1, 44; pedagogical framework for 44;

172 *Index*

role of technology 23–39; support students to integrate knowledge and skills 86; systems approach to 161

students: development 131; education for workforce 7; empowering through assessment 129; expectations 129; knowledge producers rather than consumers 125; as producers of knowledge 132

sustainability 60, 67, 89, 152, 156; AI potential 160; case studies for teaching 113, 116; growing importance of 149; UN goals 24, 152, 160

systems approach to STEM 80, 161–163

systems thinking 28, 61, 66, 146, 159, 161–163

teachers: competency framework for 130

teaching and learning: blending discipline and capability 127; changing nature of 14; HEIs using evidence-based research for 126, 136; scholarship of 136; students as knowledge producers 125

technology: aligning with learning goals and pedagogy 36; augmented reality 33; changes in, effect on STEM 9, 23–39, 159; computer 24; emergent 32; ethics for the use of 10; examples of 23–39; gaming 24, 30, 35–36, 56–57, 61, 116, 160; importance of 23–25; learning experiences using 23–25, 28–39; practical experiments 32; processes 24; professional learning for 138; role in problem solving 23; simulations 25, 30, 33, 49, 58–59, 67, 88, 101, 104–105; for solving issues 26; top ten digital 30; virtual reality 2, 24, 28, 34–35, 39, 60, 104, 139

thinking: analytical in assessment 105; creative 87, 99, 100, 141, 145, 146, 148, 157, 158; critical 31, 79, 86, 98, 99, 100, 101, 129, 134, 138, 141, 145, 146, 148, 151, 154, 157; critical in assessment 106; design 60, 79, 88, 99, 141, 159;

prevailing ways of 46; systems 146, 159, 161, 162, 163

top ten digital technologies 30

UNESCO 130

universities and other HEIs: African Leadership University in Rwanda 126; Allama Iqbal Open University 147; Curtin University 89; Flinders University 19, 27, 32, 65, 99, 109; Grand Canyon University 19; Harvard University 10; Herriot-Watt University 17; Indira Ghandi National Open University 147; Islamic University of Saudi Arabia 119; Massachusetts Institute of Technology 116; Monash University 98; National University of Galway 88; National University of Singapore 12; New Model for Technology and Engineering 105, 118; Peking University 18; Politecnico di Torino 52; Princeton University 10; Singapore University of Technology and Design 105; Universidad Politécnica de Madrid 31; Universitat Politechnica de Valencia 17, 99; Universiti Sans Malaysia 18; University of California Santa Cruz 60; University of Canberra 104; University of Edinburgh 17; University of Gloucestershire 52; University of Leeds 34; University of Leiden 35; University of Malaya 18; University of Newcastle 17, 152; University of Rwanda 14; University of the South Pacific 14; University of Western Sydney 59

VET: vocational training 8

virtual reality 2, 24, 28, 34–35, 39, 60–61, 104, 139; simulations 25, 30, 33, 49, 58–59, 67, 88, 101, 104–105; in STEM 32, 34

VR *see* virtual reality

WIL: in assessment 101, 106; technology and 33; work-integrated learning 1, 8, 51, 58, 106–107, 151, 158

workforce: student education for 7